D0662477

JACK THE RIPPER: THE SIMPLE TRUTH

Bruce Paley was born in 1949. Among his various jobs, he has been a private detective, a cab driver, and a horse wrangler, and has worked with film-makers and rock bands. He has written extensively about music and the arts, and has written numerous short stories. He is a keen photographer, and has recently taken up sculpture. He lives in London, and is currently writing a play that has nothing to do with Jack the Ripper.

Jack the Ripper

The Simple Truth

Bruce Paley

HEADLINE

Copyright © 1996 Bruce Paley

The right of Bruce Paley to be identified as the Author of
the Work has been asserted by him in accordance with the
Copyright, Designs and Patents Act 1988.

First published in 1995
by HEADLINE BOOK PUBLISHING

First published in paperback in 1996
by HEADLINE BOOK PUBLISHING

10 9 8 7 6 5 4 3 2

All rights reserved. No part of this publication may be
reproduced, stored in a retrieval system, or transmitted,
in any form or by any means, without the prior written
permission of the publisher, nor be otherwise circulated
in any form of binding or cover other than that in which
it is published and without a similar condition being
imposed on the subsequent purchaser.

ISBN 0 7472 5218 1

Typeset by Keyboard Services, Luton, Beds

Printed and bound in Great Britain by
Cox & Wyman Ltd, Reading, Berks

HEADLINE BOOK PUBLISHING
A division of Hodder Headline PLC
338 Euston Road
London NW1 3BH

For my father,
and for Rehana,
for continued love and support,
and for Lenka,
for being very special

Contents

Acknowledgements

Many people have been supportive in various ways during the years I spent researching and writing this book. Among them are Mike Lake and Wendy Brooks, for initially putting me up, and Rehana Durrani, for putting up with me while I pursued what often seemed to be a lost cause. I'd also like to thank Ann Schlachter for her kindness, Victoria Lynch, and John, Kevin, Simon and all the rest of the gang at Skinny Melink's comic shop in Lewisham, and Dez Skinn, for their interest and encouragement. I'm also grateful for the support of Paul Begg, Marc Vaulbert de Chantilly, Peter Underwood, Colin Wilson, Martin Fido, Jeremy Beadle, and Camille Wolff and Loretta Lay at Grey House Books.

Much of my research was done at the following institutions (all in London unless otherwise stated), where I generally found the staff to be very helpful and patient: the British Library; the British Library Newspaper Library, Colindale; the Greater London Record Office; the Guildhall Record Room and Library; the London Museum of Jewish Life; the Public Record Office in London and in Kew, Surrey; the Ragged School Museum; St Catherine's House; and the Tower Hamlets Library, Bancroft Road.

Foreword

If I had to recommend a single book on Jack the Ripper to someone who knew nothing about the subject, I would unhesitatingly choose this one. Bruce Paley has captured the atmosphere of Whitechapel at the time of the murders – and indeed, of London in the late 19th century – with a sense of living reality that no other writer on the case has achieved.

Bruce Paley is an American who was brought up in New York, and who worked for a time as a private detective. He first wrote to me from New York in the late 1970s. Looking through my Ripper file, which had grown to alarming proportions even at that time, I see that he was about the twentieth person to write to me with a new theory of Jack the Ripper's identity in a decade. His was certainly completely original, although it now seems so logical that it is hard to know why no one thought of it earlier.

Over the years, I have become a sort of clearing house for new theories on the Ripper. It all began in 1960, with the publication of my 'Ripper novel' *Ritual in the Dark* (which used the Whitechapel background for a series of prostitute murders), and a series of articles I wrote in the London *Evening Standard* called 'My Search for Jack the Ripper'. These led to a great deal of correspondence, which included a letter from a doctor named Thomas Stowell, who offered to take me out to lunch to reveal to me the identity of Jack the Ripper. His candidate was Queen Victoria's grandson, the Duke of Clarence, who would have become King had he not died in the great 'flu epidemic of 1893. Stowell had seen the private papers of Sir William Gull, Queen Victoria's physician, and found many dark and guarded references to the Duke of Clarence and Jack the Ripper. Stowell swore me to silence, and I observed the ban until 1970, when Stowell himself published his theory in *The Criminologist*, calling his suspect 'S'. The furore caused by the suggestion that Jack the Ripper was a 'royal' so upset Dr Stowell that he died a few days later. In fact, the Duke of Clarence was celebrating his father's birthday at Sandringham at the time of the Mary Kelly murder, which clearly exonerates him.

Clarence was the first, but by no means the most unusual, candidate suggested to me over the years; others have included Oscar Wilde's friend Frank Miles, a homosexual artist (proposed by Thomas Toughill), the novelist George Gissing (Pat Pitman), and even Lewis Carroll (Richard Wallace). But then, most books on Jack the Ripper demand a certain suspension of disbelief. One of the most widely known, Stephen Knight's *Jack the Ripper: The Final Solution*, asks us to believe that Queen Victoria's grandson, the Duke of Clarence, secretly married an artist's model, and that the murders were a conspiracy of Freemasons led by Sir William Gull to suppress this secret. *The Ripper Legacy*, by Martin Howells and Keith Skinner, suggests that Jack the Ripper was an unsuccessful barrister – Montague Druitt – who was murdered by a clique of

Cambridge homosexuals to prevent him from disgracing their secret society. (Druitt actually committed suicide by drowning.) Aleister Crowley believed that Jack the Ripper was a black magician who committed the murders as part of a magical ritual to gain godlike powers. In this company, Bruce Paley's theory seems conservative and respectable.

Bruce Paley explained to me that his interest in Jack the Ripper had been excited by Tom Cullen's *Autumn of Terror* (1965), the first book to propose the unsuccessful barrister Montague John Druitt as the Ripper (although Dan Farson had revealed his initials in a television programme as early as 1959). Druitt had been the chief suspect of the Commissioner of Police Sir Melville MacNaghten; but in his memoirs *Days of My Years* (1915), MacNaghten gets so many of his facts about Druitt wrong – stating that he was a doctor, that he lived with his family, that he committed suicide immediately after the murder of Mary Kelly – that there seems little doubt that he had merely heard a garbled story from one of his older cronies at Scotland Yard. When all MacNaghten's mistakes are corrected, Druitt simply vanishes as a viable suspect.

But as Bruce Paley read Cullen's book, he was struck by how much that final murder – of Mary Kelly – differed from the other four. The main difference, of course, was that it took place indoors, so the killer was able to take his time and indulge his sadistic obsession to the full. Another puzzle was that the door was locked, so that it had to be battered open. The solution to this problem seems to be that the door had a spring lock that closed automatically. How did Mary Kelly get in without a key (which had been missing for some time)? By leaning in through a broken window. But the fact that there *was* a missing key set Bruce Paley thinking. Could Mary's lover, Joseph Barnett, have taken it when he walked out on her ten days before her murder? Bruce went back to the original newspapers of the time, and found that Barnett stammered and contradicted himself when giving various pieces of evidence. He was next struck by the fact that the drawing of Barnett at the inquest bore a strong resemblance to three eyewitness reports of the man who had picked up Catherine Eddowes shortly before her death, describing him as a man of about 30, with fair complexion and a moustache.

But why should Barnett murder the woman with whom he was in love? As Bruce Paley studied all he could find about Barnett – by now he had moved from America to London to be closer to his sources – he began to see what to him seemed the solution. He tried it out for the first time in an article for *True Detective* in 1982, but has continued to develop it ever since.

At this point I have to admit that although that solution seems to me highly plausible, I still feel that it is no more nor less plausible than many others. In commenting on Bruce's theory in *Jack the Ripper: Summing Up and Verdict* (which I wrote with Robin Odell) I commented that we lack one vital piece of evidence that might establish whether Barnett was Jack the Ripper: whether, as a person, Barnett possessed the kind of high dominance that Paley presupposes. On the night he murdered Elizabeth Stride, the Ripper was interrupted by the arrival of a horse and cart; he hastened north to Mitre Square, and there killed Catherine Eddowes. For a man who had just been within a hair's breadth of being caught, this shows a remarkably cool nerve. This is one reason why, when James Maybrick, the Liverpool cotton broker (apparently poisoned by his wife in 1889), suddenly became a chief suspect in 1992, I felt that he might well be Jack the Ripper. Maybrick was an arsenic addict, and when taken in small quantities, arsenic has the quality of producing a 'high' of great determination and endurance – Syrian peasants used to take it before climbing mountains. And although there is a widespread impression that the 'Maybrick diaries' have been proved a fake, I know enough about the exhaustive research that has been conducted into them by Paul Feldman (producer of the video *The Diary of Jack the Ripper*) to know this is not the case.

Whoever murdered and mutilated five women in Whitechapel in 1888 was a man of high dominance – although it is possible that this only emerged when he was drunk. (Mary Kelly herself was pleasant and quiet when sober, but became a demon when drunk.) If Bruce Paley could produce a little evidence from Barnett's acquaintances to prove that he might be such a person, I would feel that he had gone a long way towards establishing his theory.

When Bruce first told me of his theory in the later 1970s, there was another thing that bothered me. If Mary Kelly was the drunken slut she seems to have been, would Barnett have been so obsessed with her that he would have been ready to kill to drive her off the streets, then to murder her in a sadistic frenzy? In fact, it was not until 1990 that I began to see that the answer might well be yes. As long ago as 1973, I had learned of the Sickert theory of the murders, finally presented by Stephen Knight in his book *Jack the Ripper, The Final Solution* (1970). On the evidence of the artist Joseph Sickert, grandson of the famous painter Walter Sickert, Knight argued that the Duke of Clarence had fathered an illegitimate child on an artist's model named Annie Crook, and that the child's nursemaid had been ... Mary Kelly. According to Sickert, it was in an attempt to silence Mary Kelly and her cronies that Sir William Gull set out to murder them all. The story was preposterous and I dismissed it in a review of the book at the time. Yet in 1990, there appeared an interesting piece of evidence suggesting that there was at least some truth in the notion that Mary Kelly had been the nursemaid of Annie Crook's child. In a book called *Sickert and the Ripper*, Jean Overton Fuller reveals that her mother knew an artist named Florence Pash, a close friend of Walter Sickert's, and that Florence Pash was certain Sickert knew the identity of Jack the Ripper, and that Mary Kelly was indeed the nursemaid of Annie Crook's baby.

I do not believe that this proves that Mary Kelly was the victim of some sinister conspiracy of the British establishment. I believe that the Duke of Clarence *did* father an illegitimate child with Annie Crook, and that Mary Kelly *was* the child's nursemaid. I believe that when Mary Kelly became the Ripper's final victim, Walter Sickert's hair must have stood on end – he must have suspected that the long arm of Buckingham Palace was involved. He told this story to his son, Joseph, who repeated it in a garbled form.

I also believe that Sir William Gull, the queen's physician, learned about this so-called connection with the final victim, and the Duke of Clarence, and that this is what he was hinting at in the papers seen by Dr Stowell – not that Clarence was Jack the Ripper.

For me, the significance of all this is that if Mary Kelly had been hired by the Duke of Clarence two or three years before her murder, then she must have seemed a decent and respectable girl, a cut above most of the working class women in Whitechapel. But Joseph Barnett also saw himself as being a cut above the ordinary Whitechapel labourer; he was, as Bruce Paley points out, better educated and more articulate than most, a person who 'took considerable pride in his appearance and grooming'. This seems to explain why, after a brief acquaintance in a pub, Barnett proposed that they live together: she must have struck him as the ideal mate. He knew she was a prostitute, and that she was prone to alcoholism, but he probably felt that this was the result of misfortune, and that living with a 'husband' with a steady job would change all that. He must have experienced a tremendous feeling of triumph when, at first, she settled down like any other housewife, and her subsequent lapses into alcoholism and prostitution must have plunged him into despair – particularly since he felt he was to blame for having lost his job. And if – as her friends insisted – she was actually contemptuous of Barnett, I can also imagine how, driven to a frenzy by her jibes on that night of November 1888 – as Bruce Paley suggests – he might well have killed her with all the violence of someone who feels completely betrayed.

Yet whether Bruce's theory is correct seems to me relatively unimportant when compared with the fact that his obsession with Barnett has led him to write the most evocative book on the period that I have ever read.

Colin Wilson
June, 1995

Introduction

When the Jack the Ripper murders so shocked and baffled London in the autumn of 1888, the concept of serial killings was virtually unknown. Detection methods were crude and unsophisticated by modern standards and, with few precedents to guide them, the police were ill-prepared to deal with what appeared to be an inexplicable string of motiveless murders. Today, they seem all but commonplace, particularly in the United States where the impersonality and anonymity granted by that country's overcrowded cities and vast expanses, and the ready availability of legal and illegal guns, are especially conducive to such crimes.

Previously, most murders were solved because some sort of connection or relationship existed between the victim and the killer and there was an obvious motive for the crime, such as jealousy, robbery or revenge. But with serial killing and other apparently motiveless murders, no such direct link existed: the victims were almost always strangers, chosen entirely at random, usually because the opportunity for the crime simply presented itself. If the killer was caught, as often as not it was due to chance or happenstance rather than to tried and true detection methods. As post-war America became home to more and more of these murders, law enforcement authorities realized that the old methods were virtually useless in combatting this new breed of killer, and that new approaches were called for. Out of this quandary was born the science of psychological criminal profiling, a process largely developed and refined in the 1970s and eighties at the FBI's pioneering Behavioral Sciences Unit in Quantico, Virginia. In a nutshell, profiling seeks to create a physical and psychological picture of the offender through analysis and evaluation of the crime scene and evidence, and knowledge gained through comparison with previous crimes of a similar nature. Probably the most experienced and celebrated practitioner of the science is the now retired veteran FBI agent Robert K. Ressler. A former army commander, FBI field agent, specialist in hostage negotiation, lecturer in abnormal and criminal psychiatry, and member of the American Psychiatric Association, the American Academy of Forensic Sciences, and the American Academy of Psychiatry and the Law, Ressler was instrumental in founding both the National Center for the Analysis of Violent Crime (NCAVC), and the Violent Criminal Apprehension Program (VICAP), two bodies which revolutionized the approach to combatting violent crime in America. Before his retirement, Ressler had become the FBI's senior criminologist and its foremost criminal profiler – it was Ressler, in fact, who initially coined the term serial killer, and later served as advisor to the author Tom Harris, whose fictitious serial killer Hannibal Lecter captured the public's imagination in the best-selling book and hit film *Silence of the Lambs*.

In an attempt better to understand the phenomenon and gain an insight into the minds of these people, Ressler interviewed hundreds of multiple murderers – a feat as yet unmatched – and as a result of his studies, was able to isolate certain characteristics common to the large majority of serial killers. Most, Ressler concluded, came from dysfunctional families, often marked by absentee fathers and distant, unloving mothers. As Ressler observed, 'potential murderers became solidified in their loneliness first during the age period of eight to 12; such isolation is considered the single most important aspect of their psychological make up.'

Most serial killers, Ressler observed, were white males in their twenties and thirties, and many tended to be intelligent men, often employed in menial jobs that fell far below their true capabilities. Many suffered from physical ailments or disabilities. Ressler also determined that the initial murderous impulse was often triggered by what he termed a pre-crime stress, such as the loss of a job or the break up of a relationship.

In 1981, the 'Ripper Project' was initiated at the Milton Helpern Centre of Forensic Sciences at the Wichita State University, Kansas, in which modern, sophisticated, scientific detection methods were applied specifically to the Jack the Ripper murders. The FBI's VICAP program was utilized, along with a computer 'profiler', and a team of experts was assembled, including a renowned pathologist, a forensic psychiatrist, two 'Ripperologists' and top FBI criminal profilers. As a result, a psychological profile of Jack the Ripper was created. Among other things, it was determined that the man who called himself Jack the Ripper was a white male, aged 28–36, who lived or worked in the Whitechapel area, and probably worked at the sort of job in which he could vicariously experience his destructive fantasies, such as a butcher. He would have come from a family with a weak, passive or absentee father, and would probably have suffered from some sort of physical disability, such as a speech impediment. He would have displayed a strong dislike of prostitutes, and during the course of the investigation he would have been interviewed by the authorities and consequently overlooked or eliminated as a suspect. His ordinary, neat and orderly appearance would not have fitted the prevailing impression of the Ripper as being an odd or somehow ghoulish-looking man.

As will be seen, of the myriad suspects thus far presented as Jack the Ripper, only one comfortably fulfills virtually all the essential criteria established by both Ressler and the Ripper Project – to a remarkably high degree – while perfectly fitting the contemporary mould of Jack the Ripper.

That man is Joseph Barnett.

1

'How these people live is a mystery'

In 1858, when Joseph Barnett was born there, the oddly named Hairbrain Court was situated 100 yards to the east of the Royal Mint, which was itself adjacent to the Tower of London. It was just north of the bustling London docks, in the shadow of the London and Blackwall Railway line, and just a short walk from the heart of Whitechapel, where the Jack the Ripper murders would take place thirty years later. Like most of the East End, it was a rundown area, a teeming labyrinth of narrow closes, alleys, passageways, yards and courts, crammed with tenement buildings populated largely by labourers and their families. Not too long before, much of the East End had been farmland and pastures, but the advent of the Industrial Revolution saw numerous factories built in the area, which resulted in an influx of workers and their families, many of them Irish and Jewish immigrants. So great was this migration that the East End quickly became overcrowded, with the result that there were far more workers than there were available jobs. At the docks, for example, 10,000 prospective labourers would show up daily for some 6,000 openings, and in some instances as many as 350 men might find themselves competing for fifteen or twenty positions, and violence often flared as a result.

At that time, the population of England and Wales had passed the twenty million mark,[1] and the British Empire was still expanding around the world, Australia and New Zealand having recently attained the status of self-governing colonies. The Crimean War, which saw Florence Nightingale revolutionize the nursing profession through her devoted care and treatment of the wounded, had been over for two years, and a mutiny begun in India in 1857 had been successfully suppressed. In Parliament, Baron Lionel de Rothschild, the first Jewish MP, was finally allowed to take his seat after an eleven-year wait. 1858 also saw Charles Dickens busy researching what was to be his next novel, *A Tale of Two Cities*, and the first presentation by the English naturalist Charles Darwin of his theory of evolution by natural selection, which would shock the world upon its publication the following year.

Joseph was the fourth child, and third son, of John and Catherine Barnett who, like thousands of their kind, had fled the poverty and famine of their native Ireland to seek a better life in London. John, who was 41 years old when Joseph was born, found work at the docks and also toiled as a fish porter at Billingsgate Market, then located just to the west of the Tower of London. Come August, however, and the Barnetts would join thousands of other East End families in journeying down to Kent to pick hops for the season. The recent expansion of the railway system had facilitated the trip, and 'Hop Picker Specials' would bring hundreds of workers from London at a time. While the hours were long and living conditions were often inadequate, the work itself was relatively easy, with the added advantage that the entire family could participate, including the children. Families would also benefit from a few weeks in the fresh country air, away from the increasing smog and pollution of London. In the latter half of the nineteenth century, respiratory ailments, in the East End and in London as a whole, were the single commonest cause of death. John Barnett and three of his sons, including Joseph, would all eventually die of lung-related ailments.

It was in Chalk, Kent, in 1849 that the Barnett's first child, Denis, was born. A second son, Daniel, followed in 1851 and a daughter, Catherine, was born two years later. After Joseph, a final son, John, was born in 1860. Except for Denis, all the Barnett children were born in Whitechapel.[2]

Working-class families tended to move frequently in those days as their fortunes fluctuated, and by 1861 the Barnetts were living in Cartwright Street, a few dozen yards from Hairbrain Court. Their neighbours there were largely unskilled or semi-skilled labourers and their families, among them a tobacco stripper, a dressmaker, a dockworker, a shoe black, a charwoman and a smith. Many were first or second generation Irish immigrants. Three years later, the family was still in Cartwright Street (though in a different building) and John, then 47, was still working at Billingsgate Market when he contracted pleurisy. He died six days later, a not untypical victim of the backbreaking working life and harsh East End conditions that prematurely aged and broke even the strongest of men.

The death of John, the chief breadwinner, in July 1864 was no small crisis for the Barnett family. As Denis, not yet 15, was still too young to find suitable work, the task of providing for the family would have fallen on John's widow, Catherine, who was probably able to maintain a minimum income by bringing home piecework, one of the few job opportunities, as will be seen, available to a woman in her circumstances. The chief advantage of such labour, in which the work could be done at home and wages were determined exclusively by productivity, was that other members of the family could contribute. It's likely that Catherine, 10 at the time of John's death, contributed on a full-time basis, and helped look after young John who was then three years old. Denis, 14, Daniel, 12 or 13, and Joseph, who had recently turned six, all attended school but probably still did their share of work in their spare time.

If John's death created financial hardships for the Barnetts, then things were to get a lot worse with the elder Catherine's subsequent mysterious disappearance. She was no longer listed as part of the Barnett family in the 1871 census; the last official record of her is as the informant on her husband's death certificate in July 1864. What happened to her remains unexplained, but there are no indications of a remarriage or any record of her death as Catherine Barnett. The likelihood is that sometime after her husband's death she went off to live with another man, taking his name as her own, and abandoning her family in the process. (Alternatively, she may have returned to her native Ireland where her death would not be included in the English records.)

It is possible that Catherine's actions were influenced by heavy drinking, or that she found herself unable to cope with the responsibility of raising five children on her own. Whatever the reasons, her disappearance, coming as it did on the heels of John's death, must have had a profound psychological affect on the Barnett children. Joseph in particular developed a speech impediment and would later display symptoms of a little-known psychological disorder recognized today as echolalia, in which a person repeats, or echoes, certain words or phrases spoken by another.[3] Common to autistics, echolalia may also be symptomatic of schizophrenia, and can occur as a personality mannerism or in anxious individuals.

It is now known that most serial killers come from dysfunctional families, marked by absentee fathers and cold, distant mothers. After personally interviewing hundreds of such killers, Robert K. Ressler, formerly the FBI's foremost psychological criminal profiler, concluded that 'potential murderers became solidified in their loneliness first during the age period of eight to 12; such isolation is considered *the single most important aspect of their psychological make up.* Many factors go into fashioning this isolation. *Among the most important is the absence of a father*' (my italics).[4]

With both Catherine and John now gone, Denis Barnett would have had no choice but somehow to assume the mantle of family breadwinner, a position he probably held (assuming that Catherine disappeared before that time) until March 1869, when he married Mary Ann Garrett, a 19-year-old local girl, in Bethnal Green. They had two sons, Dennis and John, before moving across the Thames and settling in Bermondsey. Of all four Barnett brothers, only Denis managed to escape from the East End and he was the only one to marry legally and raise a family.

It then fell to Daniel to take over as head of the family. Like his father had done before him, Daniel worked as a fish porter at Billingsgate Market, though his struggles to support his three siblings were such that by 1871 the Barnetts had moved about a mile north from the Cartwright Street area to Great Pearl Street, one of the worst streets in the East End. Marked by severe overcrowding, it would soon be condemned by the Medical Officer for Health as being unfit for human habitation. Joseph and John, 13 and nine respectively, remained in school, while Catherine, at

17, helped raise the family and run the household until her marriage later that year to the aptly named Joseph Beer who worked as a driver for a local brewery. They set up house in what is now Poplar High Street. Their attempts to raise a family were marred by the deaths of at least four of their children within a year of the births, reflecting the phenomenally high contemporary infant mortality rate, which saw one of every four children born die in their first year. At that time, diseases such as scarlet fever, measles, whooping cough, diphtheria, dysentery, tubercular meningitis and phthisis were all major causes of death, as was premature birth. Nevertheless, the Beers persevered and Catherine became pregnant several more times over a twenty-year period. At least one of their children survived into maturity, a daughter, Catherine, who died in 1960 at the age of 86, and whose descendants are alive today.

To Daniel's credit, he saw to it that his brothers Joseph and John continued to attend school. Even after the Education Act of 1870 which created the Board Schools and made schooling compulsory for all children in Britain aged 5–13, many parents still kept their children at home. In many instances, the children were already working and their incomes were necessary for the family's survival, while a weekly fee (later eliminated) of 1d or 2d per child could prove to be a significant burden on some families' budgets. Girls, who were then raised solely to become good housewives, were kept home far more frequently than boys, in order to help with domestic chores.

Part of each school's budgetary grant, however, was determined by attendance, so incentives were sought to persuade parents to send their children to school. Good attendance was awarded with certificates or medals (to impress prospective employers), while truants could be punished, often by caning. Board inspectors were sent to investigate frequent absences and were empowered to bring the absentee's parents to court though such action was rare, and in less respectable neighbourhoods, such as those found in the East End, inspectors were often reluctant to interfere in family matters.

Students that did attend school often found themselves in classes of seventy or eighty pupils, sometimes with more than one class in the same room. Girls were taught mainly domestic skills, while boys were basically schooled in the three Rs – reading, writing and arithmetic. Handwriting was taught in the copperplate style and, as will be seen, an examination of the original Jack the Ripper letter shows it to have been written in that precise hand.

Upon leaving, graduates were presented with a Scholar's Certificate that listed their abilities as well as their conduct. As there were no GCSEs or A- or O-levels at the time, a good reference was essential for almost any future employment.

In 1878, new bylaws came into effect at Billingsgate Market whereby it became mandatory for all porters to be licensed by the Corporation of the City of London. All four Barnett brothers received their licences on 1 July of that year, though like Daniel, they probably had already been working there for some time previously. According to their licences,[5] all of the Barnetts were fair complexioned and none were particularly large men. John and Daniel stood only 5ft 4ins and 5ft 6ins tall respectively, and Denis was 5ft 6ins. Joseph was the tallest at 5ft 7ins and it was recorded that he had blue eyes.

Until its recent relocation, Billingsgate was London's oldest fixed market. The name was derived, legend has it, from a Celtic king called Belin who erected a water gate on the site. True or not, Billingsgate had long been a wharf used for the landing of fish. It was rebuilt and expanded twice in the latter half of the nineteenth century, at which time it housed 180 tenants and handled over 125,000 tons of fish per annum. By that time there were 2,000 licensed porters, about 600 of whom worked regularly.

Portering at Billingsgate consisted mainly of unloading and transporting fish. It was hard, strenuous work and required considerable physical strength. Fish were generally packed in large trunks, weighing about 6½ stone, or 90 lbs, each, which porters carried about balanced on their heads. To facilitate this, they wore specially fortified hats called 'bobbins', though these didn't prevent them from becoming prematurely bald, a common job affliction caused by the constant weight and pressure on the scalp. The porters' work day began at 5.00 a.m. and was over four hours later, though those permanently employed by a market shop generally stayed on for another four or five hours, cleaning and packing fish. As Joseph Barnett worked at Billingsgate for at least ten years and was 'in decent work' as he put it,[6] it's likely that he held such a position.

Porters were paid by the piece at varying rates, so wages varied, but a steady, diligent worker could earn as much as £3 per week – a considerable sum for a labourer at the time, and one that put him at the top of his class. With 12 pence (12d) to the shilling, and 20 shillings (20s) per pound, £1 could be made to go a long way. In the 1880s, a cheap room could be had for under 5s per week, while a bed in a doss house or common lodging house cost as little as 4d per night. A pound of beef or bacon cost about 8½d, a pound of lamb breast 3½d. A half dozen eggs sold for 5d or 6d, a pound of cheese for 7½d, a pint of milk or a pound of sugar for 2d. A shilling could buy 50 oranges or 10 lbs of rice or 7 lbs of oatmeal. A nice pair of trousers went for 7s 6d, corduroys for 4s 5d; a pair of men's 'spring side', or elastic, boots was 3s, the same price as a pair of woman's high leg lace and button boots. Corsets sold for 5s per pair, men's stockings for 2s 5d. A pound of candles (still a necessity in most households as electrical services were only then being developed) cost 5½d, a pound of cold-water cleaning soap was 3d, towels were 5d or less. Most newspapers cost a penny, though some like the *Echo* were a halfpence while *The Times* sold for 3d. Posting a letter still cost a penny per ounce, and a fountain pen cost about 2s 6d. A bottle of whisky could be had for 3s 6d and a pint of beer was 2d – the same price as 10 Woodbine cigarettes – while 2½d could buy an ounce of tobacco or a cigar. An omnibus from Cricklewood to Oxford Circus was 5d, railway fares were a penny a mile, with a third-class single from London to Manchester costing 7s 5d. For entertainment closer to home, 2d could buy a gallery seat at any of a number of local music halls, which were then in their heyday.

Given his education, Joseph Barnett was probably capable of finding a better job but he may have been held back as much by the local economic situation as he was by his speech impediment and, considering the plight of many of those around him, Barnett was privileged to be working steadily, let alone earning a good wage. The East End in which he had been reared was characterized by widespread poverty and destitution, with tens of thousands of people living in deplorable conditions of degradation and squalor – this despite the fact that London was arguably the greatest city in the world, while Britain was unchallenged as the wealthiest nation on earth. The Great Exhibition of 1851, held at Crystal Palace, had ushered in two decades of unprecedented economic growth and prosperity that saw British agriculture thriving, while she led the world in industrial production, to the extent that by 1870 the United Kingdom's foreign trade was greater than that of France,

Germany and Italy combined, and almost four times that of the United States, then still recovering from the disastrous Civil War. The 1870s also saw the continued expansion of the Empire, with Fiji, Cyprus and Egypt all coming under British rule.

Yet in London, whose population had exceeded the four million mark in the 1870s, people were starving. Writers such as Charles Dickens and Henry Mayhew, among others, had previously addressed this imbalance, but one of the first to reveal the true nature and extent of the daily horrors of life in the London slums to a new generation was the novelist George Robert Sims. Accompanied by School Board inspectors, who knew their way around, Sims investigated some of the worst areas in London, likening his travels through the East End and Southwark to an exploration of some far off colonial outpost. An account of his shocking findings was serialized in *Pictorial World* in 1883 under the title 'How the Poor Live', and later released as a book.

Sims described a typical slum square encountered in his walkabout: '[It] is full of refuse, heaps of dust and decaying vegetable matter lie about here and there, under the windows and in front of the doors of the squalid tumble-down houses. The windows above and below are broken and patched.' Knocking on the door of one such abode, Sims was greeted by 'a poor woman, white and thin and sickly looking; in her arms she carries a girl of eight or nine, with a diseased spine, behind her, clutching at her scanty dress, are two or three other children.' Inside, Sims observed that 'the walls are damp and crumbling, the ceiling is black and peeling off ... the floor is rotten and broken away in places, and the wind and the rain sweep in through gaps that seem everywhere. The woman, her husband and her six children live, eat and sleep in this one room, and for this they pay three shillings a week.' Here Sims pointed the finger at slum landlords for allowing such conditions to propagate. 'As to complaining of the dilapidated, filthy condition of the room,' he wrote, 'they know better. If they don't like it, they can go. There are dozens of families who will jump at the accommodation, and the landlord is well aware of the fact.'

Sims visited one of the doss houses that proliferated in the East End. Around the time of the Ripper murders, there were 149 such registered hostels in Whitechapel alone,[7] and numerous unlicensed ones where a single bed, in a room with sometimes as many as sixty or seventy others, could be obtained for 4d per night. A double bed and more private accommodation could be had for 8d. Such arrangements were ideally suited for casual labourers, prostitutes and others who tended to live from day to day, and they and their families often lived in the same doss house for years at a time.

A useful feature of the doss house was its communal kitchen. The one Sims saw was 'a large room, where the strangest collection of human beings are crowded together. It is sheet washing day, and there is a great fire roaring up the chimney ... Tables and forms run round the room, and there is not a vacant place. Men, women and children are lolling about, though it is mid-day, apparently with nothing to do but make themselves comfortable ... Many of the men and women and boys are thieves. Almost every form of disease, almost every kind of deformity, seems crowded into this Chamber of Horrors ... an attractive face there is not among the 60 or 70 human beings in the room. Some of them only get a night in now and then as a luxury, and look upon it as a Grand Hotel episode.'

Sims also discussed the problem of school fees, showing how for many families the extra few pence each week could pose a serious financial burden. 'Where the difference between the weekly income and rent is only a couple of shillings,' he explained, 'I assure you the coppers represent so many meals.' To illustrate his point, Sims presented some typical 'case studies':

Mrs Walker – Seven children of school age, fee 2d per week each. Total earnings entire family 10s [per week]. Rent 5s 6d [per week]. Husband once good mechanic, lost employment through illness and deafness. Parish relief, none. Character good. Is now a hawker – sells oranges and fish. Children half starved. When an orange is too bad to sell, they have it for breakfast, with a piece of bread.

Mrs _____ – Five children school age; widow. Earnings 6s. Rent 3s. Respectable woman, feels her poverty very keenly.

Mrs Garrard – Eight children of school age; two always under doctor. No income. Pawning last rags. Rent 5s 6d. No parish relief. Declines to go into workhouse.

'I could multiply such instances by hundreds,' Sims lamented. 'How these people live is a mystery.'

Later that same year, Sims followed up 'How the Poor Live' with a further series of articles entitled 'Horrible London',[8] published in the *Daily News*. In these articles Sims considered some of the causes of the deplorable living conditions that he had encountered. Overpopulation, he realized, meant that the East End labour market was flooded, which kept wages down to a bare minimum, while inadequate housing for the labourers and their families had brought about the forced co-mingling of working-class families with the criminal element. Not only was this dispiriting, but also it provided a poor environment, particularly for children. This situation had come about largely as a result of the demolition of affordable working-class accommodation under the Artisans and Dwelling Act of 1875. Slums were cleared with the intention of replacing substandard buildings with affordable dwellings for the poor. In reality, however, commercial establishments rather than homes were often built on the sites, and in other instances the empty plots lay vacant for years. In some cases, when new housing was erected, the high rents were beyond the means of the workers for whom they had been intended. As such, the labourers and their families had little choice but to move to less savoury areas, where rents were cheaper. Moving to the suburbs, made feasible by the expansion of the railway system, was out of the question because of high transport fares and the fact that for many labourers it was essential that they live near their workplace. Casual dockworkers, for instance, often had to start queuing up at three in the morning, only slightly earlier than the market porters, while others such as carmen might have to report for work as early as 1.00 a.m. Home workers in the so-called 'sweated' trades, many of whom were women, also needed to be within easy walking distance of their employers.

The stunning revelations in Sims's work inspired Andrew Mearns[9] of the Orange Street Congregational Church, to undertake a similar investigation of his own, the results of which were published in October 1883 as *The Bitter Cry of Outcast London*. Mearns drew heavily on Sims's seminal work in recounting scenes and episodes of poverty and degradation. He too described a typical slum courtyard 'reeking with poisonous and malodorous gasses arising from accumulations of sewage and refuse scattered in all directions.' Of the flats therein, he found the average room to be about eight feet square, with 'walls and ceilings [that] are black with the accretions of filth which have gathered upon them through long years of neglect.'

Mearns was horrified at how some of the inhabitants lived. 'In one cellar, a sanitary inspector reports finding a father, mother, three children, and four pigs! In another room, a missionary found a man ill with smallpox, his wife just recovering from her eighth confinement, and the children running about half naked and covered with dirt... Elsewhere is a poor widow, her three children, and a child who had been dead 13 days. Her husband, who was a carman, had shortly before committed suicide... Another apartment contains father, mother and six children, two of whom are ill with scarlet fever... Here is a mother who turns her children into the street in the early evening because she lets her room for immoral purposes until long after midnight...'

Like Sims, Mearns also visited a common lodging house, which he confirmed to be 'often the resorts of thieves and vagabonds of the lowest types... In the sleeping room are long rows of beds on each side, sometimes 60 or 80 in one room. In many cases, both sexes are allowed to herd together without any attempt to preserve the commonest decency.'

Mearns was particularly affected by the widespread suffering of children. 'From the beginning of their life,' he wrote, 'they are utterly neglected; their bodies and rags are alive with vermin; they are subjected to the most cruel treatment; many have never seen a green field, and do not know what it is to go beyond the streets immediately around them, and they often pass the whole day without a morsel of food.'

18

Both Mearns and Sims agreed that State interference was necessary if conditions were to be improved, and that adequate housing for working-class families was a priority. Mearns, as a clergyman, also saw the need for greater efforts from the Church, and called for the establishment of Mission Halls in some of the worst neighbourhoods, where clergy could work with the destitute and try to bring them into the Church.

The work of Sims and Mearns in turn influenced Charles Booth, a wealthy businessman, to undertake his revolutionary socio-economic street-by-street survey of London. Booth had begun his project in Tower Hamlets[10] in 1886, though by the time his *Labour and Life of the People in London* was published five years later, it had expanded to include all of Metropolitan London (though not the City).

Where Sims and Mearns had presented harrowing, emotive accounts of individual suffering, Booth provided hard statistics which, in their way, were even more shocking. According to his findings, an astonishing 30% of all Londoners lived on or below the poverty level (which Booth defined as a weekly income of no more than 21 shillings for a moderate-sized family, i.e., one with five or six members). In Tower Hamlets the poverty rate was 35%, while in Whitechapel it was 10% higher. The highest level recorded was for St George in the East, the district covering the dock areas, where almost 49% of the inhabitants lived in poverty.[11]

The unique feature of Booth's study was his innovative 'Descriptive Map of London Poverty', in which he colour coded each street in London according to income.[12] The lowest classes, which consisted of 'loafers', the 'vicious' and 'semi-criminal' and occasional labourers, were designated by black, followed by dark blue, which largely comprised casual labourers and their families whose modest incomes left them in 'chronic want', and light blue, representing the poor where a moderate-sized family lived on 18–21s per week. Next up on the scale was purple, meaning a street with a mixture of comfortable and poor, followed by pink for the fairly comfortable who enjoyed a good regular income. Red stood for the well-to-do or middle class, while yellow indicated the better off, the upper middle and upper classes. A telling reflection of the East End's impoverishment lay in its glaring concentrations of black and blue pockets with nary a yellow block to be seen.

Despite the ground-breaking work of Sims, Mearns, Booth and others (and the national spotlight later thrown on the East End by the Jack the Ripper murders), little had actually changed by the turn of the century when the American writer and socialist Jack London was prompted to conduct his own investigation of the East End. Passing himself off as a tramp sailor, London spent six weeks living among the downtrodden East Enders in the summer of 1902, sharing their hardships, sleeping rough, working, scrounging and walking the streets with them. A former hobo himself, London felt tremendous compassion for the tramps, labourers, homeless and unemployed men and women whom he met and befriended, and was profoundly moved by the unending misery of their day-to-day existence and by their struggles to hold on to their pride and humanity. Not long afterwards, he published *The People of the Abyss*, a moving account of his experiences.

More than anyone before him, London was able to make the sorrowful plight of the East Enders palpable to his readers by presenting them as real people with character and heart, not all that different from anyone else. In one instance he described a touching moment between a labourer and his 'wife': 'She was fairly clad, for her class, with a weather worn bonnet on her grey head and a sacking covered bundle in her arms. As she talked to [her 'husband'] he reached forward, caught the one stray wisp of the white hair that was flying wild, deftly twirled it between his fingers, and tucked it back properly behind her ear... He was proud of her, standing there in the spike [workhouse] line... I found myself questioning why this man and his mate, hard workers ... should have to seek a pauper lodging.'

London himself spent some time in the Whitechapel 'spike', an institution that for many East Enders represented the final humiliation. The earliest workhouses dated back to the end of the sixteenth century, the concept being that the needy should be put to work to earn their keep. By the time they were abolished in 1929, they had come to resemble prisons more than the charitable institutions they were meant to be.

Workhouse inmates were either admitted on a long-term basis, or they could just register for a couple of nights in the casual ward, which is what Jack London did. In either case the routine was much the same, though admittance to the casual ward was limited, and prospective entrants had to queue for several hours in advance to have any chance of being admitted. Once inside, tobacco and alcohol were confiscated and families were forcibly split, including the separation of mothers from their children. London, who was admitted to the Whitechapel workhouse, found the conditions there to be extremely insanitary, and he bridled at having to bathe in water that had already been used by countless dirty men before him. Discipline was strict and the food was almost inedible, particularly a bland gruel known as skilly. Following their first night's rest, inmates were forced to perform dreary tasks, such as breaking rocks or picking oakum (the loose fibres obtained from unravelling old rope). London's job was to disinfect a mortuary.

Reinforcing the prison-like atmosphere, inmates were forbidden to leave the premises until late the following morning, by which time it was much too late for them to find any work. Overall, a deliberately unpleasant, even hostile, environment was cultivated by the wardens, ostensibly to discourage complacency in the paupers. Not surprisingly, many chose to avoid the workhouse at all costs, preferring even to be out on the streets rather than submit themselves to its cold, insensitive and dehumanizing routine.

The East End, London concluded, was 'a huge man-killing machine'. 'O dear, soft people, full of meat and blood,' he pleaded, 'how can you ever understand?'

2

'White slavery in London'

In calling the East End 'a huge man-killing machine', Jack London had not intended to minimize the plight of women, who in many instances faced even greater hardships than did men. In particular, there were few opportunities for single women – widowed or unmarried – who were on their own, especially if they had children. In Victorian England, girls were raised solely to be housewives, and apart from in domestic skills, they received little education. Nor were they given any job training, despite the fact that in the third quarter of the nineteenth century more than one out of every four women over the age of 15 worked, as did a considerable number of girls under 15.[1]

By far the largest number of women – over 40% – found what were generally relatively comfortable positions as domestic servants, while those who could worked as teachers, nurses, shop attendants, clerks and bookkeepers. But for those unqualified or unsuited to such work, the only remaining legitimate options available were menial factory and light industrial jobs, and work in the sweated trades. While many such jobs were in the textile industry, women might also work as laundresses, cigarette makers, perfumers, fur pullers, spectacle makers, surgical instrument makers, magic lantern slide makers, and so forth. Often such work was done at home and workers were paid by the piece. Wages therefore varied but for the most part were extremely low, with a ceiling of about 14s or 16s per week and no compensation for slack periods when there was little or no work. Andrew Mearns was stunned to find a tweed trouser maker who toiled seventeen hours a day for a single shilling, and a shirt finisher who earned half that amount for sewing the linings and buttons on shirts, and making the button holes, at a rate of 3d per dozen shirts, minus expenses as she had to supply her own thread. Similarly, a sack maker earned about a farthing ($^1/_4$d) per sack, a matchbox maker might clear four or five shillings a week, at a rate of 2$^1/_4$d per gross, while a pea sheller made about 10d or 1s per day in season.

George Sims described a visit to two fur pullers, an elderly woman and her daughter who cleaned rabbit skins of loose fluff and hair and other bits for a furrier: 'Floors, walls, ceilings, every inch of the one room these people live and sleep in, is covered with fluff and hair. How they breath in it is a mystery to me. I tried, and failed, and sought refuge on the doorstep. The pair, working day and night at their trade, make, when business is good, about twelve shillings a week. Their rent is four [shillings per week]. That leaves them four shillings a week each to live upon, and as there is no one else to share it with them, I suppose they are well to do folk.'[2]

Conditions in factories were often similarly unhygienic, and sometimes dangerous. As a rule, women did the lighter work, while men operated the heavier machinery or worked as clerks or supervisors, often at twice the pay that women received. One reason for this was that women were generally considered to be unreliable employees, as it was assumed that they would one day leave their jobs to marry and raise a family.

A typical workplace for women was the Bryant & May match plant in Bow, East London, which employed 1,400 girls and women. There, an average 16-year-old worker earned around 4s per week for a 10½-hour day, most of it spent on her feet, while being liable to such fines as 3d for having dirty feet or an unclean work area, or 1d for putting burnt matches on the workbench. Lateness cost a half day's pay. Employees ate in the same area that they worked in and the presence of phosphorous fumes mixing with their food resulted in a rotting of the teeth and jaw known as 'phossy jaw'. It was alleged that girls who showed signs of the disease were let go. (In some places, women could also be dismissed for having an illegitimate child, or living with a man without being married.)

In the summer of 1888, the writer Annie Besant, a founding member of the socialist Fabian society (along with George Bernard Shaw, Sidney Webb and his later wife, Beatrice Potter), published an article about the matchgirls' plight entitled 'White Slavery in London'[3] which set off a chain reaction that resulted in a mass walkout by the entire work force. Besant helped them organize, arranged for strike pay and appealed to both the public and Parliament for support. Among the press, the *Echo*, the *Star* and the *Pall Mall Gazette* responded favourably, publishing Besant's appeal for funds, though *The Times*, she noted, was particularly hostile. But public support for the matchgirls proved to be overwhelming, and management was forced to concede. Fines and deductions were abolished, wages were raised slightly, a separate dining area was arranged, and the Matchgirls Union was established. The true significance of their victory, however, lay in the fact that the strike was one of the earliest instances where weak, unskilled workers successfully challenged management. The matchgirls' example thus paved the way for similar actions, most notably the Great Dock Strike of 1889, when the cry for the 'docker's tanner' (the sixpence hourly wage they sought) rang through the streets of London, and was instrumental in the founding of the Labour Party a few years later.

But the matchgirls' action was an exceptional one, and in most workplaces the long hours, low wages and generally substandard working conditions were accepted without question. Because of this, a considerable number of otherwise 'respectable' women opted to supplement their meagre incomes through prostitution. Henry Mayhew, in his pioneering survey of London's working class and poor,[4] interviewed a number of workers in the sweated trades and found that about a quarter of them also worked as prostitutes. 'I never knew one girl in the trade who was virtuous,' one shirt finisher told him. 'Most of them wished to be, but were compelled to be otherwise for mere life.' 'Sin or starve' was the order of the day, according to William Booth, the founder of the Salvation Army, who worked extensively in Whitechapel. Booth estimated that there were as many as 60,000–80,000 full- or part-time prostitutes in London in the late 1880s (though he admitted that this figure included 'all habitually unchaste' women).[5] The Metropolitan Police, in October 1888, estimated that there were around 1,200 prostitutes in Whitechapel, and over 60 brothels. 'Entire courts are filled with thieves, prostitutes, and liberated convicts,' wrote Andrew Mearns. 'In one street are 35 houses, 32 of which are known to be brothels. In another district are 43 of these houses, and 428 fallen women and girls, many of them not more than 12 years of age. A neighbourhood whose population is returned at 10,000, contains 400 who follow this immoral traffic, their ages varying from 13 to 50.'[6]

Earnings, of course, were erratic but in a good spell a prostitute could expect to make as much in the streets in a night or two as she did in an entire week in a sweatshop. As an orphaned 16-year-old girl, who had been 'on the game' since she was 12, explained to Henry Mayhew, 'Sometimes [I made] a good deal of money, sometimes not, feasting one day, starving the next.'[7]

Although it provided a lifeline for many women, prostitution was hardly an attractive option and most turned to it only out of desperation. Not only were earnings undependable, due in part to the often fierce competition, but women were vulnerable to physical danger, and there was the ever-present threat of venereal disease (which accounted for about 500 deaths yearly in London at the time). There was also the inherent social degradation and the likelihood of estrangement from family and friends. But for many women, this was the price they had to pay for survival.

Joseph Barnett was still working at Billingsgate Market in April 1887, when he met the young prostitute Mary Jane Kelly. By all accounts, she was an attractive woman. 'She was tall and pretty,' said a neighbour, 'and fair as a lily.'[8] A former acquaintance recalled that Kelly was about 5ft 7ins tall, and stout, with blue eyes and 'a fine head of hair which reached nearly to her waist.'[9] The *Daily Telegraph* reported Kelly as having been 'of fair complexion, with light hair, and possessing rather attractive features, dressed pretty well. Usually she wore a black silk dress, and often a black jacket, looking shabby genteel in her attire, but generally neat and clean.'[10] Barnett noted that Kelly, who was 22 or 23 when they met, was 'fresh looking and well behaved'.[11]

It was Kelly's youth and freshness which set her apart from many of her compatriots. The East End was full of middle-aged women, widowed, separated from or abandoned by their husbands and estranged from their families, who had long since succumbed to the ravages of alcohol and the hardships of East End life. To such women, life was little more than a daily struggle for survival, an unbroken quest for the next drink and a bed at the end of the day. All of the Ripper victims, except for Kelly, were of that mould. Two of them had been out in the early hours of the morning, drunkenly seeking the few pence necessary for a night's bed in a doss house when they encountered the Whitechapel Murderer (as he was initially known), while a third had just been released from the drunk tank when she met a similar fate. Such women would surface time and again during the Ripper's ten-week reign of terror, speaking to the press and testifying at the various inquests. Jack London, during his sojourn in East London, encountered many such types: 'They held carouse in every boozing ken, slatternly, unkempt, bleary eyed, and towsled ... overspilling with foulness and corruption, and gone in debauch ... unspeakably repulsive ... the wrecks of society ... the living deaths – women blasted by disease and drink till their shame brought not tuppence in the open mart.'[12] Beatrice Potter, who did investigative work for Charles Booth, observed much the same thing. 'This East End life, with its dirt, drunkenness and immorality saddens me and weighs down my spirit,' she wrote. 'A woman, diseased with drink came up to me screaming, in her hand the quart pot, her face directed to the Public House. What could I say? Why dissuade her? She is half way to death ... But with her go others; and these others may be only on the first step downwards.'[13]

Despite her youth, Mary Kelly had already fallen far by the time she met Barnett. According to Barnett,[14] Kelly had come from a stable family background. Born in

Limerick, southwest Ireland, around 1864, she had as many as six brothers and at least one sister. When she was still a child, the family moved to Wales, where her father worked as a foreman in an iron works. Kelly received some formal education,[15] and at 16 she married a local collier, who was tragically killed in a mining accident only a year or two later. Kelly then went to stay with a cousin in Cardiff who was evidently a prostitute, and the widowed Kelly had little choice but to follow suit. 'She was following a bad life with her cousin,' Barnett remarked, 'who, as I reckon and as I often told her, was the cause of her downfall.'[16] It may have been in Cardiff that Kelly first started drinking heavily, and it was alleged that she also spent several months in a Cardiff infirmary for an undisclosed illness.

Around 1884, when she was 20 or 21, Kelly arrived in London, where she worked out of a West End brothel. There she met a 'gentleman' who took her on a trip to France, but for some reason Kelly cut the trip short. 'She said she did not like the part,' Barnett explained, though he could not elaborate.[17] Back in London, Kelly drifted over to the squalid East End, her descent no doubt hastened by her growing dependence on alcohol. She lived for a time in the notorious Ratcliffe Highway, and later somewhere in Stepney, with a man named Morganstone about whom little is known. Afterwards, Kelly went to stay in a lodging house run by a Mrs Carthy in Breezer's Hill, off Pennington Street, a warehouse district also near the docks, not far from where Barnett had lived as a child. At some point, Kelly's father came to London in search of her but she avoided seeing him, possibly out of shame but perhaps out of resentment, as she had once remarked to a friend that her parents had 'discarded' her.[18] Barnett also told of a brother having once visited Kelly and there was mention of an actress cousin in London whom she may have seen on occasion, but otherwise it appears that Kelly had little contact with her family.

Evidently Kelly was working out of a brothel in Pennington Street when she met mason's plasterer Joseph Fleming, with whom she went to live. Indications are that it was a serious relationship and that the couple were planning to get married.[19] Why they never did is unknown, but they seem to have remained on intimate terms long after they parted, and Fleming continued to visit Kelly even while she was living with Barnett, giving her money when he could. Both Barnett and Kelly's friend Julia Venturney noted that Kelly was 'very fond' of Fleming, though Venturney noted that he 'often abused Kelly because she cohabitated with Barnett'.[20]

Joseph Barnett said that he didn't know why Kelly and Fleming split up, but it's very likely that Kelly's drinking was a factor. Her friends and neighbours reported having frequently seen Kelly drunk and, typical of alcoholics, she was the kind of drinker who, once intoxicated, underwent a drastic personality change. '[She] often got drunk,' Julia Venturney testified,[21] while Elizabeth Phoenix, who knew Kelly from Pennington Street, recalled that when sober she 'was one of the most decent and nicest girls you could meet,' but that Kelly became 'very quarrelsome and abusive' when drunk.[22] John McCarthy, Kelly's and Barnett's landlord, concurred. 'She was an exceptionally quiet woman,' he testified at her inquest, 'but when in drink she had more to say.'[23] Barnett, for his part, tended to downplay Kelly's drinking as was his habit. 'When she was with me, I found her of sober habits,' he insisted, though he had to admit that he had seen Kelly drunk 'occasionally ... once or twice in my presence.'[24]

When Joseph Barnett first met Kelly, she was staying at Cooney's Lodging House in Thrawl Street, and was known to walk the streets around Aldgate and Leman Street. From his account of their meeting, it appears that Barnett first came to Kelly as a customer. In response to the question 'Where did you first pick up with her?' Barnett answered: 'In Commercial Street. We then had a drink together, and I made arrangements to see her on the following day – a Saturday. On that day, both of us agreed that we should remain together ... I lived with her, until I left her, on very friendly terms.'[25]

To Joseph Barnett, still single at almost 29,[26] and afflicted with a speech impediment, a young and attractive woman like Kelly must have seemed like a terrific catch, and Barnett wasted no time in asking Kelly to come and live with him.

While Kelly appears to have been less smitten with Barnett than he was with her, there were nevertheless several good reasons for her to accept his offer, the most significant of which was the fact that Barnett would be able to support her. Given the prevailing social and economic climate of the East End at the time, the value of a good, steady earner like Barnett to a woman in Kelly's position was not to be underestimated. Kelly and Barnett could live quite comfortably on Barnett's wages and she would no longer have to walk the streets – in fact, Barnett forbade her to do so. 'Joe Barnett would not let her go on the streets,' Julia Venturney stated. 'He said he would not live with her while she led that course of life.'[27] It was an arrangement that suited Kelly, and, as it turned out, the couple appeared to live almost extravagantly at times, with Barnett spoiling Kelly with gifts 'such as meat and other things, as my hard earnings would allow', as he put it.[28] According to Julia Venturney, Barnett often gave Kelly money as well. 'He was very kind to her,' she declared.[29]

Kelly was probably also swayed to some extent by

Barnett's apparent refinement. Compared to the coarser East End types that Kelly would have been used to, Barnett must have seemed cultivated and distinguished. He had been to school where he had learned how to read and write, and judging from his various statements, Barnett was fairly articulate. He also took considerable pride in his appearance and grooming, as evidenced by the contemporary descriptions and pictures of him. The *Star* noted that Barnett looked 'very respectable for one of his class',[30] while the two small published sketches of him testifying at Kelly's inquest reveal a neatly dressed, almost dapper looking man.[31] In both pictures, Barnett's features are composed, his moustache neatly trimmed. One shows a slightly round-faced man in a bowler hat, with coat and cravat, while the other depicts a slimmer looking, rather handsome fellow, his hair neatly cut, elegantly poised in a coat, waistcoat and cravat, his left elbow resting demurely on a tabletop, alongside his top hat. With the clay pipe that Barnett liked to smoke,[32] his appearance resembles that of a gentleman more than that of a common East End labourer or fish porter – a group notorious for their coarse manners.

If Barnett fancied himself as being superior to his class, then Kelly may have felt much the same about herself. Her youth, looks, background and education set her apart from most of her fellow East End prostitutes, and those who knew Kelly described her as being somewhat aloof. 'She was a young woman who never associated with anyone,' one neighbour testified, noting that she had only spoken to Kelly twice in four months, despite being on first name terms with her.[33] Another, who eventually became friends with Kelly, noted that it had taken a long time for them to get acquainted, despite being near neighbours.[34] Barnett seemed to have responded to this, in that he alone referred to Kelly as Marie Jeanette, the rather elegant if pretentious French appellation of her name, which Kelly may have picked up on her brief trip to France. To everyone else, Kelly was just plain Mary Jane.

All things considered, then, it's not surprising for Kelly to have found herself somewhat intrigued and attracted to this strange, stammering, yet dignified fish porter, who promised to look after her. Not only would he treat her well, but Kelly may have guessed, correctly as it turned out, that she would be the dominant one in their relationship, and would be able to get her way most of the time. This is not to deny the possibility that, initially at least, Kelly may have felt some considerable affection for Barnett, though it was not to last, and by the time their tumultuous relationship had run its twenty-month course, Mary Kelly had reached the point where she could no longer bear Joseph Barnett.[35]

3

'To sink lower was inevitable'

Joseph Barnett took lodgings for himself and Mary Kelly in George Street (where Barnett said he was 'known')[1] but they didn't remain there long, and within a year they moved three more times. From George Street they moved to Paternoster Row, a narrow passway that ran between Dorset Street and Spitalfields Market, on Brushfield Street. According to Barnett, they were evicted from their room there for 'going on a drunk' instead of paying their rent,[2] after which they lived in crowded Brick Lane for a spell, before settling into a tiny room at 13 Miller's Court, 26 Dorset Street, in the early part of 1888.

Although it only stretched for about 150 yards, Dorset Street had a reputation for being one of the worst thoroughfares in the East End (and therefore in all of London). On Charles Booth's poverty map, first published the following year, Dorset Street is depicted almost entirely in black, representing the lowest class, what Booth termed the 'vicious' and 'semi-criminal' element. Despite its small size, Dorset Street housed up to 1,500 people, most of whom lived in its thirteen registered (and several more unregistered) lodging houses, more than in any other street in Whitechapel except for nearby Flower and Dean Street.[3] One of the largest of these, with over 300 beds, was Crossingham's Lodging House at number 35, which was directly opposite Miller's Court.

Due to the large number of lodging houses which featured lamps hanging over their doors and in some of their windows, Dorset Street was fairly well lit at night. It was also a relatively wide street with a pub at each end. One of these, the Britannia, at the corner of Commercial Street, was licensed only to sell beer and was known locally as Ringers', after the proprietors Mr and Mrs Walter Ringer. Just across Commercial Street stood the landmark Christ Church, and on the next corner was the popular Ten Bells pub. A few hundred yards further up Commercial Street was the Royal Cambridge Music Hall, one of about thirty-five such establishments thriving in London at the time, many of them in the East End. Although they would fade from the scene in the twentieth century, due to the imposition of stringent safety regulations and growing competition from cinemas, the music halls were in their heyday in the late nineteenth century, when 2d bought a gallery seat and a night's entertainment which ranged from jugglers and comedians to animal acts and variety troupes. Charlie Chaplin, who was born in South London in 1889, later performed with one such outfit, the Eight Lancashire Lads. The Royal Cambridge, which had a seating capacity of 2,500, had been a popular East End attraction for over twenty years at the time of the Ripper murders, and it would seem likely that Joseph Barnett and Mary Kelly were among its patrons.

Just to the north of Dorset Street, fronting on Commercial Street, was Spitalfields Market, the popular fruit and vegetable market where Joseph may have found work from time to time. A bustling concern, vendors overspilled the two and a half acre enclosure, and as a result many of the surrounding streets were crowded with greengrocers' carts, coster barrows and makeshift stalls, while up until midday Commercial Street was clogged and congested with wagons and carts and assorted traffic on its way to and from the market.

In the wake of Kelly's death, a reporter from the *Observer* went walkabout through Dorset Street and its environs, recording his impressions.[4] 'The passersby are comparatively few, and of the lowest order,' he observed, as he neared Dorset Street, 'navvies, dock labourers, and the heterogeneous class living in the common lodging houses which in this quarter abound. There was one other class in evidence, and this was unquestionably prominent. A large number of ragged and degraded women, women in draggle-tailed skirts and huge hats and feathers, women in gaudy dresses and hatless, women in every stage of drunkenness – these patrolled the street by the dozens, singing their loudest and jostling one another in their degradation.' He stops for a drink in the Britannia, which is filled to overflowing with 'English, Germans, Swedes and Lascars, of all creeds and callings'. Moving on, he notes that 'the pedestrians are fewer and noisier than before, but the drunken men and the dissolute women are as notable as earlier in the evening'. He turns into Dorset Street: 'The people hanging about are not more than a dozen; but most of them are the worse for drink; the majority women. Immediately opposite [Miller's] Court are large common lodging houses. On the pavement outside this lies a gypsy woman, in her arms an infant not more than five months old. The woman is sleepy and quarrelsome, the infant crying... She moves unsteadily on, to lie down in the mud... The whole surroundings is miserable and depressing [with] the existence of such wretchedness ... and the very spectacle of so many luckless females wandering about friendless and homeless.'

A reporter from the *East London Observer* noted much the same thing: 'In truth, [Dorset] Street is almost entirely occupied with the lowest class of lodging houses – registered and unregistered – relieved occasionally by a stable or a cheap provision shop. Leading off the street are a number of small courts ... devoted to an even lower class of people than those who frequent the lodging houses – the lowest class of unfortunates. Immorality is carried on within these houses, openly and with impunity.'[5] ('Unfortunate' was the common Victorian euphemism for a prostitute.) Dorset Street was also known for street gambling and crime. 'It was a toss-up whether it or Ratcliffe Highway could claim the honour of being London's worst crime street,' a contemporary policeman recalled, 'it was known to the local people as "Do as you please".' The police were wary of entering it.[6] Said the *Daily Telegraph*: '[Dorset] Street and the adjoining Paternoster Row ... have now been given up to common lodging houses at 4d and 6d a night ... and to women who have lost every trace of womanliness. The Street and Row are places which the police state are hardly safe for any respectable person by day, and certainly not by night. In such a neighbourhood, it was impossible to rise; to sink lower was inevitable.'[7]

Miller's Court was just past the third building on the right, off Commercial Street. Entrance was via a three-foot wide passageway which led to a small clearing containing a lamp, a dustbin and a water tap, and lined with the backs of tenement houses. Number 13, the room rented by Kelly and Barnett at a rate of 4s 6d per week, was the first through the passageway on the right. It was a tiny room, only about twelve feet square, having been partitioned off from number 26 Dorset Street, a shed owned by the landlord, John McCarthy, and often used as a nightly refuge by homeless women. Because it was separated from the other rooms in Miller's Court, it had its own entrance.

Inside, the room contained little more than a couple of small tables, a chair, a small bed, and a pail and washstand. A small, tattered rug covered part of the otherwise exposed floorboards, and dirty, faded wallpaper covered the walls. The space was so cramped that, when opened, the front door would bang against the bedside table. A narrow bed was positioned against the partitioned wall, to the right upon entering, and on the wall opposite were two windows, the panes of which Mary Kelly would break in her final row with Joseph Barnett. A dirty muslin curtain hung over them. Opposite the door was a fireplace with a mirror and some pottery resting on its mantlepiece and a print hanging over it.[8] All of the furnishings belonged to the landlord.

Among the other tenants in Miller's Court, which was sometimes known as 'McCarthy's Rents', were Henry Maxwell, a night-watchman at a lodging house, and his wife Caroline, Kelly's friend and confidante Julia Venturney, who gave her occupation as a charwoman, and 20-year-old Lizzie Albrook, who was also friendly with Kelly and worked in a Dorset Street doss house, probably as a charwoman as well. There were also a couple of older women who lived on their own – Mary Ann Cox, a widow, and Elizabeth Prater, whose husband had deserted her five years earlier. Cox, described by the *Star* as 'a wretched specimen of East End womanhood',[9] was forthright about being a prostitute, and Prater implied much the same. 'It was a common thing for the women living in the tenements to bring men home with them,' she explained to the *Daily*

Telegraph; 'they could do as they pleased.'[10] John McCarthy denied having any knowledge of his premises being used for immoral purposes. 'Since [Kelly's] murder,' he declared, 'I have discovered that she was an unfortunate, and walked the streets of Aldgate.'[11] In truth, McCarthy probably had a good idea of what his tenants got up to but, like so many East End landlords, he turned a blind eye to any irregularities, so long as he got his rent.[12]

Joseph Barnett claimed that he and Kelly lived together comfortably, but their relationship was in fact punctuated by frequent and sometimes heated rows, which seemed to revolve around Barnett's attempts to control Kelly's habits and behaviour. Indications are that these were invariably sparked by Kelly's drinking, when she would become belligerent. As Julia Venturney observed, 'I have frequently seen [Kelly] the worse for drink, but when she was cross, Joe Barnett would go out and leave her to quarrel alone.'[13] A drunken Kelly is known to have smashed a couple of window panes, presumably by hurling objects at Barnett. That particular quarrel erupted when Kelly disregarded Barnett's repeated objections and brought home two successive prostitute friends of hers to stay in their tiny, cramped room. It turned out to be their final row as a couple and, rather than share his bed with these women, Barnett moved into a lodging house. Yet despite the effect it had on her personality, and the damage it inevitably did to their relationship, there are no indications that Kelly ever reduced her intake of alcohol. As their landlord John McCarthy later told the press, '[Kelly's] habits were irregular, and she often came home at night the worse for drink.'[14] If Barnett protested, it was in vain and he seems to have finally turned a blind eye to her alcoholism (as he was prone to do where Kelly's excesses were concerned), so long as she didn't drink too much in his presence. 'As long as she was with me and had my hard earned wages,' Barnett testified, 'she was sober.'[15]

The impression is that Kelly would go out drinking with her friends, but without Barnett, whose schedule at any rate would have precluded his joining them. To be at work at Billingsgate at 5.00 a.m., Barnett would have had to be up at around 4.00 a.m., and to put in a hard day's work, a solid eight or so hours' sleep would have been essential (and a hangover would have posed a considerable burden). Kelly's time, of course, was entirely her own and she would be going out when Barnett was turning in for the night. As such, their time together was kept to a minimum, which may even have helped to prolong their relationship. When a change in their circumstances later forced them to spend much of their time at home together, Kelly seems to have quickly tired of Barnett, prompting her to remark to her friend Julia Venturney that she 'could not bear' him, despite his kindness. At the same time, Kelly may have been seeking relief from Barnett's suffocating presence when she took in her two prostitute friends to stay with them.

It's difficult to imagine too that Barnett would not have been jealous of the continued visits of Kelly's former lover, Joseph Fleming, who was in the habit of giving Kelly money. Barnett knew that Kelly was still fond of Fleming, and it's not unlikely that they were still lovers; certainly, as Julia Venturney had noted, it was no secret that Fleming wanted Kelly back. Yet, regardless of Barnett's feelings in the matter, their liaisons continued openly.

There is evidence as well that Barnett was critical of Kelly's other friends, several of whom were prostitutes. Despite the fact that he had evidently sought their services in the past, and that Kelly herself had been one, Joseph Barnett harboured a strong dislike of prostitutes and didn't like Kelly associating with them. To him, they were 'immoral women', who had 'gone wrong', and led a 'bad life'.[16] He had blamed Kelly's initial 'downfall' on her prostitute cousin in Cardiff, and her subsequent return to prostitution on the two prostitute friends she took in – the latter, as will be seen, an accusation not borne out by the facts. As Julia Venturney had observed, Barnett was adamant that Kelly should not go back on the streets, and he appears to have taken a good deal of pride in having rescued her from such a life. '[Kelly] told me that she had obtained her livelihood as a prostitute for some considerable time *before I took her from the streets*' (my italics),[17] Barnett declared, further boasting that 'Marie never went on the streets when she was with me'.[18] Although this was not entirely true, there's no question that Barnett couldn't bear for Kelly to be on the streets, and he later cited her return to prostitution as one of the reasons that he left her.

Nevertheless, so long as Barnett continued to bring home a good, regular wage, the relationship endured, and the couple lived together consensually, if not altogether harmoniously. Barnett seemed resigned to accept Kelly on her terms, while their relationship allowed Kelly both stability and security as well as the freedom to more or less do as she pleased. Even their quarrels were turned to her advantage, as Barnett sought to patch things up by buying her gifts. As Barnett explained at Kelly's inquest, 'One minute rowing, and [then] for days and weeks always friendly. Often I bought her things coming home [from work], and whatever it was she always liked it. She was always glad of my fetching her such articles: such as meat and other things, as my hard earnings would allow.'[19]

4

'If any porter shall commit
any offence …'

In April 1888, when Kelly and Barnett had been together for precisely a year and had been living in Miller's Court for a few months, there occurred a precursor to the Jack the Ripper murders, when Emma Smith, a 45-year-old prostitute, was assaulted by a gang of men near the intersection of Wentworth and Osborne Streets. In a vicious attack, she was raped with a blunt instrument and later died of peritonitis. Her killer or killers were never caught. A known drunkard, the widowed Smith had lived in nearby George Street where Kelly and Barnett had first lived together.

A few months later, a second prostitute was murdered in similarly brutal circumstances. Early on the morning of 7 August, the body of Martha Tabram (also known as Martha Turner) was discovered on the first floor landing of the George Yard Buildings (in what is today known as Gunthorpe Street). Tabram had been stabbed thirty-nine times, nine of the wounds having been to the throat. The murder site was only about 100 yards from where Emma Smith had been killed, and, coincidentally, Tabram too had been living in nearby George Street at the time of her death. A heavy-set woman in her late thirties and a hardened alcoholic, Tabram had been in the East End for about thirteen years, the last ten of them spent living on and off with William Turner, a carpenter. In what would almost become a standardized case history for the Ripper victims, their relationship was soured by Tabram's heavy drinking, and Turner had left her three weeks prior to her death. Tabram's husband, a foreman furniture packer from Greenwich named Henry Tabram, had also left her because of her drinking, taking their two sons with him, and hadn't seen his wife for nine years.

On the night she was killed, Tabram had been out soliciting trade with a friend, Mary Ann Connelly, known locally as Pearly Poll, who was a lodger in Crossingham's doss house in Dorset Street. As with the case of Emma Smith, Tabram's assailant was never found.

Mary Kelly's reaction to the two local murders would have been particularly strong, due to the close identification that she must have felt with the victims, with whom she may have been acquainted. Certainly there were several distinct connections between Kelly and the two murdered women, as there would be between Kelly and each of the subsequent Ripper victims. Both Smith and Tabram had lived on George Street (which only ran for about 115 yards) where Kelly and Barnett had lived, and according to Donald Rumbelow,[1] Smith was there when Barnett and Kelly were still living there. Although it's not known if the same held true for Martha Tabram, Kelly may have known her from Dorset Street, as Tabram's friend and soliciting partner Mary Ann Connelly lived in Crossingham's Lodging House, directly opposite from Barnett and Kelly. Like Kelly, both Smith and Tabram were heavy-drinking local prostitutes who may have worked the same streets as well as frequenting the same pubs. With so many areas of their lives overlapping, their paths had to cross from time to time and if Kelly hadn't been personally acquainted with Smith and Tabram she certainly must have known them by sight.

Given the brutal circumstances of Emma Smith's murder, Mary Kelly must have felt considerable relief in the fact that she herself was no longer walking the streets, although by the time Tabram was killed this may no longer have been the case. Around that time, an event transpired that was to alter radically the course and shape of Barnett and Kelly's life together, and set in motion a sequence of events that would culminate some months later with the murder of Mary Kelly at the hands of Jack the Ripper. For reasons unspecified, Joseph Barnett, after working there for over ten years, suddenly lost his job as a fish porter in Billingsgate Market.[2] According to the market bylaws, the prime causes of dismissal were theft, drunkenness and abusive language or behaviour: 'If any Porter ... shall be guilty of dishonesty or drunkenness, or shall use any obscene, filthy, or abusive language, or otherwise misconduct himself in the market or its immediate neighbourhood, it shall be lawful for the [Governing] Committee forthwith to revoke [his licence]'.[3] Lesser infractions of the rules were dealt with by fines or suspension, and had Barnett committed anything other than the gravest offence, he undoubtedly would have received some consideration for his longevity. Even if he felt the work was beneath him, Barnett was nevertheless well aware of how privileged he was to be earning so good a wage, and with so much time behind him, it seems unlikely that he would suddenly act in so rude or disruptive a manner for it to have cost him his job. As it would seem equally out of character for Barnett to have got drunk at work, the probable explanation is that he was let go for stealing, a crime for which there was no choice but to impose the severest penalty. Given how eager he appears to have been to placate Kelly with gifts 'such as meat *and other things*' (my italics) by way of patching up one of their frequent quarrels, chances are that Barnett had been regularly smuggling fish out of the market until he finally got caught.

Whatever the cause of Barnett's dismissal, the loss of his steady, well-paying job changed everything, most especially the nature of his relationship with Mary Kelly. Although he managed to find some labouring jobs (probably at the docks) and was able to get some work around the orange markets,[4] Barnett would no longer be able to support himself and Kelly in anything approaching the comfort that they had become accustomed to. Charles Booth calculated that the average casual dock labourer earned about 6s 3d per week – a sum far below the £2–£3 a week or so that Barnett had been making at Billingsgate Market. Nor could he have earned much more jobbing around the fruit markets. With a weekly rent of 4s 6d, Barnett's earnings would scarcely have covered the couple's living expenses, let alone enabled them to afford the 'luxuries' they had got used to, such as the gifts and money that Barnett used to give Kelly, much of which, presumably, went to support her drink habit. If Kelly wanted anything other than the barest necessities for survival, she would have to come up with the money herself, which meant a return to prostitution. 'When work was plentiful,' the *Daily Telegraph* reported, 'the pair seemed to have paid their way honourably; but earnings were often irregular, and then it is to be feared that the woman resorted to the streets.'[5]

5

'She used to ask me to read about the murders'

With the loss of his job, Joseph Barnett suddenly found himself in a frustrating, even desperate, predicament: he hated Kelly to be on the streets, but had to face the fact that it was his own failure and inadequacy as a provider that had forced her back into prostitution. It was, of course, a terrible blow to his pride and self-esteem, and Barnett must have been tormented by the thought of Kelly walking the streets and sleeping with other men. Even worse, however, Barnett had to realize that by forfeiting his role as breadwinner he had relinquished what was without a doubt his greatest asset and his strongest hold on Kelly, as far as she was concerned. Even though at some point she'd grown sick of him, Kelly nevertheless continued to live with Barnett, primarily because his ability to provide for them so well had more than compensated for whatever drawbacks Kelly found in being with him. But if Barnett could no longer support them adequately, putting Kelly in the position of having to fend for herself by going back on the streets (and perhaps even having to support Barnett to some degree), they both knew that it was only a matter of time before Kelly would ask herself just what use, really, did she have for him? Kelly was slipping away, Barnett realized, but short of finding another well-paying job – a virtual impossibility given the massively high unemployment – there was little else he could do to keep her. As Barnett later explained to Inspector Abberline in a telling remark that seemed to sum up the nature of their relationship, his subsequent separation from Kelly came 'in consequence of [my] not earning enough money to give her, and her resorting to prostitution'.[1] From the time Barnett lost his job, their co-habitation had but another three months or so to run, and Kelly's life only slightly longer, though there seems little doubt that their relationship would have ended even sooner had not Jack the Ripper so severely disrupted the lives of almost everyone in the East End.

It may have been that Joseph Barnett found what he perceived to be a way out of his dilemma through Mary Kelly's strong reaction to the deaths of Emma Smith and Martha Tabram – a frightening occurrence at any time, but a particularly ominous one now that Kelly herself had suddenly been forced back into prostitution. She must have felt especially vulnerable being on the streets at that time and at some point she voiced her fears and anxieties to Barnett. 'She used to ask me to read about the murders,' he testified at Kelly's inquest, 'and I used to bring [the newspapers] all home and read them. If I did not bring one, she would get it herself and ask me whether the murderer was caught. I used to tell her everything of what was in the paper.'[2]

Here, then, was a way for Barnett to keep Kelly off the streets, and at the same time give her need of him again. Desperately afraid that he was losing her, and simultaneously motivated by an overpowering sexual jealousy (his anguish intensified by an acute sense of frustration, helplessness and low self-esteem), Joseph Barnett determined to *frighten* Kelly off the streets and at the same time force her to turn back to him for physical and emotional support. He would accomplish this by following the example of the unknown slayers of Emma Smith and Martha Tabram and savagely butcher Kelly's fellow prostitutes, leaving them lying out in the open, their guts literally ripped out, for all to see. In Barnett's mind, these women were worthless anyway, and he blamed them for Kelly's earlier (and subsequent) 'downfalls'. Later, he would compound his actions by boasting of his grisly cunning and hatred of prostitutes in a macabre series of letters to the press. But whatever Joseph Barnett's original intent, the Jack the Ripper murders quickly gained a life and momentum of their own, mushrooming into a Grand Guignol spectacle of terror on a scale far greater than anything Barnett or anyone could ever have imagined, as the East End and much of London were pitched into an unprecedented state of panic, madness and hysteria.

6

'I'll soon get my doss money...'

Jack the Ripper first struck just over three weeks after the death of Martha Tabram, no more than a few weeks at the most after Barnett lost his job. His victim was Mary Ann Nichols, a 43-year-old, hard-drinking local prostitute who had been knocking around the East End for many years. Sometimes known as 'Polly', Nichols was a short woman with greying hair and missing five of her front teeth. Like Tabram, she had been married and in fact had had five children, but her heavy drinking and irresponsible behaviour resulted in numerous separations from her husband, who finally left her for good in 1880 or 1881. Since that time, Nichols had lived for a short while with her father and had worked briefly as a domestic, until she absconded with £3 worth of goods from her employers. Mostly, though, she had been in and out of workhouses or out on the streets, having once been picked up for sleeping rough in Trafalgar Square. At the time of her death, Nichols had been dividing her time between a lodging house at 18 Thrawl Street and one called the White House in Flower and Dean Street.

In the early morning hours of Friday, 31 August, Nichols

51

was turned out of her lodgings because she didn't have the 4d necessary for a bed. It was a sum that she had already had three times that day but each time had spent it on drink. Despite the late hour, Nichols thought she'd be able to raise that amount yet again that night, telling the lodging house deputy, 'I'll soon get my doss money,' as she headed out on the streets in search of custom. At precisely 2.30 a.m. in Osborne Street, she ran into Emily Holland, an elderly woman with whom Nichols had previously lodged in Thrawl Street. Seeing that Nichols was drunk, Holland suggested that she come back with her to Thrawl Street, but Nichols still hadn't come up with her doss money. When Holland last saw her, she was staggering drunkenly down Whitechapel Road.

At 3.45 a.m., a carman on his way to work discovered Nichols' body, her eyes still open, lying in front of the gates to a stable in Bucks Row (now largely demolished). Situated just behind the Whitechapel train station, Bucks Row then ran roughly parallel to Whitechapel Road for several hundred yards, from Thomas Street to Brady Street, at one point forking around a Board School into two streets. The body lay just opposite an office building called Essex Wharf, itself adjacent to the sprawling Spitalfields Coal Depot. Also fronting on to the narrow street were a manure works, a dressmaker's, a wool warehouse, a cap manufacturer, a clergy house and several occupied ter-raced houses. Nearby was the Jews' Cemetery and the Friends Burial Grounds. Behind the stables, on Winthrop Street, was a horse slaughterhouse called Barber's Yard which was busy throughout the night, though none of the workers reported having seen or heard anything unusual. Similarly, a gateman on duty at the nearby Great Eastern Railway reported a quiet and uneventful night. Nor did the regular police patrol of the area note anything peculiar, and two residents of Bucks Row (one of whom was awake for most of the night, while the other claimed to be a light sleeper) both said that they had heard nothing out of the ordinary.[1] A doctor summoned to the scene, perhaps feeling resentful at having been awakened so early in the morning, lingered only long enough to pronounce the woman dead and order that the body be taken to the local mortuary (actually a makeshift affair in the back room of a workhouse). The small amount of blood where the body had lain was washed away.

It was only at the 'mortuary' that the true extent of Nichols' injuries became evident when it was discovered that she had suffered such severe cuts to the abdomen that her bowels were protruding. Dr Llewelyn, who had been roused from his sleep the night before, was again sent for and on the following day he conducted a thorough post-mortem. An inquest was convened that same day, presided over by Coroner Wynne Baxter and attended by Detective Inspector Frederick Abberline, who had been recalled from Scotland Yard to coordinate the investigation.

Dr Llewelyn testified in great detail as to the nature of Nichols' injuries. There were bruises on both sides of her face and two cuts across her throat, one eight inches long, the other half that length. Both were so deep that they reached to the vertebrae. There were several slashes about the abdomen, one a deep, jagged gash on the left side that ran from the bottom of the ribs almost to the pelvis. On the right-hand side of the abdomen were several cuts running downward. There were also two stab wounds to the genitals. Dr Llewelyn concluded that the killer had used a very sharp knife, about six to eight inches in length, with a thin, narrow blade, not unlike the kind used by a cork cutter or a shoemaker. The path of the wounds from left to right told him that the killer was left-handed, and it was Dr

Llewelyn's belief that he had stood in front of his victim when he struck, pressure from his hand causing the bruises on Nichols' face. It appeared that she had been swiftly overpowered, as there was no evidence that Nichols had put up much of a struggle. The police initially suspected the murder to be the work of local extortionists who preyed on prostitutes, such as the so-called 'High Rip' gang, but this theory was soon dropped in favour of a lone killer. There was also some brief speculation that the murder had been committed elsewhere, due to the small amount of blood on the spot where the body was found and the fact that no one in the immediate vicinity had seen or heard anything. As it turned out, Nichols' clothing had absorbed a good deal of blood and the idea was dismissed after considering how difficult it would have been for the killer to have carted Nichols' corpse for any distance without being observed or leaving some kind of trail.

In fact, a dimly lit, quiet and empty street like Bucks Row, just off a busy main thoroughfare, was just the sort of spot where a prostitute like Nichols would have taken someone she believed to be a prospective customer for a brief, cheap liaison. On the other hand, she may have given up on the idea of finding custom and a bed and drunkenly staggered off the main street in the hope of catching a few hours undisturbed sleep before daybreak. Either way, Nichols' intoxication and weariness, and the dark, isolated locale, made her an especially vulnerable target and the ideal victim for someone about to commit his first murder, a task further facilitated by the fact that Nichols' killer may have been a vaguely familiar local figure whose presence would have put her at ease.

Despite the fact that there were significant and considerable differences in their circumstances, the press was quick to link Mary Ann Nichols' death with the still unsolved murders of Emma Smith and Martha Tabram, giving the false impression that a single hand was responsible for all three crimes, something that helped spread the growing sense of fear and anxiety that was already beginning to take root in the East End.

The *East London Advertiser* caught the local mood in the wake of Nichols' death: 'The crowds of people which have since daily assembled at the scene of the murder have been reduced to a condition of almost abject terror. They have talked almost in whispers, and a panic-stricken cry has gone up from the inhabitants and tradesmen in the neighbourhood of Bucks Row for more police protection'.[2] 'At every street corner', noted the *Daily News*, 'gossips cluster around anybody who could give the fullest particulars of the inquest, and the end of Bucks Row is the scene of eager debate as to the probabilities of discovering the criminal. Groups of hard featured, sorrowful looking women clustered together and bent over what they supposed to be the bloodstained paving stones, and told strange stories ... Very rarely has anything occurred even in this quarter of London that has created so profound a sensation'.[3]

Both Dr Llewelyn and Coroner Baxter were of the opinion that the killer had possessed some anatomical knowledge, and with the imposing structure of London Hospital looming over the murder site just 100 yards away, the enduring image of a sinister, black-clad fiend, clutching his medical bag as he stalked silently through the shadowy, fog-filled, cobblestoned streets and alleys of Whitechapel in search of his prey, was born.[4]

And he was about to strike again.

7

'His eyes are small and glittering ...'

Jack the Ripper's second victim was 'Dark' Annie Chapman, a long-time habitué of various Dorset Street doss houses and, according to one report, a friend of Mary Kelly's.[1] In the months prior to her death, Chapman had been living in Crossingham's Lodging House at 35 Dorset Street, having previously stayed at the doss house at 30 Dorset Street. There she was known as Annie Sievey, as her common-law husband was a sieve maker known as Jack Sievey. Lately, Chapman had been keeping company with a man called Edward Stanley, believed to be an army pensioner and described as superior to the usual lodging house resident. Stanley, then serving in the militia, had been with Chapman for about two years and spent his weekends with her. When he heard of her death, he was reluctant to come forward, believing that his involvement with her made him an automatic suspect. When he did surface, however, he was able to satisfy the police as to his innocence.

Chapman was a stout woman, 47 or 48 years old, five feet tall with light brown, wavy hair going grey. She had blue eyes, a dark complexion and a distinct, flat nose. According to the *Daily Telegraph*, she was 'well formed and of good looks'.[2] Like Tabram and Nichols before her, Chapman had been married. She had had two children, one of whom was crippled and in a home, while the other lived in France. She had been separated from her husband John, a coachman in Windsor, for several years, possibly because of her drinking. Unlike the other victims thus far, Chapman wasn't an habitual drunk but she did have a fondness for rum. She liked to get drunk on Saturday nights and was easily intoxicated. As her friend Amelia Farmer recalled, Chapman 'could not take much without getting drunk'.[3]

Those who knew Annie Chapman liked her. She was described as a quiet, friendly woman who got along well with others and wasn't coarse, like so many women in her circumstances were. According to Farmer, who also lodged at 35 Dorset Street and had known Chapman for five years, she was 'a very respectable woman, [who] never used bad language'.[4] Nor did Chapman frequent the streets, only turning to prostitution now and then as a last resort.

From the time they separated, Chapman's husband gave her a regular allowance of 10s per week until his sudden death in December 1886. It was then that 'she seemed to give way altogether', according to Farmer.[5] Suddenly faced with the prospect of having to support herself completely, Chapman tried her hand at a number of things. She sold matches and flowers on the streets and would take her crochet work around the neighbourhood. On Fridays, she often went to a market in Stratford where she sold whatever she could. On the weekend that she was killed, she had hoped to borrow a pair of boots from her sister to enable her to go hopping in Kent. As Farmer testified, Chapman was 'a very industrious woman when sober'.[6]

In the early hours of Saturday, 8 September, Timothy Donovan, the deputy at Crossingham's Lodging House, turned Chapman out as she lacked the necessary 8d for her regular bed.[7] Donovan saw that Chapman was the worse for drink, though not terribly so. 'I shall soon be back,' Chapman announced, eerily echoing Polly Nichols' last words. 'Don't let the bed.'[8]

At that point, Chapman was desperate enough to take to the streets. She had spent all her money on drink and hadn't been feeling very well of late, having just spent several days in the infirmary as a result of bruises and a black eye suffered in a brawl with another woman. Some medication was later found on her person, though that may have been to treat something more serious. According to Dr George Bagster Phillips, the divisional surgeon of police who conducted the post-mortem, Chapman was suffering from a disease that affected the membranes of both her brain and her lungs – most likely tubercular meningitis, possibly meningovascular syphilis.[9] That would explain her recent pale appearance (noted by her friend Amelia Farmer in her inquest testimony) and why Chapman had been feeling too ill to make her regular Friday trip to the Stratford market. Had she done so, she might have been spared a horrible death at the hands of the man soon to be known as Jack the Ripper.

Chapman's mutilated remains were found at around 6.00 a.m. on the morning of 8 September, in the backyard of a three-storey tenement building in Hanbury Street, a narrow, busy thoroughfare that still stretches today for almost half a mile from Commercial Street to Baker's Row, near the beginning of Bucks Row. The spot where her body was found, behind number 29, was about a five-minute walk from Dorset Street and even closer to Great Pearl Street where Joseph Barnett had lived as a boy. Similarly,

Heneage Street, where Barnett lived shortly after obtaining his porter's licence in 1878, was only about 150 yards away from the murder site.

Hanbury Street was colour coded light blue and violet on Charles Booth's poverty map, meaning that the residents were a mixture of the poor and relatively comfortable. 'The neighbourhood is described as a very rough one,' wrote the *Daily Telegraph*, 'and respectable people are accustomed to avoid it. It is inhabited by dock labourers, market porters, the tenants of common lodging houses, and a certain number of cabinet makers, who supply the furniture establishments of Curtain Road ... In these squalid parts of the metropolis, aggravated assaults, attended by flesh wounds from knives, are frequently met with, and men and women become accustomed to scenes of violence. The people do not appear, however, to interfere with each other's affairs unless provoked ... Late at night, there are many scenes of degradation and immorality'.[10]

Still, Hanbury Street was an enterprising little road; the two- and three-storey buildings that were crammed into its half mile were home to a hundred, mostly small, diverse businesses. Among these were a couple of auctioneers, some bakers, a bootmaker, a bottle manufacturer, a brace maker, various carmen and cheesemongers, two churches, a cigar maker and a cigar box maker, a coach builder, some coffee houses, a cowkeeper, a cutler, a farrier, several hairdressers, a hatter, a hosier, a horsehair manufacturer, an iron merchant, a newsagent, an oil refiner, a peel manufacturer, several pubs, a rent and debt collector, a sewing school, a stick manufacturer, a surgeon, a toymaker, an undertaker, a waterproof clothing manufacturer, a veterinary surgeon and a couple of zinc workers. Several of the businesses, such as Ellis & Lazarus Friedman's Cabinet Makers, the fried fish dealer Harris Levy, the piece broker

Simon Goldberg, pickle worker David Goodman, and the tailor Isaac Goldberg among others, were Jewish concerns, reflecting the large Jewish enclave in the area.

The Jewish presence in the East End had intensified in the latter half of the nineteenth century, when tens of thousands of Jews fled the pogroms, persecution and poverty of Eastern Europe and Russia and settled in the East End, where they joined their Western European brethren, developing over the years a thriving, close-knit community. Charles Booth estimated that there were 45,000 Jews living in Tower Hamlets, with almost two-thirds of them situated in Whitechapel.[11] According to Booth, Petticoat Lane, Goulston Street, Hanbury Street, Fashion Street, Pelham Street, Booth Street and Old Montague Street were heavily populated Jewish areas.

Despite the comfort or prosperity of some, most Jews, like their gentile neighbours, weren't immune to the suffering and hardships of East End life, and Booth estimated that three-quarters of the Jewish population were moderately poor or worse. Nevertheless, this didn't spare them the wrath or resentment of the indigenous East Enders, who viewed the Jews as strange and secretive foreign intruders, who looked, spoke and acted differently from them. The Jews, as they saw it, held strange beliefs and practised bizarre, suspicious and hedonistic rites, such as the ritual slaughter of animals in food preparation. This was accomplished via swiftly slitting the beast's throat – a practice that assumed particularly sinister overtones in the wake of the Ripper murders. Furthermore, in the over-crowded East End, beleaguered by high unemployment, fierce job competition and a lack of decent, affordable housing, Jews were seen to be taking jobs away from the locals by their alleged willingness to work for lower wages, while Jewish manufacturers were accused of flooding the marketplace with inferior products that sold at cheaper prices than the quality goods produced by the English. As such, the Ripper murders released an angry tide of pent-up anti-Semitic feeling that often took violent form. The *East London Observer* was one of several papers that reported on 'A Riot Against the Jews': 'On Saturday [8 September] in several quarters of East London, the crowds who had assembled in the streets [following the discovery of Annie Chapman's body] began to assume a very threatening attitude towards the Hebrew population of the district. It was repeatedly asserted that no Englishman could have perpetrated such a horrible crime as that of Hanbury Street, and that it must have been done by a Jew – and forthwith the crowds proceeded to threaten and abuse such of the unfortunate Hebrews they found in the streets.'[12] Extra police were summoned to the scene, and though sporadic fisticuffs broke out, they managed to keep the violence under control. A few weeks later, when a cryptic message seemingly implicating the Jews in the killings allegedly appeared, Police Commissioner Sir Charles Warren ordered it immediately erased, before it could even be photographed and examined, lest it provoke further anti-Jewish outbreaks.

For a time, the police, press and public all became curiously obsessed with a Jewish cobbler said to be known locally as 'Leather Apron', a nickname derived from his work garment and one shared with many other tradesmen. Their fixation developed to the point where Leather Apron took on the stature of an almost archetypal evil. 'His expression is sinister,' warned *Lloyds Weekly London Newspaper*, 'and seems to be full of terror for the women who describe it. His eyes are small and glittering. His lips are usually parted in a grin which is not only not reassuring, but excessively repellent. He is a slip maker by trade, but does not work. His business is blackmailing women late at night. He has never cut anybody, so far as is known, but always carries a leather knife, presumably as sharp as leather knives are wont to be. This knife a number of women have seen. His name nobody knows, but all are united in the belief that he is a Jew, or of Jewish parentage, his face being a marked Hebrew type. But the most singular characteristic of the man is the universal statement that in moving about he never makes any noise... His uncanny peculiarity to [women] is that they never see him or know of his presence until he is close by them... "Leather Apron" never attacks a man. He runs away on the slightest appearance of rescue.'[13] Other accounts added that Leather Apron was also known as the 'mad nob', and that he possessed the highly unusual habit of walking without bending his knees.

It fell to the *Daily Telegraph* to provide the voice of reason. '[Leather Apron] has been repeatedly described by women who have asserted that they have been accosted by him, but it is by no means certain that all the complainants refer to the same individual. So much has been talked about Leather Apron in the neighbourhood that many persons who had never previously heard of his doings appear to have accustomed themselves to the idea that they had actually seen him'.[14]

A detective who knew Leather Apron was assigned to bring him in, and not long afterwards a frightened 38-year-old man named John Piser (or Pizer), also known as Leather Apron, was arrested. But rather than being the dangerous, leering, stiff-kneed fiend of popular imagination, Piser turned out to be a weak, frail and sickly man who spent much of his time in hospital. He stood only 5ft 4ins tall, was of slight build and said to be of dim intelligence.[15]

Although he was Jewish, Piser had been born in London and thus spoke without an accent, unlike many of his brethren. None of his alleged female victims was able to pick him out of a line-up, and those who knew Piser testified to his good character and helped establish that he was elsewhere during the times of the Nichols and Chapman murders. His innocence thus established, Piser was released the following day without having been charged, and was given the opportunity to clear his name by testifying at Chapman's inquest. But the damage had already been done and Piser continued to be harassed by people he encountered, once even being attacked in the streets. According to Paul Begg, he died in 1897 of 'gastroenteritis collapse'.[16]

Some came to the Jews' defence. 'If the panic-stricken people who cry "Down with the Jews!" because they imagine that a Jew has committed the horrible and revolting crimes knew anything at all of the Jewish horror of blood itself ... they would pause before they invoked destruction on the head of a peaceful and law-abiding people,' reasoned the *East London Observer*. 'Since the return of the Jews to England in 1649, only two Jews have been hanged for murder ... a very remarkable record. That the beast who has made East London a terror is not a Jew, I feel assured. There is something too horrible, too unnatural, too un-Jewish, I would say, in the terrible series of murders for an Israelite to be the murderer.'[17] Still, anti-Semitism lingered in the East End throughout that autumn and beyond, causing the Jewish community to announce the offer of its own reward for the killer's capture.

Number 29 Hanbury Street contained eight rooms and was home to fifteen people. The building was leased by an elderly widow, Mrs Richardson, who ran a small packing-

case manufacturing business on the premises, and let out
the other rooms. She maintained a steady clientele, some
of her lodgers having been there for as long as twelve years.
Among them were a maker of lawn-tennis boots and his
retarded son, two spinster sisters who worked as cigar
makers, a retired woman whom Mrs Richardson kept on
out of charity, and a woman who ran a cat's meat shop from
her ground floor rooms.[18] Most of the remaining tenants
worked in Billingsgate or Spitalfields Markets. 'Some of
the carmen leave home as early as 1.00 a.m.,' Mrs
Richardson explained, 'while others go out at four and five,
so that the place is open all night, and anyone can get in.'[19]
The yard where Chapman's body was found was reached
via a separate entrance, and its easy access at all hours
made it a popular spot for prostitutes to take their clients to
late at night for a quick liaison. 'I have often turned them
out,' Mrs Richardson's son, John, testified at Chapman's
inquest. 'We had them on our first floor as well, on the
landing.'[20] Mrs Richardson, who ran weekly prayer meetings on the premises, was incensed at the suggestion that
her building could be used for immoral purposes, but her
son stuck to his story, telling a *Lloyd's* reporter that the
practice had been going on for years. Annie Chapman,
apparently, had been familiar with the property and Mrs
Richardson said she recognized her as 'the dark woman
that used to come around with cotton and crochet work'.
Lest any should doubt her charitable nature, Mrs Richardson
added that she had bought such items off Chapman 'many
times when she has said that she has been hard up'.[21]

Annie Chapman's body was discovered by John Davis,
an elderly carman employed at Leadenhall Market, who
lived on the top floor with his wife. According to the
Observer, the sight of the remains caused Davis 'to go
shrieking afright into the street' to fetch the police.[22]

Inspector Joseph Chandler was the first policeman to arrive on the scene. 'I saw the body of a woman lying on the ground on her back,' he recalled. 'Her head was towards the wall ... the face turned to the right side, and the left arm was resting on the left breast. The right hand was lying down the right side. Deceased's legs were drawn up, and the clothing was above the knees. A portion of the intestines, still connected with the body, were lying above the right shoulder, with some pieces of skin. There were also some pieces of skin on the left shoulder.'[23] Said Mrs Davis, who nearly fainted at the sight: 'The poor woman's throat was cut, and the inside of her body was lying beside her ... [She] was quite ripped open.'[24]

Police surgeon George Bagster Phillips, testifying at the inquest, described the lacerations to Chapman's throat, one of which went entirely around her neck and cut into the bone, in a possible attempt to sever her head. Cause of death, he concluded, was loss of blood as a result of this wound. No cries had been heard, and as there were again no signs of a struggle, the impression was that Chapman had been taken completely by surprise and was swiftly overpowered. As Phillips saw it, the assailant first grabbed Chapman's neck and chin, partially suffocating her, before slitting her throat. The path of the cuts was again from the left to the right, and there was no doubt that Mary Ann Nichols' killer was responsible for this crime too. Phillips was in agreement with Dr Llewelyn and Coroner Baxter in believing that the killer possessed some degree of anatomical knowledge, as evidenced by his skilled removal of certain unnamed portions of Chapman's body.

Apparently hoping to minimize the lurid sensationalism that the case had already attracted and not further alarm the public, Dr Phillips wouldn't specify what the missing portions of Chapman's body were – not even to Inspector

Abberline. He was also reluctant to elaborate on the mutilations that had been inflicted on the body, arguing that the purpose of the inquest was solely to determine the cause of death and as that had already been established he saw no reason to detail any further atrocities. He did, however, brief the medical journal, the *Lancet*, in some detail. 'The abdomen had been entirely laid open,' they reported, 'the intestines, severed from their mesenteric attachments, had been lifted out of the body, and placed on the shoulder of the corpse; whilst from the pelvis, the uterus and its appendages with the upper portion of the vagina and the posterior two-thirds of the bladder, had been entirely removed. No trace of these parts could be found.'[25] The weapon responsible for this carnage, Phillips testified, was 'a very sharp knife, probably with a thin, narrow blade, and at least six to eight inches in length, probably longer'.[26] This was essentially the same description of the weapon used on Mary Ann Nichols. A cobbler's knife, such as that used by Leather Apron, wouldn't have been long enough and it was determined that the cuts hadn't been made with bayonet or anything commonly found in a doctor's kit. More likely, it was felt, a slaughter-man's knife may have been employed, though at the time no one thought to suggest that perhaps the type of knife used by Billingsgate porters to clean fish might have been responsible. Some time later, however, Dr D. G. Halsted, who was positioned at London Hospital during the time of the Ripper murders, and subsequently spent time in the North Sea with the Mission to the Deep Sea Fishermen, became convinced that this had indeed been the case. 'The great surgical skill which [Jack the Ripper] used to apply to his female victims', he wrote in his memoirs, 'could easily have been picked up by a man accustomed to boning and filleting fish.'[27]

8

'Life ain't no great things with many of us, but we don't all want to be murdered'

'Another Horrible Murder in Whitechapel!' the *Standard* had cried on 1 September, after the death of Mary Ann Nichols. 'Another Brutal Murder!' said the *Observer*, while *Reynolds Newspaper* opted for 'Another Fiendish Murder!' 'A Fourth Woman Foully Mutilated' reported the *Pall Mall Gazette* after Annie Chapman's murder (referring to the earlier murders of Smith and Tabram). This latest killing, they wrote, had created 'a painful sensation' in the East End, 'a state of wild excitement bordering on panic'. 'Ghastly', commented the *Telegraph*. 'This latest crime,' *The Times* declared, 'even surpasses the others in ferocity.' 'Yesterday morning [Saturday, 8 September],' wrote the *Observer*, 'the neighbourhood of Whitechapel was horrified to a degree bordering on panic by the discovery of another barbarous murder of a woman at 29 Hanbury Street.'

So began the sort of articles that Joseph Barnett would read to Mary Kelly at her urging. If the coverage was at times sensational and excitable, this was in part a reflection of the increasingly eerie and unsettling effect the murders were having on the community, and in part because the murders were so different from anything that had ever happened in London before, or anywhere in England for that matter. Although there could be no denying that the East End, and Whitechapel especially, had a well-deserved reputation for being a violent, dangerous and unsavoury place, murder itself was actually a surprisingly rare occurrence. In fact, in 1887, the year before the Ripper murders, out of eighty recorded homicides in London, *not a single one took place in Whitechapel*. According to statistics collected in the 'Annual Report on the Sanitary Conditions of Whitechapel' by Joseph Loane, the Medical Officer for Health, there were seventy-one violent deaths in the district in 1887, of which sixty-nine were accidental. Most were the result of suffocation, fractures and contusions, and burns and scalds. The remaining two deaths were classified as suicides, one by drowning, the other a poisoning.[1]

In all, a total of 1,602 deaths were registered in Whitechapel in 1887. The highest percentage of these came as a result of respiratory diseases, followed closely by the constitutional diseases, which included phthisis, cancer, tuberculosis, meningitis and rheumatism. Together, these two categories accounted for over 45% of all Whitechapel deaths, a figure 5½% higher than the overall London rate.

The third greatest cause of death in the district was zymotic disease, such as diarrhoea and dysentery, diphtheria, venereal disease, and measles, scarlet fever and whooping cough, with the latter three ailments claiming 109 victims between them. The next greatest killer in

Whitechapel was disease of the nervous system, such as apoplexy, epilepsy and convulsions (185 victims), followed by disease of the circulatory system (111 fatalities), and disease of the digestive system (105 deaths), which included liver disease, peritonitis, enteritis, dentition, and quinsy or sore throat. There were eighty-six Whitechapel deaths resulting from premature births or old age, and, following the aforementioned sixty-nine violent deaths, forty-six people died from urinary system diseases. All the remaining totals were in single figures. In all, the report listed twenty classes of death for Whitechapel in 1887, but out of all of these, only the homicide category showed no entries whatsoever.

Nor were that year's statistics a fluke. There hadn't been any murders in Whitechapel in 1886 either, out of sixty-eight committed in London, while the reports for 1889 and 1890 each show one murder per year in the district, out of totals of seventy-nine and seventy-four respectively for all of London.

By mid-September 1888, however, four women had died in the most grotesque and horrifying circumstances imaginable, and the murders were seen to be increasing in both frequency and ferocity. The gruesome nature of Annie Chapman's death had made it painfully clear that this was no ordinary series of murders, and East Enders could hardly be faulted for succumbing to the darker fears aroused by the chilling evil that was still out there somewhere, no doubt seeking its next victim. No one could recall anything like it having happened before. Some of the older locals remembered the 1831 murder of an Italian boy named Carlo Ferrair, or Fariere, who had eked out a living by displaying various curios such as white mice to tourists in front of St Paul's Cathedral. Ferrair was subsequently abducted by four men who murdered him and tried to sell

71

his corpse to several hospitals. One of the men wrenched the boy's jaw from his mouth and sold it to a dentist for 12s, with bits of pink gum still clinging to its teeth. Others were reminded of the exploits of the infamous graverobbers/killers Burke and Hare, or the notorious Sawney Bean family who lived in an isolated cave in rural Scotland where they waylaid travellers whom they then ate. The large interbred family – Bean and his wife produced fourteen children, who gave them over thirty grandchildren – survived this way for twenty-five years and were said to have killed over a thousand people before they were caught by King James's men and summarily executed. Without the benefit of a trial, the Bean men were dismembered, their private parts tossed into a fire, and left to bleed to death in front of their women, who were themselves burned to death.[2] Comparisons were even made with the stories of the American mystery writer Edgar Allan Poe, particularly *The Murder in the Rue Morgue* in which a series of gruesome killings turned out to have been committed by an ape. But horrifying as these and other cases had been, none of them quite roused the deep-seated terror, unprecedented mass hysteria and bizarre reactions that the Whitechapel murders produced throughout their duration and beyond.

Over the weekend of the Chapman killing, anxious, agitated crowds again gathered outside the murder site, and surrounded the mortuary where the body lay. Others besieged local police stations or packed into the Ten Bells pub on Commercial Street where Chapman was believed to have had her last drink.

The scenes in Hanbury Street were the most frenetic. Businesses were forced to close as thousands of people blocked the street, obliging the police to make frequent charges into the crowd to disperse them. 'The streets were ... swarmed with people,' reported *Reynolds Newspaper*, 'who stood about in groups and excitedly discussed the details of the murder ... Great anxiety is felt for the future. While the murderer is at large, they cannot feel safe.'[3] The crowds had come from all over London and consisted of all kinds of people. 'Thousands of respectably dressed people visited the scene [of the crime],' wrote the *Standard*, noting among them 'two prominent members of the peerage'.[4]

Some were quick to capitalize on the situation. Half-a-dozen enterprising costermongers hurriedly set up stalls in the streets and did a thriving business, while the residents of 29 Hanbury Street charged the eager throngs a penny apiece for a view of the actual murder site. Several hundred people reportedly paid the fee until the police put a stop to the practice. Nearby, the owner of a small waxworks exhibit was said to have dabbed a few strokes of red paint on to an already existing display, instantly transforming it into a popular new attraction.

Rumours passed quickly through the crowds. The most startling of these claimed that the killer had left a message on the wall of 29 Hanbury Street that read: 'I have now done three, and intend to do nine more and give myself up'.[5] Some importance was attached to the discovery of what appeared to be a trail of blood leading through the neighbouring yards in Hanbury Street, but closer examination revealed the substance to be faecal matter. When word spread that a woman had been 'ripped up' behind London Hospital, there was a mad dash to the scene, though there was nobody to be found. Another disturbance resulted from the anguished cries of a distressed woman who moaned that Chapman had been her mother. She attracted great sympathy from the assembled crowds, until they realized that she was deluded. She struggled violently with the police until a friend led her away. In nearby Whitechapel Road, another commotion was caused by an ambulance rushing towards London Hospital. Sensing another victim, an inflamed crowd pursued the vehicle, though it turned out to contain a man who had attempted suicide in an unrelated matter. Similarly, when the police apprehended a man near Commercial Street, the rumour quickly spread that the killer had been caught, causing hundreds of people to rush to the Commercial Street Police Station where they learned that the man had merely been a thief.

An incident in Spitalfields Market also attracted an animated crowd. In this instance, a man suddenly threw a woman to the ground and began kicking her and slashing wildly at her with a knife. When the police arrived, they had to rescue the man from an angry mob who were calling for him to be lynched. Incredibly, the man turned out to be blind and the woman was his regular escort. As *Reynolds Newspaper* explained, with considerable understatement, 'The blind man is described as having a most ungovernable temper'.[6]

Equally strange was what *Lloyds Newspaper* termed 'A River Mystery', when a human arm was found entangled amongst some debris floating on the Thames. A closer inspection revealed that the limb had been recently severed from the body of a young woman whose decomposed torso was found several weeks later on a building site.[7]

People saw the supposed killer everywhere. In Brick Lane, two startled passersby were singled out and attacked by a mob suspecting them of being the killers simply because they didn't like the look of them. At other times, the killer took on the sinister guise of a sneering, menacing ruffian, sometimes brandishing a long, deadly knife. In the Prince Albert pub (known locally as the 'clean house') on the corner of Brushfield and Stewart Streets, the landlady Mrs Fiddymont let her imagination get the better of her when a stranger stopped there for a quick pint. His rough appearance and the fact that his hat was drawn low over his eyes aroused Mrs Fiddymont's suspicions, as did what appeared to be spots of blood on the back of his hands. Upon seeing the 'startling and terrifying' look in his eyes, she became frightened and when the man left after downing his drink in a single gulp, Mrs Fiddymont had him followed by a patron, who reported back that the man had had a 'nervous and frightened way about him' and eyes 'wild as a hawk's'. More than likely, the man was merely a thirsty labourer employed at one of the numerous slaughter-houses in the area, whose behaviour normally wouldn't have attracted a second glance.[8]

In another instance, a woman named Lyons told of an encounter in a pub with a strange man she had met in Flower and Dean Street. She couldn't help but notice that the man had a large knife on his person, and she grew even more suspicious when he allegedly said to her, 'You are about the same style of woman as the one that's been murdered.' 'What do you know of her?' Lyons asked, to which the man cryptically replied, 'You are beginning to smell a rat. Foxes hunt geese, but don't always find 'em.' The man then hurried out of the pub and ran off. It was noted that his description tallied with that of the nefarious Leather Apron, then still at large.[9] In a Camberwell pub, a man announced to patrons that the much sought after Leather Apron was a pal of his and that he himself was in fact in possession of the very same knife that had killed Annie Chapman. At this, the frightened landlady locked herself in an adjoining room, while terrified customers scrambled into the streets. When the police arrived and arrested the man, he explained to them that he was just having a good laugh.[10] Yet another man was said to have inquired of the caretaker of Tower Subway if the killer had been caught yet, before supposedly producing a curved knife, about a foot in length. 'This will do for them,' he snickered, after which he ran off.[11] One woman told of another man with a knife who 'peered' into her daughter's face. When the woman called for help, the man assumed 'a threatening attitude', before fleeing.[12] A man fitting his description was later picked up, and it was pointed out that he also fitted the description of the man who had so frightened Mrs Fiddymont, as well as that of a man who may have picked up Annie Chapman in a pub on the night she was murdered. Needless to say, the man was able to prove his innocence. As the press noted, the 'butchery' of Chapman had driven the inhabitants of Whitechapel 'nearly crazy', leaving them 'paralysed with fear'.[13]

Not surprisingly, some prostitutes took to arming themselves. 'Two [such] poor creatures ... showed a reporter two formidable Bowie knives,' *Lloyds* reported, 'which they would unquestionably use upon any man who attempted violence of a deadly character.'[14] Explained another woman, 'whose sprightly manner and rosy cherub face belied her pessimism, "Life ain't no great things [sic] with many of us, but we don't all want to be murdered, and if things go on like this, it won't be safe for nobody to put their 'eads out o' doors."'[15] Others disagreed, welcoming an end to their misery. 'A thin woman, pale, weak, and starving, said [to a *Lloyds* reporter] with evident sincerity, "Well, suppose I do get killed, it will be a good thing for me, for the winter is coming on, and the life is awful. I can't leave it; nobody would employ me."'[16]

9

'A man with a bear-shaped brain should be avoided'

From their creation in 1829, Sir Robert Peel's Metropolitan Police Force had proved unpopular with large segments of the London masses, who viewed them as intruders and meddlers rather than as friends and protectors. As Henry Mayhew observed, 'The hatred of a costermonger for a peeler is intense. I am assured that in case of a political riot, every coster would seize his policeman.'[1] But with the advent of the Whitechapel murders, the denizens of East London looked to the police for help, though it was not to be forthcoming. Scotland Yard may have boasted the finest force in the world but it was fairly primitive by modern standards, and, essentially, the police were as baffled, helpless and confused as everyone else.

In fairness, while they weren't entirely blameless in their failure to catch the Ripper, the police did about the best they could under the circumstances, given that they were faced with the task of tracking down a lone killer who struck at random in the middle of the night without any apparent motive, before disappearing in the labyrinth of East End nooks and crannies, leaving nothing behind in the way of useful clues. So far the police had very little to work with, and besides the dearth of physical evidence, there were as yet no reliable eyewitness reports. Psychological profiling, as it is now called, was then haphazard and unrefined, particularly as the police had no known precedents to guide them. Nor had forensic science progressed beyond its earliest nascent stages, and fingerprinting was then but an intriguing idea that had yet to be applied to a criminal procedure.[2] But even with the sophistication of modern detection methods such as genetic fingerprinting, where a drop of blood can pinpoint a killer out of a field of tens of thousands, or when a single near-invisible fibre can lead to a conviction, there are still said to be scores of serial killers at large in America at any given time, and hundreds of unsolved multiple slayings. Furthermore, in recent times such multiple murderers as the Boston Strangler, the Hillside Strangler(s), the so-called 'Zodiac Killer', David ('Son of Sam') Berkowitz, John Wayne Gacy, Peter Sutcliffe (the Yorkshire Ripper), Dennis Neilsen, Wayne Williams, Ted Bundy and, most recently, Milwaukee's Jeffrey Dahmer, to name but a few, all killed many more people and over a far greater period of time than did Jack the Ripper, whose five victims were murdered over a ten-week period.

The *East London Advertiser* summarized the police predicament: '[They] have no basis to go on. They do not even know the kind of class from which to select the criminal. They have not a single notion of his whereabouts. They do not know his motive, except so far as our guessing psychologists have enabled them to decipher it. He had left no material trace, and practically no moral trace ... meanwhile, perhaps, the worst feature of the murders is the manner in which the panic seems to be growing, and it is being aggravated by scoundrels to whom murders of the

REGISTRATION DISTRICT Whitechapel

1858. BIRTH in the Sub-district of Aldgate in the County of Middlesex

No.	When and where born	Name, if any	Sex	Name, and surname of father	Name, surname, and maiden surname of mother	Occupation of father	Signature, description and residence of informant	When registered	Signature of registrar	Name entered after registration
454	Twenty fifth May 1858 4 Hairbrain Court Whitechapel	Joseph	Boy	John Barnett	Catherine Barnett formerly Hayes	Dock Labourer	X the mark of Catherine Barnett Mother 4 Hairbrain Court Whitechapel	Thirtieth June 1858	John James Harris Register	/

REGISTRATION DISTRICT Stepney

1926 DEATH in the Sub-district of St George in the East in the County of London

No.	When and Where died	Name and surname	Sex	Age	Occupation	Cause of death	Signature, description and residence of informant	When registered	Signature of registrar
	Twenty ninth November 1926 54 Lion Street	Joseph Barnett	Male	68 years	Dock Labourer	Cy Bronchitis Oedema of Lungs 16 R.M. Certified by E. J. Collins M.B.	A. Denis Present at the Death 106 Red Lion Street	Thirtieth November 1926	Charles Coombs Registrar

Joseph Barnett's birth and death certificates. Barnett died only about half a mile from where he was born.

Contemporary pictures of Barnett, from the *Pictorial News*, Nov. 17, 1888 (left), and the *Illustrated Police News*, Nov. 24 (below).

J BARNETT
THE FRIEND OF THE DECEASED

Barnett's porter's licence from Billingsgate Market, listing some of his 17 known addresses (Corporation of London Record Office).

A sample Billingsgate Market porter's licence listing some of the market's rules and by-laws. (Corporation of London Record Office)

Census reports for 1861 and 1871, showing the Barnett family (Crown copyright material reproduced with the permission of the Controller of Her Majesty's Stationery Office, Public Record Office ref. R.G. 9/274, R.G. 10/506).

Red Lion Street, Shadwell, in the 1920s, when Joseph Barnett lived there with his 'wife' Louisa (Greater London Record Office).

Commercial Street, c. 1908. The Britannia beer house, known locally as Ringer's, is on the left, at the corner of Dorset Street (Greater London Record Office).

'In a Kentish Hop Garden.' Up until the 1970s, the late summer hop picking excursion to the Kent countryside doubled as an annual holiday for many East End families (from the *Pictorial World*, Oct. 4, 1888).

A group of Jewish cabinet makers in Bacon Street, off Brick Lane, c. 1911. There was a large Jewish community in the East End, and the Ripper murders unleashed a great tide of pent-up anti-Semitism (courtesy of the London Museum of Jewish Life).

Unemployment in the East End was such that at the docks, ten men competed daily for every six casual jobs (G.R. Sims, *How the Poor Live*).

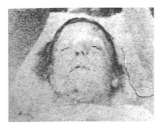

Mortuary photos of the first four victims of the Whitechapel Murderer, (clockwise, from top left) Mary Ann Nichols, Annie Chapman, Elizabeth Stride, and Catherine Eddowes.

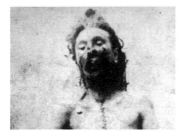

Press coverage of the murder of Mary Ann Nichols. Although Nichols was actually Jack the Ripper's first victim, the press linked her death with the earlier unsolved murders of Emma Smith and Martha Tabram (from the *Pall Mall Budget*, Sept. 6).

ANOTHER BRUTAL MURDER IN WHITECHAPEL.

THREE MURDERS WITHIN THREE HUNDRED YARDS.

NO CLUE TO ANY OF THE CRIMES,

BUCK'S-ROW, † SHOWING WHERE THE BODY WAS FOUND.

The scene on the streets after the death of Annie Chapman (*Pictorial News*, Sept. 15).

CROWDING TO THE SCENE

HANBURY ST
ON SUNDAY MORNING

Whitechapel order only suggest further opportunities of mischief. People's imaginations are at work, finding dangers where there are none. Every forbidding looking man is the object of suspicion, every unfortunate in Whitechapel fancies herself the prey of a malignant ruffian ... what is likely to happen is this: there will be more murders, and the ruffian's heels may be tripped by chance, if not by the foresight of the police.'[3]

The London police were also hampered by finding themselves in the uncomfortable position of having to operate under intense public scrutiny, due to the massive amount of publicity the Ripper murders attracted. When it became apparent that they would not get a quick result, the police found themselves subject to mounting criticism and increasingly besieged with suggestions and advice from the public and press (and even Queen Victoria herself!) as to how best to capture the killer. Although they stubbornly resisted most outside advice, as will be seen, some of these ideas were very sensible and might have made a difference had they been applied; these included calls for better lighting in some of the darker corners of the East End, the offering of a reward for information leading to the apprehension of the killer, an augmented local force, including an increased number of plain-clothes men, and the distribution of rubber-soled shoes to constables, whose boots normally made a loud, clomping sound that effectively announced their approach from some considerable distance away. It was also suggested that some of the younger, beardless PCs might act as decoys by disguising themselves as women, while one radical thinker suggested that actual female PCs be hired for just such a purpose. The use of bloodhounds to track down the killer also subsequently became the subject of a lively debate in the leaders and letters pages of the press and was one of the few ideas that the police actually took up, though with farcical results.

On the other hand, the police had to contend with a considerable number of silly and impractical proposals. One wag advised that prostitutes be armed, another sought the strategic placement of spring-operated female dummies that would automatically clasp on to anyone who molested them, while someone else thought it might be a good idea for all East Enders to register with the police before they turned in for the night.

One man, the noted alienist (a physician specializing in mental disorders) Dr Forbes Winslow, graciously offered his services to Scotland Yard. 'The first and foremost condition I propose,' he explained to *Lloyds Newspaper*, 'is [that] the matter be left entirely under my control, and an implicit compliance with my demands however strange these demands might appear.' It was Winslow's idea that some of the younger policemen disguise themselves as women, and he also suggested that the authorities contact local lunatic asylums regarding recently discharged or escaped patients. 'Homicidal mania is absolutely incurable,' he warned, adding (correctly as it turned out) that 'all the ordinary means of detection will fail, because once more, the moment [the killer's] fit or mania is passed, he becomes quite rational.'[4]

'Homicidal Mania' was also the title of a rather bizarre article that appeared in the October 1888 issue of *Fortnightly Review*. In it, one Dr Savage discussed the work of Hans Benedikt, a Viennese professor who had made a comparative study of the brains of various criminals. As the *East London Advertiser* wryly observed, 'Dr Benedikt had devoted especial attention to the cerebral development of murderers ... [and] had demonstrated satisfactorily that the brain of a murderer frequently resembles that of a lower animal "in certain definite ways". There is a strong similarity between the convolutions of a monkey's brain and those of some criminals ... According to Dr Benedikt, murderers' brains have a special likeness to those of bears. A man with a bear-shaped brain should therefore be avoided – unfortunately, there is considerable difficulty in telling the shape of your friend's brain while he is still alive.'[5]

Short of examining suspects' brains, the Metropolitan Police conducted a thorough inquiry into the death of Annie Chapman, employing an augmented force which did indeed contain a number of plain-clothes men. They visited every doss house within half a mile of the murder site – over 200 in all – and they questioned hundreds if not thousands of people. They also made numerous arrests, all of which, of course, came to nought, giving the impression that many of these were made merely to counter the growing public suspicion that the police weren't up to the job by showing that they were conducting a vigorous investigation. The satirical magazine *Punch* suggested much the same in a cartoon entitled 'Blind Man's Buff', which depicted a blindfolded constable groping helplessly about as several ruffians stood by mocking him. 'Turn round three times', the caption read, 'and catch whom you may.'[6]

In a further effort to maintain public confidence in the force, the police determined to keep up an optimistic front. There were regular reports in the press of 'important' new clues and developments, such as the one carried by *Lloyds Newspaper* not long after the Chapman murder, in which it was said 'the detective officers who are engaged on the case returned to the station more hopeful than they have been before. In reply to enquiries they said they had some fresh information, which encouraged them to hope that before next week is over, they would be able to solve the mystery.'[7]

What this new evidence was, was never revealed, but like every other lead the police professed to have, it turned up empty and both public and press began to lose patience. '[The police] are simply helpless,' *Reynolds Newspaper* concluded, speaking for many, '[and] childish in their endeavours to catch the Whitechapel ghoul.'[8]

It was becoming increasingly obvious that the police needed help. Even the celebrated detection abilities of Sherlock Holmes proved to be of no use to the beleaguered force. Arthur Conan Doyle, whose fictional detective first appeared in the *Strand* magazine the year before, was of the belief that the Ripper was a woman, or a man disguised as a woman – an unlikely if not entirely implausible theory. It indicated that Doyle, like Forbes Winslow, was at least aware that the Ripper murders represented a new and different type of crime and it was therefore necessary to abandon the old ways of thinking in favour of a fresh and different approach – something that the authorities never seemed to grasp. What impeded the police investigation more than anything was their inability to adapt and adjust to a new situation, an attitude thoroughly personified by the controversial Police Commissioner, Sir Charles Warren, who maintained an inflexible stance throughout. Warren stubbornly disdained most advice – no matter how good some of it was – and displayed a general lack of tact, understanding and imagination in his handling of the Ripper investigation.

A former army commander who had served in Palestine, Africa and India, Warren's appointment to the post of Police Commissioner in 1886 had attracted controversy early on, though it was the arrest of an innocent woman for soliciting during the Jubilee Day Festivities in 1887 that first turned the public against him. Warren's handling of that affair was said to have been 'blunt, tactless and contradictory',[9] and he was reportedly unsympathetic and unapologetic to all involved – traits he would demonstrate again and again during his tenure as commissioner. Further controversy arose later that year when Warren banned the homeless and unemployed from camping in Trafalgar Square, as Mary Ann Nichols had done. This decree led to a mass demonstration on Sunday, 13 November that turned into a battle between a 5,000 strong police coalition and a group of 20,000 homeless and unemployed, their sympathizers and supporters. The police quickly and brutally prevailed and several hundred protesters were injured or arrested. The event became known as 'Bloody Sunday'. Warren's action earned him further public animosity and the enmity of such radical-leaning newspapers as the *Star*, the *Echo* and the Liberal *Pall Mall Gazette*, as well as that of Conservative journals such as the *Daily Telegraph* and the *Daily News*. Warren also maintained strained relations with Home Secretary Henry Matthews, the police receiver Richard Pennefather, and CID head James Monro who would later succeed Warren as Police Commissioner.

The most frequent criticism of Warren concerned what was perceived to be the rigid, impractical and unimaginative military structure that he allegedly brought to the Metropolitan Police. Such an approach may have worked in the army, his detractors claimed, but it was clearly unsuited for police work. 'The conduct and direction of a criminal investigation is entirely foreign to the attributes of Sir Charles Warren,' declared the *Daily Telegraph* in the wake of Annie Chapman's murder.[10] The *Daily News* was equally blunt, correctly pointing out that the police had displayed 'no sign of an especial cunning of device to meet the terrible emergencies of the case'.[11]

Probably no paper was more scathing in its criticism of Sir Charles Warren or his force than the *Pall Mall Budget* when it printed the following satirical letter: 'Notice to Murderers: The following is a proclamation which, it is said, will in the future largely diminish the number of undetected murders: I, Charles Warren, hereby give notice that from and after this date, all loyal subjects are required, with the view of aiding the police in the discovery of crime, to leave on the body of any person they may have murdered their engraved or printed address card, or failing this, a paper with full name and address legibly written. Constables will be in attendance night and day at all police stations to receive murderers desiring to give themselves up. A list of the stations may be had on application. (issued) Scotland Yard, September—, 1888.'[12]

It was a growing lack of confidence in the police that led to the formation of vigilance committees. One had been assembled as early as the Martha Tabram killing, but the murder of Annie Chapman prompted some local tradesmen to start their own group. They met in the Crown pub in Mile End Road and elected George Lusk, a builder and vestryman, and J. Aarons, as their heads. Not wishing to alienate the police, Aarons announced that 'he wished it to be distinctly understood that he was in no way antagonistic to the police authorities, who were doing their best'.[13]

One of their first actions was to appeal to the Home Secretary to issue a reward for information leading to the arrest of the killer. The request was curtly denied. 'I am to inform you', the Home Office began a letter to the committee, 'that had the Secretary of State considered the case a proper one for the offer of a reward, he would have at once offered one, but that the practice ... was discontinued some years ago, because experience showed that such offers of a reward tended to produce more harm than good, and the Secretary of State is satisfied that there is nothing in the circumstances of the present case to justify departure from this rule'.[14]

It was a decision that only strengthened the growing local resentment towards the authorities. As the *Pall Mall Budget* reported, 'The foreman of the jury at the Bucks Row inquest ... declared his conviction that "if the victims had been rich instead of poor, a large reward would have been offered". The police were much shocked at this statement, and the coroner told the foreman that he "had no right" to make it. But right or wrong, the foreman was only giving the expression to what is a widespread belief. Ask any man in the street, or any woman in the kitchen, and that is what they will say.'[15]

It fell to the people of the East End, then, to come up with their own reward. The vigilance committee announced their intention of doing so, as did the Jewish community, still shaken by the Leather Apron fiasco and the lingering anti-Semitism it had brought to the surface. The police pitched in too, as individual members of Whitechapel's H Division came up with £50 of their own, an amount that was doubled by Samuel Montagu, a local MP. Spencer Charrington, of the brewery family, made a token contribution, and in the coming weeks the reward coffers swelled into four figures.

Meanwhile, life went on and as the days since the Chapman killing grew into weeks and October neared, the tension in the East End began to abate, and people's attention shifted from the murders as other stories filled the newspapers. In the United States, a heated Presidential election was underway. The Republican candidate, Benjamin Harrison, who proposed a tariff on foreign imports, mounted a successful campaign against the

Democratic incumbent, Grover Cleveland. At the same time, a Yellow Fever epidemic was spreading through the southern states, while in Texas two members of a gang were killed attempting a train robbery. Further to the south, one thousand armed Mexicans occupied the Texas border town of Rio Grande City, following the death of a Mexican citizen. In Europe, Romania geared up for an election, while the German army held manoeuvres in Berlin. In Rome, the unemployed were permitted their first ever open-air meeting and, in France, miners began a violent strike. In Turkey, the Sultan's palace was shaken by the murder of a black eunuch, while in Vienna, during a visit by the Prince and Princess of Wales, the remains of the composer Franz Schubert were exhumed sixty years after his death and his body was placed in a new coffin and reburied near Beethoven's grave.

In the far reaches of the Empire, meanwhile, British troops routed a poorly armed Tibetan force, killing 400 in a dispute over the Sikkim territory in northeast India. In Cyprus, a British archaeological expedition unearthed the Temple of Aphrodite at Paphos, while in Spain, British engineers won a commission to build a railway, something that had long been the province of the French.

In London, life outside the East End carried on as normal. Crystal Palace presented an aquatic fireworks display, while the Everton football club beat Aston Villa 2–1, and the Australian cricket team twice beat Surrey. In the West End, the Victorian theatre was enjoying its grand heyday. H. Beerbohm Tree was starring in *Captain Swift* at the Haymarket Theatre, while at the Lyceum the production of Robert Louis Stephenson's *Dr Jekyll and Mr Hyde*, starring the American actor Richard Mansfield, was winding up its successful run. So chillingly convincing had Mansfield's performance been that he found himself briefly accused of being the Whitechapel murderer! Preceding the main show was a short comedy called *Lesbia*, double bills being common at the time. The Gaiety Theatre was host to a production of H. Rider Haggard's *She* featuring Sophie Eyre, *The Ticket of Leave Man* was at the Olympic, while R. D'Oyley Carte's presentation of Gilbert and Sullivan's *The Mikado* was about to end its run at the Savoy. In Sloane Square, the modern Court Theatre was poised to open. One of the new small theatres then coming into vogue, it held only 700–800 people and boasted electric light throughout as well as a fireproof construction.

On the crime front, a Marylebone man was charged with throwing a fellow passenger off a train, and a Greenwich man was arrested for bigamy. In Lambeth, a woman stood accused of locking her nine-year-old daughter in a box, and a local man was remanded for attempting to slit his daughter's throat. The landlady of the Falcon pub in Clapham Junction appeared before the magistrate for having failed to keep her bull mastiff under control after it bit an employee, while in Poplar a man was said to have killed his wife by striking her with a hammer before slitting her throat and attempting to kill himself. In Durham, in the northeast, a woman was murdered in circumstances so apparently similar to the Whitechapel slayings that Dr Bagster Phillips was dispatched there to have a look, though he quickly ruled out any connection between the crimes. In London, meanwhile, as September neared its end, a curious letter was received by the Central News Agency signed 'Jack the Ripper', and purporting to be from the Whitechapel Murderer himself, though news of its existence would be held back from the public, in accordance with the writer's wishes, until he struck again. Around the same time, a drunk was released from custody after having confessed to killing Annie Chapman, but otherwise there was very little in the news about the murders, until the very end of the month when the culprit suddenly struck twice in the very same night!

10

'All was silent as the grave'

With the exception of the Bucks Row killing, three of the four murders thus far had occurred within a relatively small area north of Whitechapel Road and south from Hanbury Street, extending from Bell Lane and Crispin Street in the west, eastward to Brick Lane and Osborne Street. This was essentially the heart of Whitechapel, where the victims had lived, worked and drunk, an area that was crammed with doss houses and that included Dorset Street, Flower and Dean Street, Fashion Street, Thrawl Street, Wentworth Street, and George Street. Common sense dictated that the police concentrate their investigation within these parameters and it was probably their increased presence that prompted the killer to seek his next victim south of Whitechapel Road, where there would have been a lesser police presence, as evidenced by the fact that the man who discovered the first of the two victims killed in the early hours of 30 September had to run for several hundred yards, shouting for the police, before he found a constable.

But if the Whitechapel Murderer was seen to have

moved out of his 'regular' territory, it was to an area nonetheless familiar to Joseph Barnett, who at that point seems to have spent his entire life in the East End and had previously lived near and around both Berner Street and Mitre Square where the two new murders took place. In fact, at some time or another, Barnett had lived in some proximity to *all* of the murder sites, including Emma Smith's and Martha Tabram's, the two non-Ripper victims. When he first got his Billingsgate porter's licence in 1878, Barnett lived on Osborne Street, just near to where Smith had been attacked. George Yard, where Tabram's body was found, was just one street to the west of Osborne Street, and just south of George Street where Barnett and Mary Kelly had first lived together in 1887. Bucks Row, where Mary Ann Nichols was killed, was just under 700 yards from Heneage Street, the second address listed on Barnett's porter's licence, while 29 Hanbury Street, where Annie Chapman was murdered, lay less than 200 yards southeast of Great Pearl Street where the 13-year-old Barnett had lived. That murder site was also about 230 yards to the north of Heneage Street and less than 300 yards from Dorset Street, where Barnett and Kelly were then living. The part of Berner Street where Elizabeth Stride, the first of the two victims claimed on the night of 30 September, was killed was around 365 yards due north of Wellclose Square, the third address given for Barnett on his Billingsgate porter's licence, about 400 yards southeast of Osborne Street and some 650 yards northeast of Cartwright Street, where Barnett had lived as a child. Mitre Square, where Catherine Eddowes' body would be found later that night, was roughly 750 yards northwest of Cartwright Street and about 650 yards south of Dorset Street, where the killer's trail allegedly ended that night. Billingsgate Market, where Barnett had worked for over a decade, was about 700 yards to the southwest.[1] As it turned out, his familiarity with the area served him well, for Jack the Ripper was nearly set upon with both victims that night and each time narrowly escaped capture.[2]

Swedish born Elizabeth Stride stood only 5ft 5ins tall but among the denizens of the East End doss house circuit she was known as 'Long Liz', perhaps owing to the shape of her face. A thin woman, Stride was described by the *Daily Chronicle* as having 'sharp, somewhat pinched features, as though she had endured considerable privations of late'.[3] Dr George Bagster Phillips, however, who presided over the post-mortem, said that Stride was 'fairly nourished', and the *Chronicle* was probably unaware at the time that Stride was missing all of the teeth in her lower left jaw, which would have accounted for her 'pinched' or hollow look.

In fact, Stride was an attractive woman, dark complexioned with curly, nearly black hair, who looked ten years younger than her age. Detective Inspector Walter Dew (who later achieved fame with his capture of the murderer Hawley Harvey Crippen) worked on the Ripper case and recalled in his memoirs that Stride retained 'a trace of prettiness'.[4] Although she was almost 45 years old at the time of her death, the Press Association thought Stride was around 30, while *The Times* and *Daily Chronicle* initially estimated her age to be 35 and 40 respectively. Louis Diemschutz, who discovered the body, thought she was '27 or 28'. Evidently Stride wasn't averse to taking advantage of her youthful appearance and lying about her age; Michael Kidney, the Dorset Street dock labourer she lived with, was under the impression that Stride was in her thirties while a fellow lodger recalled Stride having told him that she was 35.

When her body was found, Stride was wearing a cheap black dress made of sateen, which was an imitation satin fabric, much like her velveteen bodice was imitation velvet, its colour having faded from black to brown. She also had on a black worsted jacket with fur trimming and a bunch of flowers pinned to it, a pair of white stockings, white stays and elastic boots. A black crêpe bonnet was found near her body, the inside stuffed with newspaper for a tighter fit. Her clothes were worn but clean and tidy; as the *Daily Chronicle* reported, Stride 'had the appearance of an unfortunate, but not one of the worst class'.[5]

There is some confusion regarding Stride's background; like Mary Kelly was thought to have done, Stride seems to have romanticized certain elements of her past, either to gain sympathy or perhaps to make her life seem more interesting or exciting than it actually was. She told friends that she and her husband had worked on the *Princess Alice*, a Thames pleasure steamer that sank in September 1878 after colliding with a coaster. Stride claimed that in the mêlée following the crash some of her teeth had been kicked out and that her husband and two of her children had been among the 600–700 people who perished in the incident. Although some papers later confirmed her story, subsequent research has all but disproved it as a fabrication, and it was recently discovered that Stride's husband may have died six years later in a Bromley hospital.[6] What does seem certain is that Stride was born Elizabeth Gustafsdotter, in Sweden in 1843 and that she worked as a domestic, and a prostitute, both before and after her arrival in London in 1866. Three years later she married John Thomas Stride, a carpenter, who opened up a coffee shop in Poplar, though the business was subsequently lost or sold and Stride afterwards separated from her husband. There were some reports of a later tryst with a policeman that produced a child, but Stride's whereabouts are essentially unknown until 1882, when she surfaced at a Flower and Dean Street lodging house. Around that time, Stride was also known to have stayed in nearby Fashion Street and Devonshire Street.

In the three years preceding her death, Stride had been living on and off with Michael Kidney at 38 Dorset Street,[7] no more than a couple of dozen yards from where Barnett and Kelly were then living. From time to time, she would go off on her own, often returning to the lodging house at 32 Flower and Dean Street. There, neighbours described her as 'quiet and sober', and 'a good natured, hard working, clean woman, who only took to the streets when she was unable to obtain employment' – much like Annie Chapman was said to have done.[8] When she could, Stride worked as a charwoman and she was a skilled seamstress as well, often doing jobs for local Jewish tailors – an arrangement facilitated by her knowledge of Yiddish. Elizabeth Stride, it seems, had a knack for languages, and besides speaking Yiddish, she was fluent in her original Swedish tongue and was said to speak English like a native with no trace of a foreign accent, even though she was already over 20 years old when she first came to England.

Exactly what prompted Stride's eventual decline from respectability is unknown but, her neighbours' opinions to the contrary, Stride is known to have had a drink problem. She had been arrested numerous times for drunkenness, sometimes under the name Annie Fitzgerald,[9] while Michael Kidney suggested that Stride's periodic disappearances were the result of drunken binges. 'She was subject to going away,' he testified at her inquest. 'During the three years I have known her she has been away from me altogether about five months ... It was drink that made her go away.'[10] (Kidney himself, however, was no teetotaller. He was said to have assaulted Stride, and had been picked up in the past for drunkenness. Upon hearing of Stride's death, he made a drunken scene at the Leman Street Police Station, where he swore that he would have committed suicide had he been the constable on whose beat the murder had occurred. Kidney also boasted that he would quickly catch the killer himself, if the police would just give him a few men to work with.)

Stride left Kidney for the final time about four or five days before her death, telling friends that they had quarrelled. Kidney, however, perhaps fearing that this might make him a suspect, denied that there had been any row and insinuated instead that Stride had merely gone off on one of her regular jaunts.

Stride took a room for herself in the Flower and Dean Street doss house, where on Saturday, 29 September she earned herself 6d by cleaning some of the rooms. But instead of using the money to pay for her nightly bed, Stride headed straight to her local pub, the Queens Head, on the corner of Commercial Street and Fashion Street. The last reliable sighting of her that night placed her back at the Flower and Dean Street lodging house, at 8.00 p.m. At that point she still hadn't paid for her bed, but it was not unusual for lodgers to wait until the last minute to do so.

Over the next few hours there were some six reported sightings of Elizabeth Stride, each time in the company of a man, or men, presumed to have been her killer.[11] But for various reasons most of these sightings are suspect. For one thing, none of the witnesses actually knew Stride beforehand, and there's no reason at any rate for so many people to have paid attention to a hitherto obscure and anonymous woman. But false or misleading eyewitness accounts (like phoney confessions) are not at all uncommon in a sensational murder case, and the Ripper killings unleashed an unparalleled wave of bizarre and extraordinary behaviour which peaked in the wake of the double murder. The unprecedented series of horrendous killings represented a tremendous upheaval in the dull and dreary routines of East End life; it was as though the Devil himself had come to Whitechapel and the streets were abuzz with a frenzied current of hysterical excitement and turmoil. As such, there was considerable local celebrity and respect to be had by someone who could claim that he or she had actually seen the notorious Jack the Ripper. One such person, an elderly grape seller named Matthew Packer, told the press and police that Stride and a male companion had bought a stalk of grapes from him shortly before her death, but not only did Packer change the details of his story several times but, as will be seen, he was to surface again after Mary Kelly's death with a strange tale of two men who approached him with supposed knowledge of Jack the Ripper's identity.

Other sightings of Stride that night had her in different places at the same time, or in the company of men of varying descriptions. A couple had Stride and her companion involved in public activities where their behaviour was sure to call attention to themselves – something that the crafty and cautious killer never would have done. Nor would he have maximized his chances of being seen by spending an hour or two in Stride's company, as other accounts alleged. One report, however, is less easily dismissed, as the eyewitness was a policeman, PC Smith, who identified Stride as the woman he had seen talking to a man in Berner Street shortly before her death. Although Smith's description of the suspect – aged 28, 5ft 7ins, dark complexion, small dark moustache[12] – is not at all incompatible with Joseph Barnett, considerable doubt nevertheless remains as to whether he had actually seen Stride and her killer. As so many people had pointed out, constables tended to signal their approach from a great distance by the loud, steady clomp of their boots on the pavement, and it's inconceivable that the killer would have allowed himself to be seen by a policeman in the company his victim-to-be only minutes before he killed her.

As it turned out, he apparently barely avoided detection at any rate. On the likely pretext of having sex with her, Stride's killer (whom she may have known, or recognized, from Dorset Street) coaxed her a few metres through the gates and into the dark courtyard adjoining the Jewish Socialist club at 40 Berner Street. Once there, he quickly grabbed her scarf from behind and tightened it around Stride's neck, stifling her cries, before wrenching her to the ground where he swiftly slit her throat. No doubt he was about to begin his usual mutilations upon the body when he was alerted by the unmistakable sounds of an approaching horse and cart, coming from the Commercial Road end of Berner Street. As there was only one way out of the yard, he had no choice but to hurry back out through the gates and turn right on Berner Street, away from the approaching horse and cart, in the direction of Fairclough Street. In this instance he was very lucky not to be seen, as it turned out that there were several people in the vicinity at the time, though none of them reported having seen or heard anything out of the ordinary.

Probably no more than a minute or two elapsed before Louis Diemschutz arrived on the scene with his horse and cart at 1.00 a.m: A hawker in cheap jewellery, Diemschutz was also the steward of the International Working Men's Educational Club, the Socialist organization made up of ethnic Jews located at 40 Berner Street. Although it was a thriving concern that had been there for several years, the club was unpopular with much of the East End Jewish community, who viewed its members as being overly concerned with matters political at the expense of maintaining their religious beliefs and traditions. The club members were mostly recently arrived Russian and East European immigrants, their thick accents and old country ways marking them (not necessarily accurately) as unsophisticated peasants and earning them the scorn and the shame of their already assimilated brethren, many of whom were from western Europe. At the same time, local residents objected to the noise that often came from the club, and no doubt the native English resented the presence of an enclave of strange looking and sounding foreigners in their midst.

Berner Street, largely coloured violet on Charles Booth's poverty map (representing a mixture of comfortable and poor), was known as a 'notorious' area. According to the *Daily Chronicle*, it was situated 'close to a district which was formerly known as Tiger's Bay, because of the ferocious character of the desperadoes who frequented it. A few yards distant [from the murder site],' the *Chronicle* noted, 'is the house wherein Lipski murdered Miriam Angel, and the neighbourhood generally has an evil repute.[13]

The Jewish club, however, was actually a very respectable establishment and, unlike 29 Hanbury Street whose yard was often the scene of illicit encounters, the club members made sure that their premises weren't used for such purposes. A flourishing, busy concern, it was the scene of meetings, debates and discussions, dances, dinners, and plays and poetry readings. The Yiddish journal *Der Arbeter Fraint* (*The Worker's Friend*) was also published on the premises.

On the night of 29 September, about ninety to a hundred members had showed up for a debate on the necessity of Socialism for Jews. When the discussion ended at around midnight, about twenty to thirty members remained behind, many of whom joined in a songfest. Others were in the kitchen, unaware that just on the other side of the wall from them, the Whitechapel Murderer was claiming yet another victim.

Although Louis Diemschutz stabled his pony elsewhere, he had returned to the club to unload his wares. He had just passed through the gates, when his pony suddenly shied. As Diemschutz later recounted,[14] 'On Saturday [29 September], I left home at about half past eleven in the morning, and returned at one on Sunday morning. I noticed the time at a tobacco shop. I had been out with some goods on a barrow, like a costermonger's, which I use at markets, drawn by a pony. I drove into the yard in Berner Street to leave my goods there. The gates were open. All at once, the pony shied towards the left. I could see there was something unusual, but I could not see what it was. I tried with my whip handle to feel what it was before I got down, and tried to lift it up with my whip but could not. I then jumped down at once and struck a match. It was rather windy and I could not get a sufficient light to see what it was, but there was sufficient light to show that it was the figure of some person. I could tell it was a woman by her dress. I did not wait to see whether she was drunk or dead. I did not disturb it, but went at once into the club and asked where my 'missus' was. I did this because I knew my wife had rather a weak constitution, and anything of that kind shocks her.'

Mrs Diemschutz, who was one of only about seven or eight women present at the club that night, took up the tale. 'I was in the kitchen on the ground floor of the club, and close to the side entrance [which led directly into the courtyard where the murder was committed] serving tea and coffee for the members who were singing upstairs. Up till then I had not heard a sound, not even a whisper. Then suddenly I saw my husband enter, looking very scared and frightened. I inquired what was the matter, but all he did was excitedly ask for a match or candle, as there was a body in the yard. I at once complied with his request, and gave him some matches. He then rushed out into the yard, and I followed him to the doorway, where I remained. Just by the door I saw a pool of blood, and when my husband struck a light, I noticed a dark heap lying under the wall. I at once recognized it as the body of a woman, while to add to my horror, I saw a stream of blood trickling down the yard, terminating in the pool I had first noticed. She was lying on her back with her head against the wall, and the face looked ghastly. I screamed out in fright, and the members of the club, hearing my cries, rushed downstairs in a body and out into the yard. When my husband examined the body he found that life, so far as he could tell, was quite extinct. He at once sent for a policeman.'

Diemschutz: 'Unfortunately, in the direction I took I could not find a policeman. I passed several streets without seeing one. I shouted as loud as I could, "police", but I could not get a policeman.'

Another club member had better luck. 'I returned back to the club at about twenty minutes to one,' said Morris Eagle, who had earlier chaired the night's discussion. 'Finding that the front door was closed, I went through the gateway that leads into the yard, and then through the back door into the club. It was rather dark, [so] I cannot form any opinion as to whether the deceased was there or not. As soon as I passed the gate into the yard, I could hear a friend of mine singing in the Russian language. On entering the club, I went up to the room, and my friend and I sang together. I had been there about twenty minutes when [another] member came upstairs and into the room and said, "There's a dead woman in the yard." I went down to the yard in a second and struck a match. I then saw a woman lying on the ground near the gate. Her feet were about six or seven feet from the gate, and she was lying by the side of the club wall. Her feet were towards the street, and her head towards the yard. Just as I was striking the match I said to her, "Get up," but when I struck the match I saw a lot of blood. On seeing the blood I was very excited, and ran away for the police. I yelled all the time I ran, "police". At the corner of Grove Street [which runs parallel to Berner Street about 400 feet to the east] I saw two constables [who] came back with me, and when we got to the yard, one of the policemen lit his lamp. He told me to go to the police station for an inspector, and he sent his fellow constable for a doctor.'

'When the police came,' continued Mrs Diemschutz, 'we were told that we must not quit the premises, and everybody was at once searched. Nothing was found to occasion suspicion, and the members were eventually allowed to go. At four o'clock the body was removed to the mortuary, and later in the morning the police washed away the bloodstains with which the side of the yard was deluged. I am positive I did not hear any screams or sound of any kind. Even the singing on the floor above would not have prevented me from hearing [them] had there been any.[15] In the yard itself, all was silent as the grave.'

PC Lamb was the first constable to arrive on the scene. 'I was in Commercial Road, between Christian Street and Batty Street [a walk of about 200 yards to the northeast of the murder site]. Two men came running to me and shouting. I went towards them, and they said to me, "Come on. There has been another murder!" I asked, "Where?" When I got to the corner of Berner Street, they pointed down the street and said, "There!" I saw the people moving about some distance down the street and ran, followed by another constable. I went into the gateway at number 40 Berner Street, and saw something lying close to the gate. I turned my light on and found it was a woman. I saw her throat was cut and she appeared dead. I at once sent the other constable for the nearest doctor, and sent a young man who was standing by to the police station to inform the inspector that a woman was lying in Berner Street with her throat cut. There was a number of people in the yard before I arrived. Deceased was lying on her left side, and her left arm was slightly under her body. The right arm was across her breast. She looked as if there had been no struggle, and she had been quietly laid down. Dr Blackwell was the first doctor who arrived, and he came ten or twelve minutes after my arrival. Dr Phillips arrived about twenty minutes after I came. When [he] was examining the body, I had the gates closed. I then went into the club and examined the hands and clothes of all those present. I went into every room, and behind the stage in the large room, and saw no marks of blood.'

Dr Blackwell: 'I consulted my watch upon arrival and it was sixteen minutes past one. The woman was lying on her left side, completely across the yard passage. Her legs were drawn up, her feet were close against the wall on the right side of the yard passage, her head resting almost in the carriage wheel rut. Her feet were three yards from the gateway. The neck and chest were quite warm, also the legs. The face was slightly so; her hands were cold. The right hand was lying on the chest, and was smeared inside and out with blood. The left hand, which was lying on the ground, contained a small packet of cachous [a breath freshener]. The appearance of the face was quite placid. The mouth was slightly open. There was a check silk scarf around the neck, the bow of which was turned to the left side, and pulled very tight. There was a long incision in the neck, which exactly corresponded with the narrow border of the scarf, the scarf being above the cut. The lower edge of the scarf was slightly frayed, as if by a sharp knife. The incision on the neck commenced on the left side, two inches and a half below the angle of the jaw, and almost in a direct line with it. The cut nearly severed the vessels of that side, and cut the windpipe completely in two, and terminated on the opposite side one inch and a half below the angle of the right jaw, but without severing the vessels on the right side.

'Probably the man took hold of the silk scarf at the back of it, and pulled the woman backwards, and cut her throat, while in the act of falling, or on the ground. As the scarf was round her neck there would have been room to put the hand in and pull it tight. It would be difficult to pull a scarf sufficiently tight to prevent a person [from] making any noise, but the cut would be almost instantaneous, and there would not be much time for her to cry out. I don't think she had been dead more than ten minutes to half an hour before my arrival. She would have bled to death comparatively slowly on account of the neck being cut and the artery not being completely severed. Dr Phillips came about ten minutes to half an hour after my arrival.'

'I was called at twenty minutes past one to Leman Street,' recalled Dr Bagster Phillips, 'and I was sent down to Berner Street to a yard at the side of a club house. There I found the body of a woman which had already been examined by Dr Blackwell, who had arrived sometime before me. On 1 October at 3.00 a.m. at St George's Mortuary, Dr Blackwell and I made a post-mortem examination of the body. We found the body fairly nourished. Over both shoulders, especially the right from the front aspect, under the collar bones and in the front of the chest, there is a bluish discolouration. The cut on the neck, taking it from left to right, is six inches in length, the incisions commencing two and a half inches in a straight line below the angle of the jaw, and three-quarters of an inch over undivided muscles, and then becoming deeper – about an inch – dividing the sheath and the vessels, and then ascending a little, divides between two cartilages, the cut being very clean, but indicating a slight direction downwards, through the resistance of the denser tissue of the cartilages. The carotid artery on the left side, and the other vessels contained in the sheath were all cut rough, save the posterior portion of the carotid. The cut tails off to about two inches below the right angle of the jaw. The sheath of the vessels is entire. It is evident that the haemorrhage, which probably will be found to be the cause of death, was caused through the partial severance of the left carotid artery.

'The lower lobe of the [left] ear was torn, as if from forcibly removing or wearing through of an earring, but it was thoroughly healed. The right ear had been pierced for an earring, but had not been so injured. The left lung had old adhesions to the chest wall. Both lungs were unusually pale. There was a small substance of fat outside the muscular substance deposited on the heart. The heart was small. I found undigested food in the stomach apparently consisting of cheese, potatoes and farinaceous [starchy] particles. All the teeth on the lower left jaw were absent.

'I found in the pocket of the underskirt the following articles: a key, as of a padlock, a small piece of lead pencil, a pocket comb, a broken piece of comb, a metal spoon, half a dozen large, and some small, buttons, a hook off a dress and some small pieces of newspaper.

'The cause of death was undoubtedly from the loss of blood from the left carotid artery, and the division of the windpipe. I will defer saying anything about the kind of weapon the injuries were inflicted with till I consult my colleagues in the other case.'

The 'other case' that night was the murder of Catherine Eddowes, whose severely mutilated torso was found at 1.46 a.m. in Mitre Square, a distance of less than one thousand yards as the crow flies. Given that it's known that the killer left Berner Street at around 1.00 a.m. and that he arrived at Mitre Square about half an hour later, it's possible to trace the likely route that he took to get there. Assuming, as the evidence indicates, that Louis Diemschutz's arrival in his horse and cart at 1.00 a.m. forced the killer to abandon Elizabeth Stride's body, then his objective would have been to get off Berner Street and out of the immediate vicinity as quickly as possible (though not so quickly as to call attention to himself). This would be best achieved by keeping to the darker, narrower, less travelled streets whenever possible. With Diemschutz approaching from the north, he had no choice but to head south on Berner Street, probably turning left onto Fairclough Street (as a right-hand turn would have led him to the wider and therefore potentially busier Backchurch Lane). The next street he came to was Providence Street, a short, dark, narrow street where he was less likely to encounter anyone. If he continued directly southwards so as to put as much distance between himself and the murder site in the least amount of time, he would have gone down Elizabeth Street and briefly into Pinchin Street, before crossing the London and Blackwall Railway tracks. This would have placed him close to the northeast corner of Wellclose Square where Joseph Barnett had once lived and very near to the streets where he had spent a good deal of his childhood. If he continued due south, he would have come to the wider St George Street, a good 500 yards from the scene of the crime. Here, in the comfort and security of familiar surroundings, he could briefly pause to catch his breath and regroup his senses. A right-hand turn would then take him into Upper East Smithfield Street, past the Cartwright Street of Barnett's youth and past the Royal Mint, to his right, and the Tower of London, to his left. From there, he probably followed the road northwards into the Minories, which took him to Aldgate High Street. Immediately to his left was Duke Street, with its narrow covered passage leading to Mitre Square. At this point he had travelled for about a mile and a half on his circuitous route from Berner Street and, given his brisk pace, it would have been about 1.30 a.m., only a few minutes before witnesses spotted Catherine Eddowes talking to a man in Duke Street, outside the passage leading to Mitre Square, a few minutes before she was killed.

In fact, what brought Jack the Ripper to Mitre Square may have been the presence of the Orange Market, as the adjoining St James Place was locally known. Although his sadistic craving was unsated as he hadn't been able to mutilate Elizabeth Stride's body (and, as will be seen, he had failed to get his victim's ears for the police, as he had promised in his letter to the Central News Agency), the Ripper wasn't necessarily seeking another victim, as he would have been well aware that the streets would soon be aswarm with police. Rather, he had probably only intended to distance himself from the scene of the crime and take a safe route home, when he had the ingenious idea of heading towards the nearby Orange Market to try to find some casual work – after all, what better way to explain his presence in the vicinity at that hour, if need be? Several people were already in the Orange Market gearing up for the next day's business, and as it is known that Barnett had occasionally sold oranges since losing his job at Billingsgate

Market, he may have even previously worked in the Orange Market itself and dealt with some of the many fruit merchants located in the surrounding streets.[16]

But he hadn't counted on meeting Catherine Eddowes, making her way unsteadily down Duke Street having just been released from a police holding cell for drunks. They were probably acquainted with one another from Dorset Street, as Eddowes had often stayed in the empty shed that was literally next door to Barnett's and Kelly's room. In her weakened, weary condition, Eddowes presented a particularly vulnerable target. Jack the Ripper abandoned all thoughts of market work and instead set out to finish the job he had only begun on Elizabeth Stride.

11

'She was in the habit of giving way to drink'

Throughout her life, 'jolly' was the word most often used to describe Catherine Eddowes, known as Kate to her friends. 'She was a jolly woman,' recalled one of her sisters, '[who] would often take part in a bit of singing or dancing when any was going on.'[1] She had a 'jolly disposition' her uncle concurred, noting that even when young, Eddowes liked to keep late hours.[2]

Forty-six years old at the time of her death, Eddowes was originally from Wolverhampton, one of a dozen children born to George Eddowes, a tinplate stamper, and his wife Catherine, a cook at a local hotel.[3] By the time she was 13, both of Eddowes' parents had died, at which time she was taken in by an aunt. Around the age of 20, she hooked up with Thomas Conway, a former soldier who drew a pension and apparently either wrote or sold biographical adventure books. Although they never married and would separate periodically, their relationship endured for seventeen years and they had three children, two boys and a girl, before they parted for good in 1880, largely because of Eddowes' heavy drinking. Although not an habitual

107

drunkard, Eddowes enjoyed her alcohol and tended to drink beyond her limit, at which time she invariably became quarrelsome and abusive (much like Mary Kelly did). This pattern of behaviour particularly irked her daughter, Annie Phillips, then married to a gunmaker and living in Bermondsey. Phillips, who didn't read the papers much, had disassociated herself from her mother, and it was several days before she heard of her death. The statement she subsequently gave reflects the bitterness and animosity Phillips felt towards her mother, despite the fact that at the time they fell out Eddowes had just nursed her daughter through a difficult pregnancy. 'It is two years or more since I saw my mother,' Phillips told the press. 'Since then I have not only not seen her, but have heard very little of her. I have not asked after her, in fact, though I am told that she has tried to find me. We did not part on good terms, that is the truth. She was attending me during my confinement, and she went out and got too much to drink, which caused unpleasantness. She was in the habit of giving way to drink ... It was in consequence of her drinking habits that she and my father [Conway] separated ... They could never agree, because she gave way to drink, [and] he is a teetotaller.' Perhaps realizing that she sounded cold and ungrateful towards her recently deceased mother, Phillips added, as an afterthought, 'I should like to say again that she was always a hard-working woman, and that except for her taking too much to drink, I never knew her to do anything wrong.'[4] Others added that Phillips regarded her mother as a 'persistent scrounger', and had deliberately not given her mother her new address when she moved from Bermondsey to Southwark. Similarly, Eddowes' former 'husband' Thomas Conway collected his army pension under a pseudonym so Eddowes wouldn't be able to trace him.

Not long after her separation from Conway, Eddowes took up with the market worker John Kelly. The relationship lasted for seven years, up until Eddowes' death. Described as 'a poorly clad labourer, thick set and dark', and 'a quiet, inoffensive man [with] sharp, intelligent eyes',[5] Kelly was devoted to Eddowes. 'He appears to feel the murder of the woman deeply,' noted the *Daily Chronicle*, 'for he feels they were always the best of friends'.[6] William Wilkinson, a lodging house deputy who knew the couple for seven years, spoke of their strong relationship. 'They lived on very good terms,' he testified at Eddowes' inquest. 'They had a few words now and again, when Kate was in drink, but not violent quarrels.'[7] Wilkinson added that they paid 'pretty regularly' for their bed, and that as far as he knew, Eddowes never walked the street – in fact, Kelly wouldn't allow her to. As the *Pall Mall Budget* explained, the couple had 'gone through many hardships together, but while she was with him, [Kelly] "would not let her do anything wrong"'.[8] 'She had a rough and ready manner,' a friend of Eddowes' recollected, but was otherwise 'respectably conducted'.[9]

John Kelly had worked for a fruit salesman for twelve years, until poor health (he had a kidney ailment and a nagging cough) apparently cost him his job. When he could, he jobbed about the East End markets, while Eddowes, for her part, hawked things in the streets, and sometimes did cleaning jobs for some of the Jewish families. Most of the time, the couple shared a bed at a lodging house at 55 Flower and Dean Street, though when they couldn't manage the 8d fee for a double bed, they either split up to try their luck separately or signed in together at the workhouse in Shoe Lane, Mile End. At other times, according to *Lloyds Newspaper*, Eddowes 'slept in a shed off Dorset Street, which is a nightly refuge of some ten to twenty homeless creatures who are without the means of paying for their beds'.[10] Although Lloyds didn't give the exact address of the shed, the *Daily Telegraph* later reported that it was in fact located at 26 Dorset Street – the very same address where Joseph Barnett and Mary Kelly then lived.[11] As *Lloyds Newspaper* subsequently explained: '[13] Miller's Court is really the back parlour of 26 Dorset Street, the front shop being partitioned off and used for the storage of barrows, etc. This was formerly left open, and poor persons often took shelter there for a night; but when the Whitechapel murders caused so much alarm, the police thought the spot a temptation to the murderer, and so the front was securely boarded up.'[12] Eddowes also gave an address of 6 Dorset Street when she pawned a pair of boots in the name of Jane Kelly, shortly before her death.

Although mechanization and the decline of the British hop industry effectively put an end to the tradition, in the late nineteenth century 'hopping' was at its peak As many as 80,000 Londoners, many of them from the East End, descended upon the hop fields of Kent in August and September for a couple of months work and a respite from the stress and travails of city life. For many East Enders, the trip was regarded as a holiday. Although living conditions were often inadequate and the work lasted from dawn to dusk, the work itself was relatively easy and the entire family, from the young to the elderly, could participate. Jack London tried his hand at it and called it 'woman's work', though when the writer George Orwell gave it a try, he found that there was a knack to it, and that more experienced hands could pick the hops far faster than he could and therefore earn more money.

Shortly before her death, Catherine Eddowes and John

Kelly went to Kent on a hopping excursion, but they couldn't find any work and were forced to 'hoof it' (walk) back to London. Probably they had left it too late in the season, when casual work was scarce. They returned to London on Thursday, 27 September. That night they slept in the Shoe Lane workhouse casual ward. On Friday, Kelly found a few hours work for which he earned sixpence, while Eddowes pawned a pair of his boots which brought them an additional half crown (2s 6d). From these funds they purchased some tea and sugar before going their separate ways, Kelly taking a single bed in the Flower and Dean Street doss house, Eddowes sleeping again at Shoe Lane. They met early the next morning for breakfast, then spent the rest of their money on drink. Broke again, it was decided that Eddowes would try to find her daughter Annie in order to get some money from her. It was 2.00 in the afternoon of Saturday, 29 September; Eddowes promised Kelly that she would be back in a couple of hours, but he was never to see her alive again.

Although Eddowes never did find her daughter, she somehow managed to scrape together enough money to get drunk on, and at 8.30 that evening she was found passed out on the pavement in Aldgate High Street. She was taken to Bishopsgate Police Station in Wormwood Street, where she later gave her name as Mary Ann Kelly of 6 Fashion Street.

By 1.00 a.m. on Sunday, 30 September, Eddowes was deemed sober enough to be released and upon leaving the station was seen heading in a southeasterly direction. By then she must have been near exhaustion, tired, hungry, hung over and weak from her ordeal, as reflected by the fact that she only managed to travel about a quarter of a mile in a space of half an hour.

At 1.30 a.m. PC Edward Watkins' regular beat took him though Mitre Square, at which time all was well.

At 1.35 a.m. three Jewish traders left their club at 16–17 Duke Street. It was a bright night, the moonlight illuminating the otherwise dimly lit street. As a police house-to-house enquiry later revealed, the men noticed a man and a woman standing talking outside Church Passage, a narrow alleyway about nine or ten yards across the road from them, that led to Mitre Square. Two of the men paid the couple no further attention, but one of them, Joseph Lawende, a cigarette dealer, had a better look at them. Although he didn't see the woman's face, he was later able to confirm that it had been Catherine Eddowes by her clothing. Eddowes was rather distinctively clad that night with her beaded, green and black velvet trimmed black straw bonnet, black, imitation fur trimmed jacket, and chintzy, flower-patterned dress. Nor did Lawende catch more than a passing look at the man, but it was enough to enable him to give the police a fairly detailed description to which they attached considerable importance – so much so, that the police solicitor interrupted Lawende's inquest testimony to request that he not make his description public, presumably to allow the police time to search for the man without tipping him off. As the *Evening News* reported, '[The police] have no doubt themselves that this was the murdered woman and her murderer,'[13] and as it turned out, Eddowes was killed only minutes later and but a few dozen yards away.

In particular, Major Henry Smith, then Acting Commissioner of the City Police, in whose jurisdiction Eddowes' murder had occurred, was convinced after personally interviewing Lawende that he was telling the truth. 'This was without doubt,' he later recorded in his memoirs, 'the murderer and his victim.'[14] Despite the fact that the

Whitechapel murders were the most sensational, dramatic and exciting event to have occurred in the East End within anyone's living memory, to Smith's surprise, Lawende and his friends seemed uninterested in the case and were only marginally aware of it. They weren't seeking the spotlight or individual glory like so many others were, and had not in fact come forward with their story – rather they had only been ferreted out by the subsequent police house-to-house inquiry. As such, Smith could see no reason for the men to be lying about what they had seen. Smith had also failed to sway Lawende from his story with trick questions, and he was impressed by Lawende's insistence that he would probably *not* be able to recognize the man should he see him again.

The description Lawende gave to the police was of a man about 30 years old, standing 5ft 7ins or 5ft 8ins tall, of medium build, with a fair complexion and a moustache – *an exact description of Joseph Barnett in every particular.*

As it turned out, the same couple was also seen only a minute or two later, about ten minutes before the discovery of Eddowes' body, according to the *Daily Telegraph*, 'in the covered passage leading to [Mitre] Square, by two persons who were in the [adjoining] Orange Market, and closely observed the man'.[15] Their description was essentially identical to Lawende's, that of a man of about 30, with a fair complexion and a fair moustache.

This was probably the only time that Jack the Ripper was actually seen in the company of one of his victims, and the descriptions given to the police by two independent eyewitness accounts precisely fit Joseph Barnett in every aspect.[16]

12

'The Juwes are The men That Will not be Blamed for Nothing'

At around 1.41 that same morning, PC James Harvey went down Church Passage, stopping short of entering Mitre Square. He noted nothing out of the ordinary, though he probably did little more than take a quick glance about, for not only had Eddowes and her killer already entered Mitre Square by then, but she had probably already been killed. The square itself was fairly well lit with five lamps, but one of them had dulled, pitching the southeast corner into darkness, and this is where Eddowes' body was found. Chances are the killer was still there as well but Harvey just didn't see them.

At 1.46 a.m. PC Watkins' regular patrol brought him back to Mitre Square, his heavy footsteps most likely warning Eddowes' killer off (if PC Harvey hadn't already done just that), providing him with his second narrow escape of the night. Had Watkins been wearing rubber-soled shoes, as had been suggested, then he may very well have caught Jack the Ripper in the act.

By the light of his belt lantern (called a Bull's Eye), PC

Watkins spotted Eddowes' body. She was lying on her back in a pool of blood. Her throat had been cut, and her clothes were pushed above her waist, revealing deep wounds to her abdomen through which her bowels were protruding. As the City police carried no whistles, Watkins fetched George Morris, a former constable and now the night-watchman at the tea warehouse across the square, and sent him for help. Said Morris: 'About a quarter to two o'clock the policeman on the beat came and knocked at the door of the warehouse ... He said, "For God's sake, man, come out and assist me; another woman had been ripped open." I said, "All right, keep yourself cool while I light a lamp." Having done so, he led me to the southeast corner, where I saw a woman lying stretched upon the pavement with her throat cut, and horribly mutilated. I then left the constable, Watkins, with the body while I went into Aldgate and blew my whistle, and the other officers soon made their appearance. The whole shape of the woman was marked with blood upon the pavement ... [she] was so mutilated about the face I could not say what she was like.

'The strangest part of the whole thing', Morris continued, 'is that I heard no sound. As a rule I can hear the footstep of the policeman as he passes by every quarter of an hour, so the woman could not have uttered any cry without my detecting it. It was only last night that I made the remark to some policeman that I wished the butcher would come around Mitre Square, and I would soon give him a doing, and here, to be sure, he has come and I was perfectly ignorant of it.'[1] Morris, however, wasn't alone in his ignorance. As it happened, a City policeman lived in one of the houses that backed onto Mitre Square, though he slept soundly through the night. Similarly, numerous other people were about the area as well, including some street cleaners and several traders gearing up for the popular Sunday market in Middlesex Street, Petticoat Lane (then called the Middlesex Market), all of whom reported having heard nothing unusual that night. In fact, the extraordinary silence that cloaked the crimes gave rise to the rumour that the killer had chloroformed his victims, though this was later disproved.

George Morris succeeded in finding PC Harvey, who had just passed through the area. He in turn summoned PC Holland, on patrol nearby, who fetched Dr William Sequeira whose surgery was close by. Dr Sequeira agreed to leave the corpse untouched until the arrival of the City police surgeon Dr Frederick Gordon Brown, who got to the scene at around 2.20 a.m.

At about the same time that Dr Brown was examining Catherine Eddowes' body in Mitre Square, PC Alfred Long's patrol brought him through Goulston Street, about 350 yards north of Mitre Square. At that time he noticed nothing unusual, though when he passed through the street again some thirty minutes later, he made a startling discovery. Lying on the pavement in front of the entrance to numbers 108–119 was a folded blood and faecal stained piece of cloth which was later shown to have come from Catherine Eddowes' apron and which the killer had used to wipe clean his hands and knife. Even more startling was the curious message chalked on the wall nearby – 'The Juwes are The men That Will not be Blamed for Nothing' (sic).[2] It was said to have been written in a good round hand, with the capital letters standing about three-quarters of an inch high, and the little letters proportionately smaller.[3] Upon hearing of its existence, Metropolitan Police Commissioner Sir Charles Warren, urged on by Superintendent Thomas Arnold, head of H Division (Whitechapel), ordered the message to be erased immediately, fearing that it might provoke further anti-Semitic violence.

Not surprisingly, Warren's decision was met with considerable protest. Major Henry Smith and Detective Constable Daniel Halse, also of the City Police, among others, argued that if the message must be erased, then it should at least first be photographed, as it was a potentially valuable piece of evidence in a case that was thus far distressingly lacking in clues. Acknowledging the validity of Warren's argument, they suggested that perhaps only the word 'Juwes' might be erased, or that the message be covered up and guarded until a photographer arrived. But Warren displayed a consistent unwillingness to consider any 'outside' advice, and he had the message obliterated before a picture could be taken. Warren defended his hasty and ill-considered decision in a letter to the Home Secretary, Henry Matthews (which, inadvertently, said much about the ineffectiveness of the police). 'It was just getting light,' he wrote, 'the public would be in the streets in a few minutes, in a neighbourhood very much crowded on Sunday mornings by Jewish vendors and Christian purchasers from all parts of London. There were several police around the spot when I arrived, both Metropolitan and City. The writing was on the jamb of the open archway or doorway visible to anybody in the street and could not be covered up without danger of the covering being torn off at once.[4] A discussion took place whether the writing could be left covered up otherwise, or whether any portion of it could be left for an hour until it could be photographed; but after taking into consideration the excited state of the population in London generally at the time, the strong feeling which had been excited against the Jews and the fact that in a short time there would be a large concourse of the people in the streets, and having before me the report that if it was left there the house was likely to be wrecked ... I considered it desirable to obliterate the writing at once ... I do not hesitate myself to say that if the writing had been left property would have been wrecked, and lives would probably have been lost'.[5]

Much has been written about the oddly worded message, with its strange spelling of the word Jews and its confusing double negative.[6] Both Smith and Warren agreed that its intent was to cast suspicion on the Jewish community, in which case the message might be interpreted as an insinuation that the Jews were responsible for the killings but wouldn't face up to it, or that people wouldn't be blaming the Jews unless they had a good reason to do so.

But there was only scant circumstantial evidence that the message had actually been written by the killer, and as graffiti wasn't uncommon in the area it could conceivably have been written by anyone with a piece of chalk and a grudge. Nor does the timing point to the Ripper. Catherine Eddowes' body was discovered at around 1.46 a.m., yet neither PC Long nor Detective Halse saw the message or the piece of apron when they passed through Goulston Street at around 2.20 a.m. If they are to be believed, it would mean that the killer (who happened to have a piece of chalk on his person) spent over half an hour in the vicinity with bloodied hands and the blood and faecal stained knife in his possession, while the police closed in on the scene of the crime and combed the area for him – hardly a credible proposition. And why then leave such a vague or tiny message? What's much more likely is that neither Long nor Halse had noticed either the small piece of apron or the tiny scribble their first time around. If the *People* was correct in reporting the size of the lettering, then the whole message couldn't have been much larger than the breadth of a human hand, and could have been easily overlooked in the darkness. PC Long later admitted that this might have been the case, while a small, folded piece of cloth lying on the ground may very well have been similarly overlooked. As for the authorship of the message, what is much more likely and plausible is that it had actually been written *by* a Jew. The broken English, poor spelling and awkward syntax all indicate a foreign hand, in which case the message is more sensibly interpreted as a warning to the gentile community that the Jewish people would not continue to stand idly by while being victimized and accused of a crime that they most certainly did not commit.

In the end, however, it all proved to be inconsequential. The message was too vague and uncertain to be of any real significance, and whatever the interpretation, it revealed nothing about the killer or his motivations and provided no help for the police in better understanding or apprehending him.

The only possible use of the message would have been for the police to compare the writing to that on the Jack the Ripper letters, the first of which had already been received by the press but had not yet been released to the public. A positive result would have given the police their first definite clue and provided them with a focus for their investigation but, due to Commissioner Warren's panicky and irresponsible decision to destroy the message before it could be photographed, that possibility was lost to the police forever.[7]

When PC Watkins' loud footsteps signalled his approach to Mitre Square from Mitre Street, the killer had little choice but to flee the way he had come, back through Church Passage and into Duke Street. The only alternative means of exit led directly to the Orange Market in St James Square, where there were already several people about, gearing up for the Sunday market. Knowing that the square and its surrounding streets would soon be aswarm with police, his priorities were to get out of the immediate area without drawing attention to himself, and then to take the quickest and safest route home. With that in mind, the killer probably went from Duke Street briefly into Houndsditch and from there into Gravel Lane, where a warren of dark, winding streets and alleys took him across Middlesex Street and into the long yard behind the Brunswick Buildings which fronted onto Goulston Street. If he found a back way in through one of the buildings, he could then afford a brief respite in which to catch his breath, calm himself down and clean some of the blood from his hands and knife. Having sliced a small piece off Eddowes' apron for this very purpose before he fled, he would have briefly buffed his hands with it before folding it as he ran it up and down the blade of his knife, discarding the cloth behind him as he emerged from the entrance to numbers 108–119 Goulston Street. From there, if Major Henry Smith is to be believed, the killer headed straight to Dorset Street, a few hundred yards directly to the north, where he washed the remainder of the blood off his hands.

As the Mitre Square killing fell within his jurisdiction, Major Smith had been summoned to the scene, and when news of the bloody apron and chalked message reached him, he proceeded to Goulston Street. From there, he determined the killer's likely route and wound up in Dorset Street, where he came across a bloodstained sink. As he recalled in his memoirs, 'The assassin had evidently wiped his hands with the piece of apron. In Dorset Street, with extraordinary audacity, he washed [his hands] at a sink up a close, not more than six yards from the street. I arrived there', Smith lamented, 'in time to see the bloodstained water.'[8] There the trail ended, and while Smith didn't give the precise location of the sink, there was in fact a tap situated in Miller's Court, literally right in Joseph Barnett's backyard.

At the inquest into her death, Dr Frederick Gordon Brown, the City police surgeon, spoke at great length of the injuries suffered by Eddowes. It was his opinion that she had been taken completely by surprise and had died without putting up a struggle. As he saw it, her assailant had first wrestled Eddowes to the ground, where he inflicted a long, deep cut across her throat, which resulted in her immediate death from haemorrhaging. Kneeling over the right side of her body, he then began his ritual mutilations, cutting and dismembering her body to a far greater extent that he had thus far done with any of his previous victims. Eddowes' abdomen had been cut open from the groin to the breastbone, with a two-foot length of her intestines having been pulled out and placed over her chest and shoulder.

Even more gruesome was the fact that her left kidney and uterus had been removed from her body. Her face had also been severely disfigured with cuts and slashes, and the tip of her nose and a piece of one of her ears had been sliced off. In severing a portion of Eddowes' ear, the killer was evidently trying to keep the promise he had just made in one of his still secret letters to cut off his next victim's ears and send them to the police, though in his haste to leave the scene he had to leave it behind. As Dr Brown testified, 'the lobe of [Eddowes'] right ear was cut obliquely through,' adding that while he was undressing her body, 'the missing piece of ear dropped out of the clothing'.[9]

Dr Brown estimated that it had taken at least five minutes for the killer to perform his fiendish operation, and he was of the opinion that he had been somehow familiar with the position of the body's internal organs, as a person accustomed to cutting up animals might be.[10] Dr Brown also confirmed that the piece of cloth found in Goulston Street matched the remains of Eddowes' apron, and he stated that the killer wouldn't have had very much blood on his person, as the mutilations to Eddowes' body had all been inflicted after her death.

Although her penchant for drink proved to be her undoing, Catherine Eddowes was basically a decent woman who strove to maintain a certain level of dignity and respectability in her life. Of all the Ripper victims, only she was not known to have walked the streets, and her two known relationships with men lasted for a total of twenty-four years. Her family had turned against her, but Eddowes' friends and acquaintances all spoke of her with genuine fondness and respect, telling how she displayed a zest for life in spite of the hardships she endured. In the end, like all of the victims, Eddowes was as much a casualty of the brutal and heartless East End environment that also spawned the man who killed her. When she was buried on Monday, 8 October, thousands of people jammed the streets to view the small funeral cortège, which consisted of an open hearse, its plain coffin bedecked with wreaths, followed by two carriages of mourners and a wagon load of Eddowes' peers, who refused to acquiesce in the sombre gloom of the occasion by defiantly dressing in their normal, everyday gear. An anonymous benefactor paid the burial expenses.

13

'I am down on whores...'

The double murder stunned the East End like nothing before it, but there was an even more startling development with the revelation that the Central News Agency had received a letter, and a follow-up postcard, purported to have been written by the killer himself. Addressed to 'The Boss, Central News Office, London, City', and postmarked 27 September, a Thursday (two days before the double murder), it was written in red ink in a neat, copperplate hand and signed Jack the Ripper, the first use of that infamous *nom de plume*. It read as follows:

25 Sept. 1888

Dear Boss
    I keep on hearing the police
have caught me but they wont fix
me just yet. I have laughed when
they look so clever and talk about
being on the right track. That joke
about Leather Apron gave me real

fits. I am down on whores and
I shant quit ripping them till I
do get buckled. Grand work the last
job was. I gave the lady no time to
squeal. How can they catch me now.
I love my work and want to start
again. You will soon hear of me
with my funny little games. I
saved some of the proper *red* stuff in
a ginger beer bottle over the last job
to write with but it went thick
like glue and I cant use it. Red
ink is fit enough I hope *ha ha*.
The next job I do I shall clip
the ladys ears off and send to the
police officers just for jolly wouldnt
you. Keep this letter back till I
do a bit more work then give
it out straight. My knifes so nice
and sharp I want to get to work
right away if I get a chance.
Good luck.
              Yours truly
              Jack the Ripper
Dont mind me giving the trade name.

wasnt good enough
to post this before
I got all the red
ink off my hands
curse it.
No luck yet. They
say Im a doctor
now *ha ha*.

The postcard, smeared with ink and undated, was post-marked 1 October, a Monday, and read as follows:

> I wasnt codding
> dear old Boss when
> I gave you the tip.
> Youll hear about
> saucy jackys work
> tomorrow. double
> event this time
> number one squealed
> a bit couldnt
> finish straight
> off. had no time
> to get ears for
> police thanks for
> keeping last letter
> back till I got
> to work again.
>   Jack the Ripper

The letter and postcard, believed to be the first of their kind, were the most extraordinary features of an already unique and incredible case, yet at first they were regarded as a hoax and received only passing mention in the press. The first news of their existence came in the evening papers of Monday, 1 October, and was repeated in the morning editions on the following day. *The Times* coverage on Tuesday, 2 October was typical, a single paragraph on page six, column three: 'Two communications of the most extraordinary nature both signed "Jack the Ripper" have been received by the Central News Agency, the one on Thursday last [27 September] and the other yesterday morning.' The report reprinted a few passages from both the letter and the postcard but offered little elaboration except to note that 'no doubt is entertained [by the police] that the writer of both communications, whoever he may be, is the same person'.

Over the next few days, while coverage of the double murder dominated the press, the letters themselves received scant attention. 'The general opinion,' reported the *Daily Chronicle*, 'is that they were written by an idiotic practical joker.'[1] Others, however, weren't so sure. 'The writing of the previous letter immediately before the commission of the murders,' one press report argued, 'was so singular a coincidence that it does not seem unreasonable to suppose that the cool calculating villain who is responsible for the crimes has chosen to make the post a medium through which to convey to the press his grimly diabolical humour.'[2]

On 4 October, while neglecting to mention the Jack the Ripper letters at all, *The Times* carried an interesting letter from one Fred W. P. Jago, who suggested that the smeared thumbprint that was on the postcard be compared to the thumbprints of any murder suspects, as 'the surface markings on no two thumbs are alike'. While fingerprinting would go on to revolutionize the detection industry, at the time it was little more than a curious new concept, and it would be several years before the method was actually used in a criminal case. Had someone shown the imagination or initiative to try Jago's suggestion, however, the case may very well have been solved after the police briefly took Joseph Barnett into custody following Mary Kelly's murder.

While the press and authorities equivocated, the name caught on with the public, and by 5 October the *Daily Chronicle* reported that the name 'Jack the Ripper [has become] the sobriquet by which the murderer is now almost universally known'. By then, Scotland Yard was receiving an average of twenty 'Jack the Ripper' letters per day, and the Central News Agency soon reported getting some thirty to forty such letters daily. In no time at all, according to some sources, the combined figure reached as high as 1,000 letters per week, including those offering advice and suggestions as to how the killer might be caught. Decades later, they were still coming.[3] Most of the copycat letters were obvious, transparent imitations of the first 'Dear Boss' letter. In trying to appear authentic, the writers repeated such key words and phrases as 'Boss' and 'get to work', and mimicked the original letter's mocking, taunting tone. Several of these were covered with crude drawings of knives, skulls, coffins and various mysterious symbols. Others were the outgrowths of personal feuds, such as one sent to a man named Jack Porns, which read 'This is to give you notice that I intend to rip your fat little belly next week. A man so infernally conceited and such a liar as you deserves no mercy at the hands of Jack the Ripper.'[4]

Some were light doggerels:

> 'I'm not a butcher
> I'm not a yid
> Nor yet a foreign skipper
> But I'm your own lighthearted friend
> Yours truly, Jack the Ripper'

went one oft quoted example, which made reference to the various contemporary theories as to the Ripper's identity. Another, sent to Dr Thomas Openshaw of the Pathological Museum at London Hospital, closed with the rhythmic verse:

'O have you seen the devle
with his mikerscope and scalpul
a lookin at a kidney
with his slide cocked up'

One letter, signed John Ripper, was sent to the Bryant
& May match plant in Bow, East London, the site of
the famous matchgirls strike earlier that year. 'I hereby
notify that I am going to pay your girls a visit,' it read,
'I am going to see what a few of them have in their
stomachs.'[5]

The most gruesome communication of all was the
cardboard box received on 16 October by George Lusk, the
co-head of the Whitechapel Vigilance Committee. Opening
the box, Lusk discovered a piece of what was apparently a
human kidney, ostensibly the one that had been removed
from Catherine Eddowes' corpse. In an accompanying
hastily scrawled, unsigned note addressed 'From Hell',
the writer boasted of having 'fried and ate' the rest of the
kidney.

Whether or not this was actually Eddowes' missing
kidney has never been satisfactorily determined. The
disappearance of the organ was public knowledge, so in
theory it could have been sent by anyone with a twisted
sense of humour who had access to human or animal body
parts, such as a morgue attendant, medical student or
slaughterhouse worker. At the same time, the sloppy hand,
poor spelling and grammar, were notably different from
from the neat, laboured and more educated hand of the
'Dear Boss' letter.[6]

But were any of these communications actually from the
killer himself? The general consensus today seems to be
that they weren't, that the letters were hoaxes, possibly the
ploy of an unscrupulous journalist. But a close examination

of the evidence indicates otherwise and leaves little room
for doubt that the initial 'Dear Boss' letter and the follow-
up postcard had indeed been written by the man who had
just killed Elizabeth Stride and Catherine Eddowes, and
Mary Ann Nichols and Annie Chapman prior to that.[7]
These letters are too smug, too cocky, too self-assured and
too accurate in their predictions not to have been written by
the killer. For them to have been penned by anyone else
would have entailed the most extraordinary series of
coincidences and the most audacious luck. Going back to
the Emma Smith murder, the killings had occurred at
apparently random intervals, so there was no way for
anyone other than the actual killer to predict accurately
that there was about to be another murder. Yet the writer
of the 'Dear Boss' letter is so confident of his claims that he
asks that his letter be kept from the public until he can keep
his promise to strike again; after all, how better to prove
that he is genuinely who he says he is? Indeed, had the
double murder not followed so closely on its heels, the
letter would have lost much, if not all, of its impact. It
would have been rendered meaningless and probably been
all but forgotten.

Nor was there any way that anyone but the killer himself
could have known that he would try to do something as
bizarre and unprecedented as clipping off his victim's ears;
certainly no one could have simply guessed that this would
happen. As Dr Brown testified, the attempt was indeed
made. A piece of Catherine Eddowes' ear had been sliced
off but had apparently got lost in the folds of her clothing,[8]
and in his haste the killer was forced to flee the scene
without it. 'Had not time to get ears for police', he
explained in the postcard.

That the letter and postcard were written by the same
person is beyond question, as evidenced by the several

references in the latter to the former, the similar handwriting, and the peculiar words and phrases common to both, such as Boss and, most especially, the pen name Jack the Ripper. The letter, dated 25 September, was received by the Central News Agency on Thursday, 27 September, over two full days before the double murder which occurred in the early hours of Sunday, 30 September. As requested, it had been held back and news of its existence hadn't yet been made public when the postcard was received on Monday morning, 1 October, according to the press reports. Although undated, the evidence confirms that the postcard had been written sometime on Sunday. 'You'll hear about saucy jackys work *tomorrow*', the postcard says, meaning Monday, when news of the killings would be in the papers (having occurred too late in the day to make the Sunday editions). It has been argued that because the postcard was franked 1 October, it could have been written and posted on that day, after the story had hit the morning papers, but as the postcard had been received on Monday morning, it had to have been written and posted on the Sunday, before the story broke. As there were no postal collections on Sunday, anything mailed on that day would bear a Monday postmark. At that time, only the killer would have known both the contents of the 'Dear Boss' letter, as well as the details of the double murder, most particularly the fact that the killer hadn't been able to get his victim's ears, as had been promised.

It's curious too that the writer noted in the postcard that 'Number one [Stride] squealed a bit', when everyone in the vicinity at the time subsequently claimed to have heard no such cry. But why say it then, unless it was true? As only the killer could have known, Elizabeth Stride must have managed a brief, stifled cry before she was overcome, which – Mrs Diemschutz claims to the contrary – was probably drowned out by the boisterous singing coming from the adjacent Socialist club. As the *People* pointed out, 'neighbours stated that the noise [from the club] would effectively have prevented any cries for help being heard by those around'.[9]

Both former Chief Constable of the CID Sir Melville Macnaghten and former Assistant Commissioner of the CID Dr Robert Anderson were convinced that the letters were the work of an unscrupulous journalist, his motive ostensibly to sell more newspapers. Both men claimed knowledge of the culprit's identity, though neither was inclined to name him publicly, even twenty years after the events. Both men also rather pompously claimed that they knew who the Ripper was, though they were equally reluctant to point the finger or supply any evidence in support of their claims.[10]

But neither Anderson nor Macnaghten was personally involved in the day-to-day developments of the Ripper murders, and neither was in fact even on the case during the time that the Jack the Ripper letters were written and received.[11] Nor does their claim that a journalist had written the initial correspondence make much sense. For one thing, what newspaper was he alleged to have worked for? If employed by a specific paper – say the *Star*, as has been claimed[12] – why weren't the letters sent to that particular paper? With almost thirty different daily and weekly newspapers in London at the time, readership competition was extremely fierce, so the procurement of so spectacular and important a document as the letter would certainly have represented a major journalistic and sales coup, besides potentially boosting the career of the writer himself. But the original letters were sent to the Central News Agency, an independent service organization which forwarded news of the letters to their various subscriber papers, none of whom considered the material important enough to be worthy of more than a brief mention, and most of whom doubted their authenticity.

So if this mysterious fellow wasn't trying to sell newspapers and wasn't after personal gain, his motive must have been for the sheer mischief of it. While such actions are by no means unheard of – a taped message received during the Yorkshire Ripper case purporting to be from the killer turned out to be a costly hoax – all the evidence points to the conclusion that the original Jack the Ripper letters had indeed been written by the killer himself, while not a shred of hard evidence exists to support any claims to the contrary.[13]

Accepting that the letters were genuine, what then was their purpose? Why had they been written? Did they merely provide an opportunity for the killer to revel anonymously in his sadistic glee, or did they contain a more sinister, underlying message? And why were they sent to the press rather than to the police? Just who were they aimed at?

To begin with, the letters did indeed serve as an outlet for the killer to bask in the spotlight of his sudden infamy. If he had been something of a nonentity beforehand – one of the faceless masses struggling to survive yet another day in the brutal East End environment – in a few short weeks he had become the most feared and notorious, even celebrated, person in the entire country. Every day he read about himself and his deeds in the newspapers and, single-handedly, he had pitched the East End into a state of turmoil bordering on hysterical panic. He could almost feel the fear, see it in women's eyes. 'Jack the Ripper' was the subject of every pub, workplace and street corner conversation, the chilling *nom de plume* conjuring up nightmarish images from the darkest recesses of the mind. 'Men feel that they are face to face with some awful and extraordinary freak of nature,' the *East London Advertiser* wrote, touching upon this supernatural dread. 'So inexplicable and ghastly are the circumstances surrounding the crimes ... that the mind turns instinctively to some theory of occult force and the myths of the Dark Ages ... ghouls, vampires, bloodsuckers and all the ghastly array of fables which have been accumulated throughout the course of centuries take form, and seize hold of the excited fancy. Yet the most morbid imagination can conceive nothing worse than this terrible reality; for what can be more appalling than the thought that there is a being in human shape stealthily moving about a great city, burning with the thirst for human blood, and endowed with such diabolical astuteness as to enable him to gratify his fiendish lust with absolute impunity.'[14]

For Joseph Barnett, born into poverty and unfairly saddled by fate with an inhibiting stammer, and most recently having to face the ignominy of being fired from a menial job that had been far beneath his true capabilities to begin with, here at last was confirmation of his superiority. On top of everything else, he had made fools of the police and outwitted all the so-called experts. And as he certainly couldn't confide in anyone, the press briefly became a vehicle through which he could satisfy his need for recognition and safely boast and gloat of his power and cunning.

At the same time, however, the letters were a direct warning to Mary Kelly to stay off the streets. Like many women in the East End, Kelly lived in fear of the Ripper, but more than most, she had good reason to do so. At that point, Mary Kelly must have felt as if the murders were closing in on her: all four of the most recent victims had lived, drunk and worked in the same streets as Kelly did and, except for Mary Ann Nichols, all of them had direct ties to Dorset Street where Kelly and Barnett were living, as did Martha Tabram whose close friend, the prostitute Mary Ann Connelly, lived just opposite them at Crossingham's doss house, 35 Dorset Street. Annie Chapman, who was reported to have been a friend of Kelly's,[15] had also lodged at Crossingham's, and had previously lived at 30 Dorset Street; Elizabeth Stride had lived at 38 Dorset Street, while Catherine Eddowes sometimes slept in the empty shed at 26 Dorset Street, directly adjacent to the room Kelly shared with Barnett. These were Mary Kelly's colleagues and some of them, at least, were probably her friends. All had been hideously butchered, and now that she was back on those very same streets, Kelly couldn't help but feel particularly vulnerable as she realized that she herself might very well be the killer's next victim.

Joseph Barnett, of course, was aware of Kelly's dread and anxieties, particularly as she had him regularly buy the newspapers, so as to keep up with the latest developments in the case. 'She used to ask me to read about the murders,' he later testified, 'and I used to bring [the newspapers] all home and read them. If I did not bring one, she would get it herself and ask me whether the murderer was caught. I used to tell her everything of what was in the paper.'[16] It was because of this that Barnett sent the Jack the Ripper letters to the press rather than to the police or anyone else, and to the Central News Agency in particular, who would syndicate the news to all of the major newspapers. By doing so, Barnett knew that their bloodcurdling message was guaranteed to reach Mary Kelly; he would read it to her himself! 'I am down on whores,' the letter read, leaving no doubt as to who 'Jack the Ripper' was after, 'and I shant quit ripping them till I do get buckled. Grand work the last job was . . . How can they catch me now. I love my work and want to start again. You will soon hear of me with my funny little games ... My knifes so nice and sharp I want to get to work right away if I get a chance ... Yours truly, Jack the Ripper.' How could Mary Kelly, or anyone in her position, not be terrified? If Barnett's efforts thus far hadn't been enough to dissuade Kelly from walking the streets, then the simultaneous sensations of the horrific double murders and the ghoulishly macabre letters were sure to do the trick.

Indications are that Barnett's ploy was successful, as the immediate effect of the 'Dear Boss' letter, coming as it did on the heels of the double murder, was to empty the East End streets. 'It is not too much to say that the unfortunate creatures who ply their wretched vocation in the streets are paralysed with fear,' wrote the *Daily Chronicle* several days later. 'How much so this is the case is attested by the deserted condition of the East End thoroughfares after half past twelve [when the pubs had shut], and the unbroken solitude in which the side streets, alleys and backways slumber.'[17] Four days later, the *Star* reported much the same thing: 'The terror of the murderer still haunts the wretched women who walk the Whitechapel streets ... there were very few about after the public houses closed... The locality was almost entirely deserted.'[18] The *Echo* concurred: 'From the deserted condition of the streets there is no doubt the state of panic into which the frequenters of the streets by night in this neighbourhood have been thrown into continues undiminished.'[19] A full nine days later, little had changed. 'Miles of streets in the neighbourhood of Whitechapel', the *Star* observed, 'may now be traversed at night without ever meeting a female.'[20]

The evidence shows that, as intended, fear had finally got the better of Mary Kelly, who now kept closer to home, particularly after dark. As *The Times* reported after her death, Kelly had been 'in the habit of nightly going to a public house at Fish-Street Hill, but Sgt. Bradshaw, on making inquiry at the house in question, found that she had not been there for upwards of a month past' – or since about the time of the double murder.[21] Nor had Kelly and Barnett paid any rent since that time either – further indication that she no longer walked the streets. Like it or not, Kelly was now entirely financially dependent on whatever scant earnings Barnett could manage from the docks or fruit markets. Not coincidentally, there followed the longest gap without a killing since the Ripper had first struck on 31 August – an interlude that would soon come to a shattering end when Mary Kelly herself became the fifth, and final, victim of Jack the Ripper.

14

'The very fact that you may be unaware of what the Detective Department is doing is only the stronger proof that it is doing its work with secrecy and efficiency'

News of the double murder spread rapidly through the East End, and by Sunday morning, 30 September, thousands of people had gathered at the scenes of the two crimes. 'Never did ill news travel faster than yesterday,' the *Star* noted, 'while dwellers in other parts of the metropolis were enjoying a Sunday morning's licence for laying abed, the entire East End was in a furore of excitement . . . streams of all sorts and conditions of men poured incessantly in the direction of Berner Street and Mitre Square.' The fact that the police had cordoned off the murder sites and had obliterated any traces of a crime having been committed, were no deterrent to 'the sensation seeking crowds [who] seem to gather some satisfaction from mere proximity to the spot where the curtain had last been raised on the terrible series of tragedies.'[1] 'Down to as late an hour as ten o'clock on Monday night,' the *People* reported, 'large crowds of people continued to assemble around the spots where the murders of Sunday were perpetrated, and so great was the crush at Mitre Square, that it was found requisite to keep a considerable number of extra constables on duty.'[2] As the *Star* wryly noted, 'no one could say that there were not enough police in the East End today'.[3]

It was an apt remark, one reflective of the growing lack of faith on the part of most East Enders in the concern and abilities of the authorities to protect them and look after their interests. In Victoria Park around a thousand people rallied to call for the resignations of Metropolitan Police Commissioner Sir Charles Warren and Home Secretary Henry Matthews, while a similar gathering took place in Mile End Waste. The Vigilance Committee organized nightly volunteer patrols of its own, equipping their men with truncheons and whistles and issuing them with galoshes to soften their footsteps, as many people thought the police should have done. The Committee also appealed again to the Home Office to break with protocol and offer a reward for information leading to the arrest of the Whitechapel Murderer. These were special circumstances, they argued, and as all other methods had thus far failed, it was hoped that the lure of financial gain might prompt someone with useful information to come forward, who would have otherwise been fearful or reluctant to do so. But if for no other reason, the Committee pleaded, a reward should be offered as a gesture of good faith, to demonstrate that the government was indeed equally concerned with the welfare of all of its citizens, regardless of their socio-economic status. Once again, the Home Office stubbornly refused to alter its policy, while further refusing the Committee's request to present their petition to the Queen. Hoping to circumvent the red tape that seemed to be inhibiting the government, the *Financial Times* collected the sum of £300 from its readers, which it forwarded to the Home Office to be used as a reward. The cheque was promptly returned, accompanied by a letter stating the tiresomely familiar refrain that 'if Mr Matthews was of the opinion that the offer of a reward in these cases would have been attended by any useful result, he would himself have at once made such an offer'.[4] The City Police, however, unhindered by such stringent policies, announced the offer of a £500 reward of its own, while various private bodies, such as the Royal Engineers, Tower Hamlets Battalion, came up with further substantial reward offers. Readers of *The Times* and other newspapers pledged donations to a reward fund, though some expressed their resentment at having been asked to do so, arguing that it was the government's duty to deal with such matters, rather than its citizens. Similar sentiments were voiced in a petition to the Home Office signed by over 200 local businessmen and merchants, which stated that 'the universal feeling prevalent in our midst is that the government no longer insures the security of life and property in the East of London'.[5]

Further criticism of the police's handling of the case came from the Whitechapel District Board of Trade who noted a drastic drop in evening trade, as women especially now feared to venture out alone at night, while others were reluctant to stay in Whitechapel for even a short amount of time. In a meeting on the evening of 1 October, the Board among other things questioned the efficiency of the police, noting that only hours after the double murder a local post office was broken into and robbed, right under the noses of the police. The Board also questioned the alleged police policy of regularly moving constables from one district to another, and called upon Commissioner Warren and Home Secretary Matthews to 'locate and strengthen the police force in the neighbourhood'.[6]

Rather than take the opportunity to reassure the people of the East End that the police were indeed aware of their plight and were making every possible effort to deal with the situation, Commissioner Warren countered the Board's claims with a characteristically brash, tactless and ill-considered reply that, in the eyes of his critics, revealed him to be a petulant and immature authoritarian, oversensitive to criticism and entirely lacking in sympathy for or understanding of the needs of the people of the East End. In his letter to the Board,[7] Warren defended the structure and efficiency of the police, and chastised the Board for the inadequate lighting that existed in parts of the East End, before going on essentially to blame the victims for being murdered. Although he claimed that a large reserve force had been drafted into Whitechapel, Warren then contradicted himself by saying that an augmented force would serve little purpose 'so long as the victims actually but unwittingly connive at their own destruction ... [as they] appear to take the murderer to some retired spot and to place themselves in such a position that they can be slaughtered without a sound being heard'.

Nor was Warren above applying some inverted logic. 'You will agree with me,' he proposed, 'that it is not desirable that I should enter into particulars as to what the police are doing in the matter. It is most important for good results that our proceedings should not be published, and the very fact that you may be unaware of what the Detective Department is doing is only the stronger proof that it is doing its work with secrecy and efficiency.'

Only briefly in his lengthy letter did Warren see fit to mention that 'every nerve has been strained to detect the criminal or criminals, and to render more difficult further atrocities'. Otherwise, Warren's claims of police efficiency were laughable in the light of the six recent unsolved murders (including Smith's and Tabram's); and his inability or unwillingness to adjust his force to meet the new situations presented by the murders, along with his refusal to admit or accept the responsibility or blame for the police's inability to catch the murderer, only served to substantiate his critics' claims that he was unsuited for the job of Police Commissioner. As a cartoon published in *Fun* at the time demonstrated, Warren was ready to blame everyone and everything but himself for the police's failures.

In the meantime, the police kept busy with tried and true methods. They conducted a house-to-house search of the area (which turned up Joseph Lawende), and questioned hundreds of people. Ten thousand handbills were distributed throughout the East End, requesting information about the murders, and copies of the 'Dear Boss' letter were circulated, in the hope that someone might recognize the handwriting. More police were drafted into the area, including a number of plain-clothes detectives who combed the streets and pubs looking for clues and information. As the Vigilance Committee also had their own men doing the same, a Keystone Kops scenario sometimes resulted. According to the *Echo*, 'In several instances some of the plain-clothes men who were strange to the neighbourhood were on Saturday watched by members of the Vigilance Committee, while they in turn came under the scrutiny of the detectives'.[8]

The police also continued to make fruitless arrests, picking up people almost at random, it seemed, or merely for looking different or acting 'suspiciously'. In Covent Garden, a well-dressed man was taken to the Bow Street Police Station and questioned simply because he was carrying a small black bag, and a number of doctors were picked up in similar circumstances. In another instance, the police staked out a laundry for three days after a man brought in some bloodstained clothes to be cleaned. The man was arrested when he came to claim his garments, but was able to prove that he was a waiter and had cut his hand on a glass. In Whitechapel, a man arrested after being spotted walking about in female garb turned out to be a reporter hoping to find the Ripper himself. Another man disguised as a woman, who was picked up in Hampstead after brandishing knives, was subsequently released, while in Croydon the police checked out reports of yet another man in female attire who was supposedly seen entering the woods on each of the murder nights. In Shoreditch, a man was found prowling the streets with a bayonet; like the reporter, he too claimed to be on the lookout for Jack the Ripper. Suspects were arrested as far away as County Derby and Belfast, Northern Ireland, while in Bishops Stortford, a man arrested on suspicion of being the murderer objected to being searched and refused to remove his hand from his pocket. As it turned out, only a spectacle case was found on his person. In Glasgow, a man calling himself Jack the Ripper II was arrested after threatening a woman with a knife. More than any previous crimes, the Ripper murders seemed to bring out the cranks and crazies, few of whom were more unhinged than the man who strolled into the King Street Police Station, claiming that he'd lost a black bag. According to the *People*, the man 'began to talk about the women being murdered in Whitechapel, and offered to cut off the sergeant's head'. Not surprisingly, the man was eventually determined to be 'a very dangerous lunatic'.[9]

As ever, the police found themselves inundated with advice on how they should best operate. At the height of the Ripper frenzy, they were said to be receiving about a thousand letters per week, with those not purportedly from Jack the Ripper himself telling the police how they could catch him. Even the coroner, Wynne Baxter, found himself the recipient of over a hundred letters suggesting ways to catch the murderer. 'I daresay,' he remarked at Elizabeth Stride's inquest, 'all would like to have the police under their control.'[10] Newspapers were similarly deluged, and their letters pages often became a lively forum for discussion on what might be done to bring the culprit to justice. Most days saw at least three or four letters on the subject in most newspapers, sometimes more. Many of these, of course, proposed the same ideas as before, such as an augmented police force, constables on the beat to wear rubber-soled shoes, the use of decoy constables and the employment of bloodhounds. These were still among the more sensible ideas but, as often as not, the proposals were silly or impractical. One writer suggested that funds be diverted from the School Board to the police department, while another called for the dispersal of the inhabitants of crime-ridden areas such as Dorset Street, though he neglected to consider where these people would be dispersed to.[11] It was also suggested that the police photograph the eyeballs of the Ripper victims, in the belief that the image of the last thing that they saw – i.e., their killer – would be imbedded on their retinas (and it was alleged that this was done in the case of Mary Kelly).

Many people speculated about the murderer's motive, sometimes concocting bizarre scenarios. One had it that the killer had been plotting all along to frame an innocent person with evidence from one of the crimes, so as to turn him in for the reward monies, which had soared as high as £1,200 in the wake of the double murder. Coroner Baxter had gone on record to state his belief that the women had been killed for the procurement of their bodily organs, while others thought that the murders were the work of a deluded religious zealot. It was suggested that the killer might spend his time around dissecting labs, or undertakers' parlours, or that he may be suffering from syphilis. Others wondered if he may have been castrated or otherwise disfigured, though previously the opposite had been suggested. 'The Marquis de Sade was an amiable looking gentleman,' the *Pall Mall Gazette* had reasoned, 'and so, possibly enough, may be the Whitechapel Murderer.'[12] Doctors, of course, continued to be targets of suspicion, and at one point the killer's ability to overcome his victims swiftly and silently gave rise to the speculation that the killer may have been using a drug such as chloroform to overpower them, though this theory was disproved when no trace of such a substance was found in the post-mortems.

The belief that an Englishman was incapable of committing such atrocities was deep-seated, often overspilling into racist and xenophobic diatribes reflective of the times, when few questioned the morality of British colonialism. Two such letters were published in *The Times* on 4 October. In one, a writer who signed himself NEMO, theorized that the murders were probably the work of 'a Malay, or other low-class Asiatic, coming under the general term of a Lascar, of whom, I believe, there are many in that part of London'. Such a person would appear outwardly normal, NEMO continued, 'but when the villain is primed with his opium, or gin, and inspired with lust for slaughter and blood, he would destroy his defenceless victim with the ferocity and cunning of the tiger'. The other letter was from a Covent

Garden man who, after a considered dismissal of robbery, revenge, the procurement of bodily organs, 'the gratification of animal passion', and homicidal mania as possible motives, concluded that the killer had to be a foreigner, as there was no record of an Englishman ever having committed such a gruesome series of murders. Furthermore, he reasoned 'the celerity with which the crimes were committed [was] inconsistent with the ordinary English phlegmatic nature'.

Many people pointed an accusatory finger across the pond at the United States, citing the usage of such Americanisms as 'Boss' in the Jack the Ripper letters. The Germans, too, fell under suspicion, as, according to one Australian writer, they were known to kill people so as to be able to wear their victim's skins as disguises.

Commissioner Warren grumbled that most of the correspondence repeated the same unimaginative suggestions, but several good ideas had been proposed, some of which, had they been implemented, may have led to the killer's capture. As we have seen, had PC Watkins, for instance, been wearing rubber-soled shoes, which would have enabled him to enter Mitre Square in silence, he might very well have caught Jack the Ripper in the act of butchering Catherine Eddowes; and had someone taken up Fred P. Jago's idea of comparing suspects' thumbprints to the one on the Jack the Ripper postcard, a match might have been made when Barnett was later taken into custody. Nor is there any way of knowing what useful information might have been procured by an early reward offer, or what results might have been achieved by the hiring of female detectives, as had been suggested. Likewise, the effectiveness of plain-clothes men and the infiltration of the criminal underworld by the police, as suggested, have long since been proven, while police efficiency would undoubtedly have been increased had they listened to the letter writer who proposed that the Met have a detailed procedural drill worked out in advance, so as to enable them to act in the most expedient manner when the next murder occurred – something that should have appealed to Warren's military mindset.

One idea that was embraced by Warren – to his later embarrassment – was the employment of bloodhounds. A letter writer to *Lloyds Newspaper* had suggested their use as far back as 9 September, just after Annie Chapman had been killed. He pointed out that they had proved effective some twelve years earlier, in tracking down the Blackburn child murderer, Fish, and the call for their use was subsequently echoed by dozens of letter writers, particularly after the double murder. 'Why are not bloodhounds tried?' argued a typical letter. 'At the very worst, they can fail [in which case] the public will at least have the grim satisfaction of knowing that not a stone is left unturned to run the felon to the ground.'[13]

Several newspapers took up the idea but not all were convinced that the dogs would be able to function effectively in the city streets. As the *Echo* explained, 'The first difficulty ... will be to get them on the right scent, and once that is done, there is the thousand and one cross scents that will run over the track, so that there can be no assurance of their following the same person.'[14]

Nevertheless, Warren seemed keen on the idea, and hoping, perhaps, to allay some of the criticism he was receiving by demonstrating the police's commitment to finding the killer, he procured two dogs, Barnaby and Burgho, from a Scarborough breeder. Several trial runs were held, with Warren himself even acting as the bait in a couple of them, much to the delight of some of his critics. The dogs initially performed well, it was agreed, but

Warren suffered a further ribbing when it was erroneously reported that they had got lost while on a practice run. 'Telegrams have been dispatched to all the Metropolitan Police Stations,' the *Daily Chronicle* wrote, 'stating that if seen anywhere, information is to be immediately sent to Scotland Yard.'[15] In actuality, as it was later discovered, the bloodhounds hadn't got lost at all, but had rather been returned to their owner when it was determined that, as feared, they wouldn't be able to function effectively in the crowded city streets. But Warren's own men were unaware of this, as was the general public, and when the police arrived at Miller's Court after Mary Kelly's murder, they waited for over two hours for the dogs to arrive before it was ascertained that they wouldn't be coming.

At one point, a couple of weeks after the double murder, the police seem to have become convinced again that Jack the Ripper was a Jew. As Assistant Metropolitan Police Commissioner Dr Robert Anderson, recently returned from holiday, was of the belief that the killer was being shielded by the close-knit Jewish community, it may have been he who instigated the house-to-house search of Jewish homes (though what the police expected to turn up at so late a date is unknown, as by then the killer would have had ample time to dispose of any incriminating evidence).

The idea that Jack the Ripper was a Jew was not in itself an unreasonable one, given the large Jewish population in the East End. With their thick foreign accents, their apparent unwillingness to assimilate into the community at large, and their strange dress, behaviour and customs, the Jews had long since aroused the suspicion of their gentile neighbours, and been subject to bizarre rumours, both in England and abroad. The *People* told of the trial some

149

years earlier of an Austrian Jew named Ritter, for the murder of a Christian woman who had suffered mutilations said to be similar to those inflicted upon Annie Chapman's body. 'At the trial,' the *People* reported, 'numbers of witnesses deposed that among certain fanatical Jews there existed a superstition to the effect that if a Jew became intimate with a Christian woman he would atone for his offence by slaying and mutilating the object of his passion. Sundry passages of the Talmud [the Jewish Holy books] were quoted which, according to the witnesses, expressly sanctioned this form of atonement. The trial caused an immediate sensation, and Ritter, being found guilty, was sentenced to death.' A court of appeal, however, ruled that Ritter had been the victim of anti-Semitism and he was eventually cleared, though not before he had spent over three years in prison. As the *People* stressed, 'There is no doubt that the man was innocent.'[16]

All things considered, it was only logical for the police to want to take a closer look at the Jewish community, though they may have been somewhat influenced by the wave of anti-Semitism that the murders had unleashed, as evidenced by the earlier Leather Apron fiasco and the anti-Jewish riots in the East End streets. In fact, Major Smith of the City Police later suggested that Dr Anderson was himself an anti-Semite, given his reckless talk of Jewish conspiracies and cover-ups. 'The conclusion we came to,' Anderson had written in the original, serialized version of his memoirs, 'was that [Jack the Ripper] and his people were low-class Jews, for it is a remarkable fact that people of that class will not give up one of their number to gentile justice ... the only person who ever had a good view of the murderer at once identified him, but when he learned that the suspect was a fellow Jew, he declined to swear to him.'[17] While there is no denying that various ethnic minorities, be they Jews, Gypsies, Asiatics or whomever, often resent what they consider to be interference from outside agencies into their affairs, Anderson neglects to take into account that in such instances the ethnic community would deal with the situation itself and dispense its own form of justice. For Dr Anderson to suggest that the Jewish community would stand idly by while one of its own committed the most horrific series of murders that London had ever seen, is not only ridiculous, but insulting and irresponsible.

Anderson's case is further weakened by the fact that he again offers no details, facts or evidence to back up his claims, but rather pompously expects his account to be accepted at face value. As such, there is no way of knowing if he ever considered the possibility that his mysterious witness may have refused to commit himself to a positive identification because he could not be sure that this was the same person he had seen. Researchers have concluded that Anderson's witness was probably either Joseph Lawende or Israel Schwartz, a Hungarian Jew who may have seen Elizabeth Stride tussling with a man in Berner Street shortly before her death, while another man looked on. But Lawende had insisted from the outset that he would not be able to identify the man he had seen with Catherine Eddowes outside Mitre Square, and there is some confusion regarding the details of Schwartz's story, possibly due to his inability to speak English. An account of Schwartz's story carried in the *Star* differs significantly from the version he gave to the police, though either way, it's inconceivable to think that Jack the Ripper would risk fighting in the streets with one of his victims shortly before murdering her, and in front of at least one onlooker, possibly two. What Schwartz probably witnessed was a domestic dispute, as he apparently first believed.[18]

If Dr Anderson was anti-Semitic, his prejudices weren't

quite as shamelessly bold as those of the reverend Dr Tyler of Mile End, Newton, who railed openly, if euphemistically, against Jewish immigration. 'What London has to fear,' he declared in a sermon at the Aldergate Street Young Men's Christian Association, 'is the importation of the scum of other countries – Russians and Poles come here in considerable numbers. It is from the dregs of society that society has most to fear.'[19]

The house-to-house search of Jewish homes began on or around 16 October, over two full weeks after the double murder. According to the *Star*, it was conducted with a notable lack of tact and sensitivity. '[The police] demand admission to every room,' the paper reported, 'look underneath the beds, and peer into the smallest cupboards. They ask for the production of knives, and examine them.' One woman described her experience dealing with the police. 'I came home from work yesterday,' she told the *Star*'s reporter, 'and as soon as I opened the street door, two men came up and said "Do you live in this front room?" "Yes," I said. "We want to have a look at it." "Who are you and what do you want?" "We are police officers, and we come to look for the murderer." "Do you think I keep the murderer here, or do you suggest that I associate with him?" I replied. They answered that it was their duty to inspect the rooms. I showed them into the room. They looked under the bed, and asked me to open the cupboard, where I keep plates and things. It is not more than two feet wide, and one in depth. They made an inspection of that also. "Do you think", I said, "that it is possible for a man, or even a child to be hidden in that small space?" They made no answer, and walked out. Then they went next door, and inspected those premises.'[20]

Needless to say, the search turned up empty, as did all other avenues of investigation, and the *Daily Chronicle* noted the force's low morale. 'The police are absolutely hopeless of any practical result attending their enquiries,' they reported. 'No attempt is made to disguise the fact that arrest following arrest, and all equally fruitless, have produced in the official minds a feeling almost of despair.'[21]

15

The night-watchman 'was not a little astonished to read that he had been murdered that morning'

The Ripper murders seemed to be a magnet for the bizarre. A week after recounting the ordeal of the Austrian Jew, Ritter, the *People* turned to Vienna as the source of the superstition regarding so-called 'Thieves Candles'. According to German underworld lore, the paper revealed, such candles, made from certain bodily organs, had the power of pitching those exposed to their light into a deep slumber, so as to enable them to be easily robbed. Although it had its roots in the seventeenth century, the superstition was said to be still prevalent in certain German criminal circles.[1] (Equally outlandish was the motive for the murders later allegedly expounded by Aleister Crowley, the famed British occultist, who was 13 years old at the time of the Ripper murders. Apparently Crowley proposed that the location of the victims' bodies formed a five-point star, the completion of which would enable the murderer to achieve a state of invisibility.)

Several psychics and spiritualists came forward to help the beleaguered police. In Cardiff, an elderly woman held a seance in which she and her companions summoned the spirit of Elizabeth Stride. 'After some delay it came', the *Echo* reported, revealing to them the identity of the Ripper, a middle-aged man who lived in Commercial Street, or Road, and was part of a gang of twelve.[2] The *Echo* that evening also reported on another seance, held in Bolton, which also produced information about the killer. According to that medium, he had 'the appearance of a farmer, though dressed like a navvy, with a strap around his waist and peculiar pockets. He wears a dark moustache, and has scars behind the ear and in other places. He will (says the medium) be caught in the act of committing another murder.'[3]

The most celebrated spiritualist connected to the Ripper case was Robert James Lees, the renowned author of several books on spiritualism and said to have been favoured by Queen Victoria herself. While it's uncertain what Lees' actual involvement in the case might have been, it appears that on several occasions he had vivid visions of the killer and his victims which he reported to the police, who, not surprisingly, regarded him as a crackpot. Lees allegedly later saw the man from his visions on a bus and followed him to a prestigious West End address, where it was discovered that the man was a physician. The police were summoned, the story goes, at which time the doctor's wife revealed that her husband had been suffering from blackouts and memory loss, and that on several occasions of late he had returned home with unexplained blood on his clothes and scratches on his person. Accordingly, he was committed to an asylum, after which the murders ceased.[4]

Another strange incident began with an alleged pre-moni tion experienced by a Holborn woman at the very hour that Elizabeth Stride was being murdered by Jack the Ripper. 'As I was lying in bed,' Mrs Mary Malcolm testified at Stride's inquest, 'a strange pressure passed over me, and there were like three distinct kisses given over my face ... this occurrence was like a presentiment to me about my sister.'[5] Although Stride's body had already been tentatively identified, Mrs Malcolm's insistence that the murdered woman was her sister, Elizabeth Watts, resulted in a good deal of confusion, as she didn't appear to be a crackpot or hoaxer. The respectable looking wife of a tailor, Mrs Malcolm appeared to all concerned to be absolutely sincere in her testimony, and it was noted that she bore a strong resemblance to Elizabeth Stride.

According to Mrs Malcolm, who told her tale with considerable grief, her 'sister' had been married to a wine merchant from Bath, who left her when he discovered that she was carrying on with one of his employees. 'Long Liz', as she was known, then took up with a man who owned a coffee shop in Poplar, who was later shipwrecked. Since that time, apparently, she had been drinking heavily and living an immoral life in the East End. 'I have had a great deal of trouble with her,' Mrs Malcolm lamented, 'she once left a baby naked outside my door.'[6] Nevertheless, she had tried to look after her sister and they would meet each week, at which times Mrs Malcolm would give her sister money. It was when she failed to turn up for their regular meeting one week that Mrs Malcolm had become concerned.

As it turned out, Mrs Mary Malcolm was a seriously deluded woman and her entire story was a fantasy, evidently concocted out of what she had read in the papers about Elizabeth Stride and details culled from the life of her real sister, who came forward and spoke to the Central News Agency. 'Mrs Malcolm who gave evidence at the inquest is my sister,' she revealed, 'but I have not seen her for years, [and she] has never, as she swore, given me any money. I never used to meet her, nor [have I] kept a coffee house in Poplar. I may take a drink now and then, but my sister never saw me in drink.'[7] Mrs Stokes, as she was then known, went on to relate a sad and harrowing history of her own. Her marriage to the wine merchant Watts had ended when he went to America without her, where he later died. Watts' friends, who had opposed the union because of the bride's poverty, allegedly took her two children from her and had Mrs Watts committed to a lunatic asylum. Upon her release, she married a sailor named Sneller, who was later shipwrecked. After she was left destitute when her late husband's pension was stopped, Mrs Sneller, as she then was, made an attempt to regain possession of her children, only to find herself again committed to a lunatic asylum. Upon her release, her story went, she married the bricklayer Stokes, with whom she still lived.

When the authorities sought Mrs Malcolm to confront her with the appearance of her real sister, she was nowhere to be found.

The East End, meanwhile, remained on edge. 'The most trifling incident suffices to create a disturbance, if not a panic,' the *Daily Chronicle* observed.[8] One such occurrence took place in Islington a few days later, when a man and woman were arrested on a routine drunk and disorderly charge. As the *Echo* reported, 'Somehow the idea got abroad that the male prisoner was Jack the Ripper, and that the woman was his accomplice... Soon an extraordinary and excited crowd had assembled. A mounted policeman on patrol saw the mob approaching in the distance, and he at once galloped off to render further assistance. This fact appeared to give the arrest an element of importance, and by the time that the prisoners were inside the lock-up, there were quite two thousand people in Upper Street. A number of constables were sent out to clear the thoroughfare, and this was quickly affected, on the people being assured that no important arrest had been made.'[9]

A similar scene ensued in Wentworth Street in the East End, when a Polish butcher accidentally stabbed himself in the abdomen with his own knife. Word quickly spread that the man had been attacked by Jack the Ripper, and by the time the police arrived, several hundred people had already gathered around the shop, and followed excitedly as a cab took the injured man to nearby London Hospital.

Another story that made the rounds had it that the Ripper had been nabbed in the act of stabbing a night-watchman in Shadwell. When a large crowd besieged the Shadwell Police Station, they were told that there was no basis whatsoever for the story and that it was a complete fabrication. As the *Daily Chronicle* noted, the night-watchman involved 'was not a little astonished to read that he had been murdered that morning'.[10]

A bizarre footnote to all the madness was provided when a neatly wrapped package was discovered on the building site of a new police station being erected on the Thames Embankment. When opened, it was found to contain the decomposed remains of a female torso – a headless, armless and legless trunk. It was later determined to be the remains of the same woman whose severed arm had been found in the Thames several weeks earlier, though her identity was never established.

16

'I am not an actual dog...'

If every cloud has its silver lining, then the one benefit of
the Ripper murders was the attention they called to the
East End. Suddenly, with the eyes of the nation – indeed,
of the world – focused on Whitechapel, the appalling
conditions that had festered and propagated there for so
long could no longer be ignored or denied. As the young
fledgling playwright and critic George Bernard Shaw
quipped, 'The Whitechapel murderer has been so successful in calling attention for a moment to the social question
[of the East End].'[1]

Others, of course, had long sought to expose and
alleviate the harsh realities of life in the East End, but any
significant changes to come about were few and far
between. Annie Besant had achieved an important break-
through in helping to organize the successful matchgirls
strike, and Beatrice Potter had, with others, got the government to investigate the so-called sweating system of labour.
Considerable as such developments were, they did not
address the underlying problems of high unemployment,
overcrowding and inadequate housing that had combined

to make the East End so brutal and inhospitable a place to begin with. But the Ripper murders prompted a great cry for social reform that forced people to consider these factors and others. 'The veil has been drawn aside,' wrote the Conservative *Morning Post* in the wake of Annie Chapman's murder, 'that covered up the hideous condition in which thousands, tens of thousands, of our fellow creatures live ... in the very heart of the wealthiest, healthiest, the most civilised city in the world. We have all known for many years that the deplorable misery, gross crime and unspeakable vice – mixed and matted together – lie just off the main roads that lead through the industrial quarters of the metropolis... Parts of our great capital are honeycombed with cells, hidden from the light of day, where men are brutalised, women are demonised, and children are brought into this world only to be inoculated with corruption, reared in terror, and trained in sin, till punishment and sin overtake them too... Amid such gross surroundings, who can be good? Who can rise to anything better?'[2]

Several days later, *The Times* published a letter signed 'S.G.O.'[3] that elaborated on some of the points made by the *Morning Post*. 'Londoners could no longer turn a blind eye to the existence of tens of thousands of our fellow creatures begotten and reared in an atmosphere of Godless brutality,' S.G.O. declared. Such conditions were self-propagating, he argued, in that children reared in such environments had little choice but to follow along the same path to crime and vice. One way of alleviating such conditions, he suggested, would be to re-channel some of the considerable monies being used to spread the Gospel and 'convert the heathens' in various colonial outposts, and to put the funds to better use closer to home.

S.G.O.'s plea provoked a considerable and largely sympathetic response, though some papers, such as the Conservative leaning *Morning Advertiser*, took a defensive stance. 'S.G.O. hardly gives us the credit we deserve for what has already been done,' they wrote. 'The fact remains that well-to-do London has not, for many years, at any rate, been indifferent to the needs of the poor.'[4]

Among the letters received by *The Times* was a thoughtful series of proposals, written by the Reverend Samuel Augustus Barnett (no relation to Joseph), the Vicar of St Jude's Church. A long-time crusader for social reform, Barnett was also warden of Toynbee Hall, the Commercial Street Settlement House, where he organized frequent concerts, art exhibitions, lectures and discussions, in an attempt to bridge class barriers and bring 'high culture' to the East End. In his letter to *The Times*, Barnett spoke for many when he declared that '[the] Whitechapel Horrors will not have been in vain if at last the public conscience awakes to consider the life which these horrors reveal. The murders were, it may almost be said, bound to come.'[5]

Barnett went on to outline a four-part plan which he believed would improve conditions in the East End while acting as a deterrent to further killings. Unafraid to speak his mind, and ruffle a few feathers in the process, Barnett criticized the police for allowing some criminal activities to go unchecked in certain parts of the East End, and called for a larger and more efficient force. Secondly, Barnett saw the need for better lighting and sanitation, suggesting that funds for this purpose be diverted from some of London's wealthier neighbourhoods. The third of what Barnett called his four practical suggestions called for the removal of the many slaughterhouses that blotted the East End, 'for the sake of both health and morals'. Lastly, Barnett saw the need for more responsible landlords, who wouldn't turn a blind eye while their tenants openly engaged in illegal activities, as many did. Barnett stressed that most of Whitechapel was actually as orderly as any place in London, and that most East Enders had high moral standards. Most of the evil in the area, he believed, was concentrated in the notorious quarter mile that included Dorset Street, Fashion Street, Flower and Dean Street and Thrawl Street, and Barnett urged prosperous landlords to buy up properties in this area. 'They might not secure great interest,' he reasoned, 'but they would clear away evil not again to be suffered to accumulate.'

Although he may have sounded idealistic, Barnett was realist enough to acknowledge that his ideas wouldn't actually 'do away with evil' altogether, and probably wouldn't even be implemented. And although he chose to take a more secular approach in dealing with the East End's problems, Barnett believed that ultimately, real change came down to individual people, who must 'find their strength in God'.

The MP Henry Brudnell Bruce saw overcrowding as the source of the East End's problems, and like the Reverend Barnett, he pointed an accusatory finger at unscrupulous landlords and at the laws that allowed them to overfill tenement and lodging houses while charging unjustly high rents.

Reverend F. W. Newland of Canning Town, blamed the East End's miseries on drink, claiming that one out of every six houses on any given street was licensed to sell beer, wine or spirits. On one Saturday night, he counted over 1,500 people entering a single pub in just three hours, while at another pub the figure was 2,000. Reverend Newland believed that it was up to the church to provide viable recreational alternatives to going to the pub, and he also proposed that the church hold regular week-night services.

One writer to the *Star*, Samuel Hayward, addressed the problem of homelessness, and touched on the deficiencies of the workhouse, which released inmates from the casual wards too late in the day for them to find work. Hayward sought funding for the purchase of shelters which would have more liberal hours.[6] Similarly, another group, calling itself the Whitechapel Committee, acquired an abandoned mansion, called Harlow House, which they converted into a shelter for destitute women. 'The only passport required [for admission],' declared its co-founder, R. H. Winter (along with J. L. Dale), 'will be the abject poverty of the applicants, who will be ... allowed to leave between 5.00 a.m. and 7.00 p.m., to enable them to obtain employment.'[7]

Hayward estimated that there were 15,000 homeless people in London, one of whom described his life on the streets in an article written for the *Echo*, eerily resonant of today's situation. 'We are an actual fact in society,' the writer, 'F.H.', declared, 'the despair of reformers and the misery of ourselves. For us there is no hope of better things'. F.H. went on to recount a typical autumn night on the London streets: 'It has just gone midnight. I have been wandering aimlessly about during the evening ... but the wind sweeps with bitter coldness up the river, and the hurrying clouds warn me that the open air will be bad lodging tonight ... if I wish to raise the four pence for the rare luxury of a bed, there is no time to waste ... Just down the south end of the bridge, there used to be some sheltered seats outside the church, but when they found that we used them at night they removed them did these good people of Christchurch.' Still hoping to raise the money for a bed, F.H. heads for the Strand, where he encounters only resentment. 'I don't suppose that I am a very desirable looking companion for anyone, for my coat is in tatters, my feet show through rents in my boots, and it would be impossible for a human face to wear a very good favoured expression under my conditions, but for all that, I am not an actual dog, as every passer by seems to think me. Even the vendors of matches and various trifles despise me and deride my appearance.' Abandoning the hope of raising any money, F.H. opts for a night under the arches near Waterloo Bridge. 'Here and there someone in a similar plight to myself, with head bent down against the wind, and hands thrust deeply into such pockets as his mass of rags can boast, is making doggedly for his accustomed haunt. And I, too, go to my rest – such a rest as Christian England provides for her outcasts in this most enlightened age.'[8]

Another benefactor to the East End needy was the half Jewish, half Irish Thomas Barnado, who began his work with children in Stepney. Like S.G.O., Dr Barnado saw that children had little hope of growing up physically and morally untainted in a slum environment, and he thus arranged for the boarding of destitute children with country families. At one point, Dr Barnado visited the lodging house at 32 Flower and Dean Street, where it is said he spoke to Elizabeth Stride, whose body he later viewed in the morgue. It was, in fact, as a direct reaction to the Whitechapel murders that Dr Barnado set up his registered common lodging houses for children, and by the time of his death in 1905, almost 60,000 children had passed through his homes. Dr Barnado's work continues in his name today.

Also a friend to the East End's poor was the evangelist General William Booth, whose Christian mission in Whitechapel later became the Salvation Army. Booth's initial intent was to provide a hostel with affordable food and lodging for the very needy, though his plan met with considerable hostility when it was claimed that his premises represented unfair competition against local cafe owners and landlords, and that they were frequented by many people who could actually afford better. It was further alleged that Booth's hostel attracted the destitute from other parts of London, who would then remain in Whitechapel where they would be a burden to the community. Later there would be those who criticized the religious indoctrination that was the price of a cheap bed and meals, but there was no denying that Booth provided much needed relief, and within a short time his hostel had fed and lodged thousands of men, and would go on to become an international organization.

For all that was accomplished, however, conditions in the East End were slow to improve, as evidenced by Jack London's sojourn in the area over a decade later, when he found the East End to be as dire, harsh and inhuman a place as it had ever been. It would remain so for some time yet to come.

17

'Whatever you do, don't go wrong and turn out as I have'

The eerie climate of fear and hysteria that had assumed a stranglehold over the East End in the wake of the back-to-back sensations of the double murder and the lurid Jack the Ripper letters, was slow to abate, boosted in part by the shocking 'kidney' letter and parcel received by George Lusk on 16 October, the victims' inquests, and the ongoing debate in the press about how the killer might be caught. With four murders in the past month, and six overall, there was little doubt that he would strike again and, almost three weeks after the double murder, the East End streets remained relatively deserted. But while this may have been exactly what Joseph Barnett had wanted, Kelly's enforced retirement from the streets had unforeseen consequences, and rather than prolonging their relationship, as Barnett had hoped, it only served to hasten its end. Previously, when Barnett was fully employed, their differing schedules allowed Kelly the freedom to do more or less as she pleased, while only having to contend with Barnett for a few hours each day. But all that changed when Barnett lost his job: not only did he now spend much of his time at home, but the loss of his income denied Kelly the funds to go out drinking nightly with her friends, as she had been doing. The situation may have been alleviated somewhat when Kelly's return to prostitution presumably brought in some money, but when the double murder put an end to that, Kelly found herself virtually trapped with Barnett – a man she could no longer stand – in their cramped and claustrophobic twelve-foot square room. If they had frequently quarrelled before, their enforced togetherness under such trying circumstances could only have aggravated the existing tension between them.

Given the situation, Kelly was probably seeking a diversion and relief from Barnett's stifling presence when she disregarded his objections and took in her prostitute friend Julia to stay with her and Barnett, on or around 27 October.[1] This represented a great intrusion into Barnett's life; not only did Julia's presence necessitate the three of them having to co-exist in so small a space together, but it also meant that either they all crammed into the tiny bed or that one of them – undoubtedly Barnett – would have to sleep on the floor. Barnett may have also feared that Julia's presence might encourage Kelly to go back on the streets.

The company of someone Kelly could talk to and confide in must have been a great comfort to her, for no sooner did Julia leave than Kelly immediately took in a second friend, Maria Harvey, to stay with them, on 30 October. It has been suggested that Kelly may have been having a lesbian affair with Julia and/or Mrs Harvey, which would have certainly been a further affront to Barnett.[2] In any event, it proved to be more than Barnett could bear; he had grudgingly tolerated Julia's presence for two or three days, but faced with the sudden appearance of a second woman in their home, Barnett put his foot down. It appears that he gave Kelly an ultimatum: that either Mrs Harvey leave or he would. But if it was a show of bravado, Barnett had misread the situation and Kelly, who was reputedly drunk at the time, called his bluff. At 5.00 or 6.00 p.m., the couple engaged in a violent, heated row in which objects were hurled, breaking two window panes, and blows may have been struck, the end result of which saw Barnett move out, taking a bed in nearby Buller's Lodging House, promising to return when Mrs Harvey had gone.[3] It was also at this time, evidently, that the key to their room went missing, an event that was to assume considerable significance in the light of subsequent events.

If there had been any question before as to who was the dominant one in their relationship, Barnett's departure following their confrontation left no doubt that it was Kelly – indeed, although Barnett had long been the main provider for the couple, Kelly had persuaded Barnett to rent their Dorset Street room in her name, perhaps in anticipation of just such an occurrence.

Shortly after Kelly's death, Barnett gave his version of the circumstances surrounding their quarrel in a statement he made to the press.[4] 'We lived comfortably until Marie allowed a prostitute named Julia to sleep in the same room,' he explained. 'I objected, and as Mrs Harvey afterwards came and stayed there, I left and took lodgings elsewhere. I told her that I would come back if she [Mrs Harvey] would go and live somewhere else ... She only let them in the house because she was goodhearted, and did not like to refuse them shelter on cold, bitter nights.'[5]

Without Barnett and his income – however meagre it may have been – Kelly now had no choice but to return to regular prostitution, in order just to survive. 'Since Joe Barnett left her, she obtained her living as an unfortunate,' Caroline Maxwell, a neighbour, testified at Kelly's inquest.[6] In actuality, Kelly had probably already begun to venture back out on to the streets. As the impact of the double murder receded from memory and the weeks went by without a new one, Kelly may have felt that it was safe enough to risk the occasional job, particularly as Barnett still wasn't earning enough money to suit her needs. Barnett admitted as much to Inspector Abberline not long after Kelly's body was found, with his initial statement that 'in consequence of not earning sufficient money to give her, and her resorting to prostitution, I resolved on leaving her'. A few days later, however, Barnett no longer saw himself as being responsible for Kelly's return to prostitution, but rather put the blame squarely on her friends. 'Marie never went on the streets when she lived with me,' he told the Central News Agency. 'She would never have gone wrong again, and I should never have left, if it had not been for the prostitutes stopping in the house.'[7]

Despite the violent nature of their parting, Barnett and Kelly were quickly back on good terms. Whatever animosity Kelly felt towards Barnett, she couldn't deny that he had been very good to her. Not only had Barnett provided them with the security and stability of a steady roof over their heads, while so many of their ilk existed on a day-to-day basis in lodging houses or worse, but he kept Kelly off the streets, and treated her kindly, spoiling her with gifts and giving her money. 'We were always good friends,' Barnett testified,[8] and this was corroborated by Maria Harvey, who remarked to Inspector Abberline that Barnett and Kelly 'seemed to be on the best of terms' when she saw them together on Thursday evening, 8 November, only hours before Kelly's murder.[9] Barnett had visited Kelly the very next day following their break-up, and he continued to see her on an almost daily basis thereafter, giving her money when he could, no doubt biding his time until Maria Harvey left and he, presumably, would move back in with Kelly.

Unbeknown to Barnett, however, Mary Kelly saw things differently. Barnett's departure, after eighteen hectic months of co-habitation, marked a turning point in Kelly's life, and provided a much needed time for reflection, an opportunity for her to consider her predicament. To begin with, despite his kindness towards her, Kelly was undoubtedly glad to be free of Barnett's austere and suffocating presence. So long as he brought home a good regular wage, Kelly could tolerate him and their constant arguing, particularly as their time together was limited. But now that he could no longer support her, there seemed to be little reason for Kelly to stay with a man she could neither get along with nor bear being with. As far as Kelly was concerned, Joseph Barnett had outlived his usefulness and there was no reason for her to take him back.

On the other hand, Kelly was now alone and worse off than she had ever been. For a young, educated and attractive woman who had come from a stable family background, she had fallen very far indeed. At only 24 or 25 years old, Kelly was an alcoholic and a low-class prostitute, with no money to speak of and no prospects for the future. She lived in one of the worst streets in the East End, notorious for its squalidness, violence and crime, in circumstances barely superior to those who had to struggle for their nightly bed. However, unless Kelly could somehow come up with the six or so weeks back rent that she owed, then she would soon be in that predicament herself – a dismal, frightening prospect, with winter fast approaching and the ever-present spectre of Jack the Ripper still looming ominously over the East End. Not surprisingly, Kelly's friends found her very despondent at this time, given to despair and possibly even contemplating suicide. 'About the last thing she said to me,' Kelly's young friend and neighbour Lizzie Albrook recalled, 'was "whatever you do, don't go wrong and turn out as I have." She had often spoken to me this way,' Albrook remembered, 'and had warned me against going on the street as she had done. She told me, too, she was heartily sick of the life she was leading, and wished she had money enough to go back to Ireland where her people lived.'[10]

Another friend of Kelly's told the Press Association of a similar encounter. 'I saw Kelly on Thursday night [8 November],' Kelly's friend Margaret remembered. 'She told me she had no money, and intended to make away with herself.'[11]

On top of everything else, there was the possibility that Kelly was pregnant, though this has never been confirmed.[12] If true, it would have only posed yet a further hardship to Kelly. Despite the fact that she was a Catholic, when faced with the prospect of struggling to support herself through several more months of pregnancy, and the burden of rearing of a child on her own, Kelly would have had little choice but to have an abortion. As to who the father was, it's difficult to determine. Joseph Barnett, of course, is a candidate, as would be Kelly's former beau Joseph Fleming. However, if, as alleged, Kelly was in her third month of pregnancy at the time of her death, then conception would have occurred sometime around early to mid-August. At that time, Barnett had probably already lost his job, prompting Kelly's return to the streets, in which case the father may very well have been an anonymous customer.

In any case, she couldn't tell Barnett. If he found out that Kelly was pregnant and believed that the child was his, he would have certainly fought with her to keep it and would have bitterly opposed Kelly's plans for an abortion. He may have even thought that having a child might be just the thing to keep them together. If, on the other hand, Barnett

Press coverage of the double murders (*Pictorial News*, Oct. 6).

Reproduction of the 'Dear Boss' letter, and follow-up postcard, which, new evidence shows, couldn't have been written by anyone other than the actual killer.

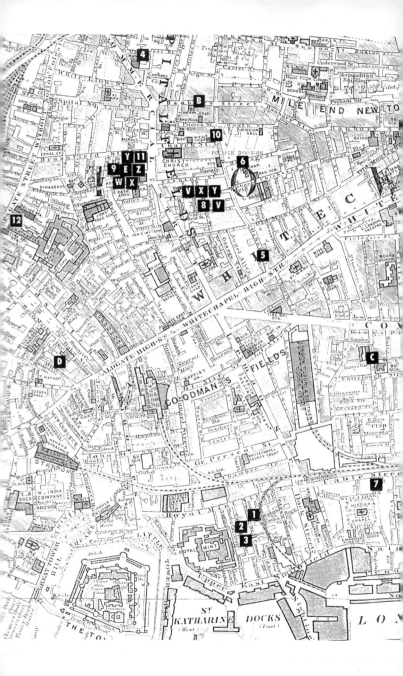

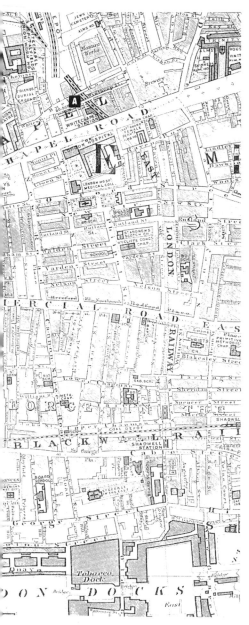

1862 Map of East London

KEY

Known addresses of Joseph Barnett through the time of Mary Kelly's murder:

1. 1858, 4 Hairbrain Court.
2. 1861, 2 Cartwright Street.
3. 1864, 8 Walton's Court, Cartwright Street.
4. 1871, 24½ Great Pearl Street.
5. c. 1878, Osborne Street.
6. c. 1878, St. Thomas' Chamber, Heneage Street.
7. c. 1878, North East Passage, Wellclose Square.
8. 1887, George Street.
9. 1887, Paternoster Court, Dorset Street.
10. 1887/88, Brick Lane (precise location unknown).
11. 1888, 13 Miller's Court, 26 Dorset Street.
12. 1888, New Street, Bishopsgate Street.

Murder sites of Jack the Ripper victims:

A Mary Ann Nichols, Bucks Row.
B Annie Chapman, 29 Hanbury Street.
C Elizabeth Stride, 40 Berner Street.
D Catherine Eddowes, Mitre Square.
E Mary Kelly, 13 Miller's Court, 26 Dorset Street.

Victim's addresses around the time of their deaths:

V Mary Ann Nichols, 18 Thrawl Street, Flower and Dean Street.
W Annie Chapman, 35 Dorset Street.
X Elizabeth Stride, 38 Dorset Street, 32 Flower and Dean Street.
Y Catherine Eddowes, 26 Dorset Street, 55 Flower and Dean Street.
Z Mary Kelly, 26 Dorset Street, 13 Miller's Court.

Causes of Death.	1st Quar.	2nd Quar.	3rd Quar.	4th Quar.	Total
All causes	437	336	395	434	1602
ZYMOTIC DISEASES.					
1 Small Pox { Vaccinated...	..	...	...	...	...
Unvaccin't'd	...	...	...	...	...
No statement	...	...	...	...	...
2 Measles	27	16	6	3	52
3 Scarlet Fever	3	3	10	11	27
4 Typhus	...	...	...	...	.
5 Relapsing fever	...	...	...	...	...
6 Influenza	...	...	...	...	...
7 Whooping cough	6	3	3	18	30
8 Diphtheria	1	2	...	3	6
9 Simple, continued and ill-defined fever	...	1	...	...	1
10 Enteric fever	...	3	...	4	7
11 Simple cholera	...	1	...	...	1
12 Diarrhœa, dysentery	4	8	64	4	80
13 Remittent fever	...	...	...	...	...
14 Hydrophobia	...	...	...	...	...
15 Glanders...	...	...	...	...	...
16 Cow pox and effects of vaccination	...	...	...	...	...
17 Venereal affections	3	3	1	4	11
18 Erysipelas	2	...	3	1	6
19 Pyæmia and Septicæmia	...	...	3	...	3
20 Puerperal fever	1	...	...	...	1
21 Other Zymotic diseases	...	...	...	1	1
22 Thrush	...	...	..	1	1
23 Worms and other Parasitic diseases	...	...	...	...	...
24 Starvation, want of breast milk	1	...	..	1	2
25 Alcoholism	...	1	3	...	4
26 Rheumatic fever and rheumatism of heart	...	1	...	3	4
27 Rheumatism	...	...	1	2	3
28 Gout	...	...	...	...	.
29 Rickets	...	...	...	1	1
30 Cancer	10	10	13	8	41
31 Tabes Mesenterica	1	5	18	5	29
32 Tubercular Meningitis	2	3	5	...	10
33 Phthisis	45	36	40	38	159
34 Scrofula, Tuberculosis	6	1	2	5	14
35 Other constitut'l diseas's	25	17	35	24	101
36 Premature birth	11	6	5	5	27
37 Atelectasis	...	...	1	...	1
38 Congenital malformatns	...	...	...	1	1
39 Old age	15	18	13	13	59
40 Apoplexy	2	6	1	10	19
41 Epilepsy	...	3	1	5	9
42 Convulsions	9	13	10	20	52
43 Other diseases of brain and nervous system	32	24	25	24	105

Causes of Death.	1st Quar.	2nd Quar.	3rd Quar.	4th Quar.	Total
44 Diseases of organs of special sense	...	1	...	...	1
45 Diseases of circulatory system	28	24	17	42	111
46 Croup	8	9	4	2	23
47 Bronchitis	79	32	25	60	196
48 Pneumonia	33	21	16	35	105
49 Pleurisy	...	1	1	6	8
50 Other respiratory dis'es	7	13	9	13	42
51 Dentition	10	12	12	6	40
52 Quinzy, sore throat	...	...	...	...	...
53 Enteritis	...	...	...	...	...
54 Peritonitis	...	2	2	...	4
55 Diseases of liver	1	...	2	4	7
56 Other diseases of digestive system	14	15	15	10	54
57 Diseases of lymphatic syst'm & ductless glands	...	1	...	...	1
58 Diseases of urinary sys'm	12	12	11	11	46
59 Diseases, generative system	3	...	1	3	7
60 Accidents at childbirth	2	1	2	3	8
61 Diseases of locomotive system	...	1	...	2	3
62 Diseases of integumentary system	...	1	2	1	4
VIOLENT DEATHS. Accident.					
63 Fracture and contusion	7	4	2	4	17
64 Gun-shot wounds	...	...	...	...	...
65 Cut, stab	...	...	...	...	.
66 Burn and scald	1	1	4	5	11
67 Poison	...	...	...	...	...
68 Drowning	1	1	...	2	4
69 Suffocation	24	...	6	4	24
70 Otherwise	...	...	...	3	3
Homicide.					
71 Murder & manslaughter	...	...	...	...	...
Suicide.					
72 Gun-shot wounds	...	...	...	...	...
73 Cut, stab	...	...	...	...	...
74 Poison	...	...	...	1	1
75 Drowning	1	...	...	...	1
76 Hanging	...	...	...	...	...
77 Otherwise	...	...	...	...	...
78 Other causes	...	...	1	2	3

Death statistics for Whitechapel for 1887. Despite a not undeserved reputation for violence, not a single murder occurred in Whitechapel in the year preceding the Ripper murders – out of a total of 80 for all of Metropolitan London (Tower Hamlets Library).

Over two weeks after the double murder, the police initiated a house to house search of Jewish homes (*Pictorial World*, Oct. 25).

Sir Charles Warren, the controversial Metropolitan Police Commissioner, whose stubborn refusal to consider new ways of apprehending the Whitechapel Murderer hampered the police investigation (*Pictorial News*, March 20, 1886).

A pitched battle between Warren's police force and unemployed demonstrators in Trafalgar Square in 1887 became known as 'Bloody Sunday' (*Illustrated London News*, Oct. 29, 1887, courtesy Tower Hamlets Library).

The Middlesex Street Market, a Sunday morning, c. 1895. Most of the traders were Jewish. The cryptic 'Juwes' message appeared in nearby Goulston Street (Greater London Record Office).

Fish-Street Hill, c. 1910. According to the police, Mary Kelly was known to frequent a pub there. The street was a busy thoroughfare for traffic from nearby Billingsgate Market; note the fish porter on the far left, balancing a trunk of fish on his head (Greater London Record Office).

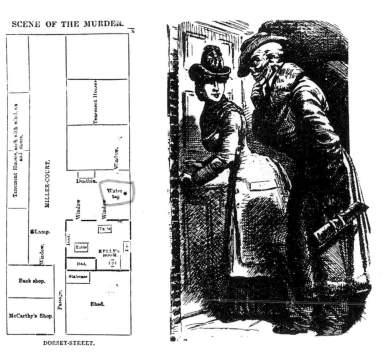

SCENE OF THE MURDER.

MILLER-COURT.

Tenement House, each with windows and doors.

Tenement Houses

Dustbin.

Water tap

Window

Window

Window

Lamp.

Window

Table

Table

KELLY'S ROOM.

Bed.

Back shop.

Staircase

Passage.

Shed.

McCarthy's Shop.

DORSET-STREET.

Press coverage of the death of Mary Kelly. Note the water tap in Miller's Court, possibly the one Major Smith of the City Police tracked the Ripper to on the night of the double murder, and the shed adjoining Kelly's room, where Catherine Eddowes used to stay.

THE NARROW COURT AND KELLY'S "HOME."

Jack the Ripper spent several hours butchering Mary Kelly, after which he was never heard from again (Crown copyright, Public Record Office).

somehow knew that he could not have been the father, then it's likely that he would have been enraged at what could only be seen as the physical evidence of Kelly's unfaithfulness and disloyalty. Either way, Kelly would have gone to considerable lengths to keep her condition secret from Barnett, and it may have been a significant factor in her decision not to take him back.

On Thursday, 8 November, nine days after Barnett's departure, Kelly spent the afternoon drinking with her friend Maria Harvey at Harvey's new lodgings. Harvey had stayed with Kelly until Tuesday, 6 November, after which she took a room a few dozen yards down the street from Kelly, in New Court, Dorset Street. There is some confusion as to their precise movements that afternoon as Mrs Harvey gave two different accounts of their time together. In a statement to the press made on Saturday, 10 November,[13] Harvey stated that she and Kelly were drinking together in her New Court room until around 7.30, at which time Kelly headed off towards Leman Street, possibly seeking trade. In her inquest testimony, however, Harvey indicated that she and Kelly had been drinking in Kelly's room in Miller's Court, and that she herself left at around five minutes to seven, when Barnett stopped by.[14] Either way, Kelly was in her room when her friend Lizzie Albrook dropped in for a visit. 'The last time I saw her,' Albrook told the press, 'was on Thursday night, about 8.00, when I left her in the room with Joe Barnett.'[15]

Barnett fixed the time of his visit with Kelly as having taken place between 7.30 and 8.00 p.m. '[I] told her I was very sorry I had no work,' he told Inspector Abberline, 'and that I could not give her any money.'[16] Barnett did not say what else they talked about over the next half hour or so, but as Mrs Harvey had last stayed with Kelly two nights earlier, Barnett had probably come there expecting to move back in with Kelly, as he had told her he would. But this never happened, as Kelly had presumably determined in his absence not to take him back, effectively ending their conjugal relationship.[17] Whether she tried to reason with Barnett, assuring him that they could still be the best of friends, if no longer lovers, or pleaded for some more time before making a final decision about his moving back, or whether alcohol got the better of her and she bluntly told Barnett that they were finished, that he was no longer of any use to her, is strictly a matter of conjecture. In any case, Barnett would have been stunned, if not devastated, by Kelly's decision and must have spent the remainder of his time with her pleading and arguing in vain for her to reconsider. So distraught was he, that he apparently turned directly to his brother, Daniel, for support. It's known that Daniel met with Kelly later that evening, perhaps to appeal to her on Joseph's behalf, possibly over drinks in the Horn of Plenty pub in Dorset Street.[18]

Kelly was next seen that evening at around 9.00 p.m. Leaving Miller's Court, she stopped for a brief chat with her neighbour, Elizabeth Prater.[19] Where she went next is unknown, but between 10.00 and 11.00 p.m., she was spotted by Maurice Lewis, the Dorset Street tailor who claimed to have known Kelly for five years. According to a statement he gave to the press,[20] Lewis saw Kelly in the Horn of Plenty where she was drinking with some companions, among them her friend Julia and a man identified as 'Dan', described as an orange seller with whom Kelly had recently been living. Obviously this is a description of *Joseph* Barnett, but as there are no other reports of him having been with Kelly at this time and it is known that Joseph's brother Daniel did meet with Kelly later that night, it seems that either Lewis and/or the reporter he

176

spoke to somehow mixed up the identities of Joseph and Daniel Barnett (an error possibly compounded by the familial resemblance shared by the brothers).[21]

According to Lewis, Kelly subsequently went off with a respectably dressed man, presumably a client. Such a man was described as having approached Kelly by her friend Margaret, when the two of them reportedly met around 10.30 that night in Dorset Street, and Kelly complained to Margaret of being destitute and spoke of committing suicide. Not long after, according to Margaret, the man offered Kelly money and she went off with him.[22]

At 11.45, Kelly was seen entering her room with 'a short, stout man [of about 36], shabbily dressed ... [with] a blotchy face, and a full, carroty moustache', by her neighbour Mary Ann Cox, a widow and fellow prostitute, who lived at 5 Miller's Court. The man was carrying a pot of ale and Cox noted that Kelly was 'very much intoxicated'. 'I said, "Good night, Mary,"' Cox testified, 'and she turned round and banged the door. She said, "Good night. I am going to have a song." As I went in [to my room], she sang "A violet I plucked from my mother's grave when a boy". I remained a quarter of an hour in my room and went out. Deceased was still singing at one o'clock when I returned. I remained in the room for a minute, to warm my hands, as it was raining, and went out again. She was singing still, and I returned to my room at three o'clock. The light [in Kelly's room] was then out, and there was no noise.'[23]

It must have been around that time that Joseph Barnett returned to Mary Kelly's room to plead with her to take him back, letting himself in by reaching through the broken window pane and manipulating the lock (the alternative method of entry he and Kelly had devised since the key had gone missing). Since his earlier meeting with Kelly, Barnett had probably spent the time anguishing over her loss and he may have been drinking.[24] At some point, his brother Daniel probably reported back to him that he had failed to persuade Kelly to reconsider her decision. Afterwards, Barnett returned to Buller's Lodging House where he lost himself in a game of whist before retiring. Over the next few hours, however, it seems that Barnett worked himself into such a desperate emotional state that, despite the late hour, he felt that he had to speak to Kelly at once. Leaving Buller's unseen, Barnett headed for his final confrontation with Kelly, hoping to persuade her to change her mind and take him back. But if he had expected Kelly to accommodate him, he was mistaken. She had been drinking the entire day and well into the evening, and when last seen only a couple of hours earlier had been very drunk indeed. She couldn't have had more than a couple of hours' sleep when Barnett unexpectedly appeared in the room, demanding that she talk to him. Hung over and groggy, fatigued and emotionally exhausted, Kelly would have been in no mood or condition for a discussion or argument with Barnett. Although precisely what may have passed between them can, of course, never be known, it's possible that, again, Kelly first tried to reason with Barnett, perhaps pleading with him to come back the next day when they might better talk, before becoming exasperated, at which point she gave vent to all the anger, hostility and frustration that had been building up within her for the past several months. With no thought of sparing his feelings, Kelly probably made it clear to Barnett that she despised him, that without his income he was of no use to her at all, and that there was no chance of them ever reuniting. She may have even told Barnett that she had never loved him, and perhaps went so far as to mock him for his inadequacy (and if she was, indeed, pregnant that may have been another point of contention between them). Whatever did occur, it proved to be more than Barnett could bear and he snapped, allowing Kelly only the time to emit a faint, startled cry of 'Murder!' and to throw her hands up feebly in defence, as he thrust the sheet over her face and slit her throat, before plunging into a maniacal frenzy that lasted up to several hours. Among other atrocities, Barnett slashed Kelly's face beyond recognition, cut off her breasts, sliced parts of her flesh down to the bone, and removed her heart, liver, spleen, uterus, kidneys and a large portion of her intestines, taking the heart with him when he left, though that ultimate ghoulish atrocity only recently came to light; as with the possible fact of Kelly's pregnancy, it was evidently considered just too horrible for the public to bear.

As it turned out, Kelly's cry was heard by at least two of her neighbours in Miller's Court, sometime between 3.30 and 4.00 a.m., though such was the nature of life in Dorset Street, that neither person paid it any mind. As one explained, such cries were 'nothing unusual in the street. I did not take any particular notice'.[25] Another neighbour, Mary Ann Cox, testified to hearing a man leave the court at about 6.15 a.m. but she too paid it no mind.[26]

18

'The sight I saw was more ghastly even than I had prepared myself for'

Friday, 9 November was Lord Mayor's Day, an occasion of pomp and pageantry dating back to 1189. Although the post, like today's monarchy, has since evolved into a more ceremonial role, in earlier days the Lord Mayor was an integral part of the City of London's corporate and financial machinery, and to this day the Lord Mayor may, technically, refuse the King or Queen entry into the City.

The highlight of the day has traditionally been an elaborate stately procession through the City and Westminster. Although the Lord Mayor-elect, James Whitehead, had hoped to play down some of the more garish aspects of the pageant, he still didn't escape criticism for the ostentatious displays of wealth flying in the face of the dire poverty of the East End, which adjoins the City. The police also anticipated disturbances from the unemployed and socialists but in the end it was Jack the Ripper who stole the show.

On the morning of the ninth, a light drizzle was falling after the heavy rain of the night before. At that point, Mary Kelly owed 29s in back rent, having not paid anything since around the time of the double murder. With Barnett now gone, John McCarthy, the landlord, probably feared that Kelly might 'do a runner' and disappear without paying what she owed. With that in mind, he sent his employee, Thomas Bowyer, to Kelly's room to try to collect some money from her. 'Arrears are got as best you can,' he explained at Kelly's inquest.[1] Had McCarthy been less anxious, Kelly's body might have lain undiscovered in her room for several more days.

Thomas Bowyer told what happened next. 'Knocking at the door, I got no answer,' he testified, 'and I knocked again and again. Receiving no reply, I passed round the corner by the gutter, about where there is a broken window ... I put my hand through the broken pane and saw two pieces of flesh lying on the table.' Sickened by the sight, Bowyer averted his eyes. 'The second time I looked,' he continued, 'I saw a body on [the] bed and blood on the floor. I at once went very quietly to Mr McCarthy ... and I told him what I had seen. We both went to the police station.'[2]

'The sight I saw was more ghastly even than I had prepared myself for,' McCarthy told the press. 'On the bed lay the body as my man had told me, while the table was covered with what seemed to be lumps of flesh.'[3]

At the Commercial Street Police Station, McCarthy and Bowyer spoke to Inspector Beck who accompanied them back to Miller's Court. The first thing he did was to seal off the immediate area, a simple task as Miller's Court was separated from Dorset Street by a narrow, covered passageway. He then summoned assistance and sent a telegram to Commissioner Warren advising that the bloodhounds be immediately sent to the scene. Like practically everyone else except for the Commissioner, Beck believed that the bloodhounds were standing by at the ready.

Dr George Bagster Phillips, the police surgeon, was among the early arrivals. 'I was called by the police on Friday morning at 11.00,' he recalled. 'As the door [to Kelly's room] was locked, I looked through the lower of the broken window panes and satisfied myself that the mutilated corpse lying on the bed was not in need of any immediate attention from me, and I also came to the conclusion that there was nobody else on the bed, or within view, to whom I could render any professional assistance.'[4] Phillips consulted with Inspector Beck and it was agreed that the room should not be entered until the bloodhounds arrived. In the meantime, the window frame was removed and a police photographer took several pictures of the remains, one of which survives to this day, testament to the demented savagery of the man who called himself Jack the Ripper.

Dr Phillips was soon joined by his assistant and by Drs Bond, Brown, Duke and Gabe. Dr Gabe let it slip to the press that a certain, unnamed organ was missing from the body. Meanwhile, word of the latest atrocity had spread quickly through the East End streets and an agitated crowd was already gathering. Numerous police converged on the site as well, among them Assistant Commissioner Dr Robert Anderson, Chief Inspector West, Inspector Reid, Chief Constables Monsell, Howard and Roberts and Inspector Abberline, who arrived at around half past eleven. 'Never before had so many men been dispatched from Whitehall,' the *People* reported. 'The scene in the narrow courtway leading to the house was one of extraordinary excitement. The whole space was closely packed with detectives and quite a small army of plain-clothes constables were located in Dorset Street, within an astonishingly short space of time.'[5]

Into the midst of this scene came Joseph Barnett, sometime in the early afternoon. 'I heard there had been a murder in Miller's Court,' he later told the press, 'and on my way there I met my sister's brother-in-law, and he told me it was Marie. I went to the Court and there saw the police inspector and told him who I was and where I had been the previous night.'[6] Barnett then peered through the open window to view the body and confirmed that it was Kelly. John McCarthy had also confirmed Kelly's identity.[7]

The police took Barnett to the station where he was interviewed by Inspector Abberline. 'They kept me about four hours,' Barnett told the press, 'examined my clothes for bloodstains, and finally finding the account of myself to be correct, let me go free.'[8] According to the *Daily Telegraph*, Barnett told the police that he 'was at [Buller's] Lodging House in New Street, and was playing whist there until half past twelve when he went to bed'.[9]

Although the police, as usual, made a few fruitless arrests, Barnett's detention may have been the inspiration for a curious story that appeared the next morning in the *Eastern Post and City Chronicle*. 'An arrest has been made,' they reported, 'and it is so far satisfactory to learn that this is not supposed to be another of the series of Whitechapel murders which have caused so much sensation in the past. It is reported that the cause of the dreadful crime was jealousy. First reports, however, are always more or less conflicting.'[10]

Indeed they were. The *Star* blamed this in part on a lack of cooperation from Sir Charles Warren's Metropolitan Police, whom they accused of suppressing information.

(Major Smith's City Police were regarded in a much more favourable light.) 'The result of the police reticence,' wrote the *Star*, 'has been the creation of a market for false news, and the actual facts of this latest horror [Kelly's murder] differ with each narrative of the revolting details.'[11] This was also due to the fierce competition between newspapers, who often printed hearsay and uncorroborated reports in their rush to get their stories out. As such, Joseph Barnett was variously referred to as Joseph Kelly, James Kelly, John Kelly, Joseph Barrett, Dan and, ominously, Jack. Among other inaccuracies, Kelly was falsely reported as having had a six- or seven-year-old child living with her, and it was elsewhere claimed that she was an accomplished artist. In one report she was said to be known as 'Ginger' due to the colour of her hair, while another story claimed that she was known locally as 'Fair Emma', though there was never any mention of these names anywhere else.

At 1.30 p.m. Inspector Arnold arrived in Miller's Court with the news that the bloodhounds wouldn't be coming after all. They would have been of little use in any case. By the time Kelly's body was discovered, it was 'broad daylight', their handler later explained, 'and the streets [were] crowded with people. The only chance the hounds would have would be in the event of a murdered body being discovered, as the others were, in the small hours of the morning, and being put on the trail before many people were about.'[12]

With the news that the bloodhounds weren't coming, there was no longer any need to refrain from entering Mary Kelly's room. As the door was locked, Inspector Arnold ordered it to be broken down and landlord John McCarthy did this himself with a pickaxe.

The locked door remains one of the more confusing but

none the less significant mysteries of the Ripper case, for if the door to number 13 had been locked with the key, as it appears to have been, then that would mean that Jack the Ripper had somehow come into possession of the key to Mary Kelly's room, which had recently gone missing.

Inspector Abberline said that that wasn't the case, though his logic appears to be that Jack the Ripper couldn't have had the key to Kelly's room because it had already disappeared. 'Barnett informs me that [the key] has been missing for some time,' he testified at Kelly's inquest, 'and since it has been lost [he and Kelly] have put their hands through the broken window and moved back the catch. *It is quite simple*.' (My italics).[13] But if it was as easy as that, why then did the police have to break down the door to get into the room? Surely with so huge an assemblage of police on the scene, among them the Assistant Commissioner, several Chief Constables and Inspectors, and numerous detectives and constables, one of them should have been able to figure out Barnett's alternative mode of entry, particularly as the removal of the window frame provided both an unobstructed view of the premises and easier access to the lock. Anyone sticking his head through the window would have seen that the lock was within easy reach and surely someone would have thought to try to jiggle it open. Furthermore, the fact that Barnett viewed the body by looking through the window means that he arrived on the scene before the door had been broken down, in which case he could have shown the police his alternative means of entry – assuming that he was aware of the situation. Even so, John McCarthy would undoubtedly have known that such a means of entry was possible and he certainly would have preferred to save himself the trouble and expense of smashing down the door to one of his own properties – unless the door had indeed been locked with a key, in which case Barnett's method of entry wouldn't have been possible, leaving the police no other choice but to order McCarthy to break down the door. As Donald Rumbelow concluded, 'Someone had a key and used it, which is why the door had to be forced.'[14]

If the door had indeed been locked with the key, the question arises as to how it happened to come into the possession of Jack the Ripper. Barnett's and Kelly's alternative mode of entry only became possible after the window panes had been broken during their violent row, which means that the key had to have disappeared at around that time. While it is possible, though unlikely, that Mary Kelly happened to find it at the last minute, conveniently enabling her unknown assailant to lock the door behind him when he left, what is far more likely and plausible an explanation is that Joseph Barnett took the key with him as security when he moved out, knowing that its possession guaranteed him access to Kelly's room, regardless of what her wishes might be. So long as the key was missing, Barnett realized, Kelly would have to rely upon their alternative mode of entry, which meant that he would be able to enter the room at any time he wanted simply by reaching through the window and manipulating the catch – a mode of entry he presumably employed in the early hours of Friday, 9 November.

Mary Kelly's room was described as 'a tenement in itself' in one press report, and as a 'wretched hole' in another.[15] 'The furniture consisted of the bed upon which the body was stretched,' the *Standard* reported, 'which was placed next to a disused washstand in the corner behind the door, and opposite the two windows, in the smaller one of which there were two panes of glass broken. A man's coat was put across there to keep out the draught. Close to the larger window stood a table, and another table of smaller size was placed between it and the bed, and it was upon this that the flesh stripped from the body was heaped ... Next to the fireplace was a cupboard.'[16] 'The only attempts at decoration,' according to the *Pall Mall Gazette*, 'were a couple of engravings, one "The Fisherman's Widow" stuck over the mantlepiece; while in the corner was an open cupboard, containing a few bits of pottery, some ginger beer bottles, and a bit of bread on a plate.'[17]

Dr Phillips was among the first to enter the room. 'On the door being opened,' he testified, 'it knocked against a table which was close to the left-hand side of the bedstead, and the bedstead was close against the wooden partition. The mutilated remains of a woman were lying two-thirds over, towards the edge of the bedstead, nearest the door. Deceased had only a linen undergarment upon her, and by subsequent examination I am sure the body had been removed, after the injury which caused death, from that side of the bedstead which was nearest to the wooden partition previously mentioned. The large quantity of blood under the bedstead, the saturated condition of the palliasse [mattress], pillow, and sheet at the top corner of the bedstead nearest to the partition, leads me to the conclusion that the severance of the right carotid artery, which was the immediate cause of death, was inflicted while the deceased was laying at the right side of the bedstead, and her head and neck in the top right-hand corner.'[18]

Dr Bond detailed how they found Kelly's body in his post-mortem report: 'The body was lying in the middle of the bed, the shoulders flat, but the axis of the body inclined to the left side of the bed. The head was turned on the left cheek. The left arm was close to the body with the forearm flexed at a right angle and lying across the abdomen.

'The right arm was slightly abducted from the body and rested on the mattress, the elbow bent and the forearm supine with fingers clenched. The legs were wide apart, the left thigh at right angles to the trunk and the right forming an obtuse angle with the pubes.

'The whole of the surface of the abdomen and thighs was removed and the abdominal cavity emptied of its viscera. The breasts were cut off, the arms mutilated by several jagged wounds and the face hacked beyond recognition of the features. The tissues of the neck were severed all round down to the bone. The viscera were found in various parts viz: the kidneys with one breast under the head, the other breast by the right foot, the liver between the feet, the intestines by the right side and the spleen by the left side of the body. The flaps removed from the abdomen and thighs were on a table.

'The bed clothing at the right corner was saturated with blood, and on the floor beneath was a pool of blood covering about 2 feet square. The wall by the right side of the bed and in a line with the neck was marked by blood which had struck it in a number of separate splashes.'[19]

Following the preliminary examination of Kelly's body in her room by Drs Phillips, Bond and the others, the remains were placed in a much used, 'dirty and scratched' coffin for removal, according to *The Times*. 'The news that the body was about to be removed caused a great rush of people from the courts running out of Dorset Street,' that paper continued, 'and there was a determined effort to break the police cordon at the Commercial Street end. The crowd which pressed round the van was of the humblest class, but the demeanour of the poor people was all that could be desired. Ragged caps were doffed and slatternly looking women shed tears as the shell, covered with a ragged looking cloth, was placed in the van. The remains were taken to the Shoreditch Mortuary where they will remain until they have been viewed by the coroner's jury.'[20]

The *People* told what happened next. 'The photographer who had been called in to photograph the room and the body, removed his camera from the premises at half past four, and shortly afterwards a detective officer carried from the house a pail with which he left in a four-wheel cab. The pail was covered with a newspaper and was stated to contain portions of the woman's body. It was taken to the house of Dr Phillips, 1 Spital Square. The windows of the room where the crime was committed were boarded up, and a padlock put on the door. The streets were patrolled by the police all the evening, and no one was allowed to loiter near the place. The neighbourhood was like a fair on Friday night, and the excitement and hubbub has filled the streets with thousands of idlers attracted by morbid curiosity.'[21]

On Saturday, 10 November, Dr Phillips presided over the post-mortem examination on Mary Kelly's corpse, a task that took them some six and a half hours, so savagely had the body been mutilated. The shelter of Kelly's room had given the Ripper the time and opportunity to indulge in and give vent to his darkest, deepest fantasies, and as a result, he spent several hours frenetically slicing and slashing at Kelly's corpse. The remainder of Dr Bond's post-mortem report, which had disappeared from the Public Record Office, was recently returned anonymously to Scotland Yard, and is reproduced here:

'The face was gashed in all directions, the nose, cheeks, eyebrows, and ear being partly removed. The lips were blanched and cut by several incisions running obliquely down to the chin. There were also numerous cuts extending irregularly across all the features.

The neck was cut through the skin and the other tissue down to the vertebrae, the 5th and 6th being deeply notched. The skin cuts in the front of the neck showed distinct ecchymosis.

The air passage was cut at the lower part of the larynx through the cricoid cartilage.

Both breasts were removed by more or less circular incisions, the muscles down to the ribs being attached to the breasts.

The intercostals between the 4th, 5th, and 6th ribs were cut through and the contents of the thorax visible through the openings.

The skin and tissue of the abdomen from the costal arch to the pubes were removed in three large flaps. The right thigh was denuded in front to the bone, the flap of skin, including the external [organs?] of generation and part of the right buttock. The left thigh was stripped of skin, fascia and muscle as far as the knee.

The left calf showed a long gash through skin and tissues to the deep muscle and extending about five inches above the ankle.

Both arms and forearms have extensive and jagged wounds.

The right thumb showed a small superficial incision about one inch long, with extravasation of blood in the skin and there were several abrasions on the back of the hand [moreover?] showing the same condition.

On opening the thorax it was found that the right lung was virtually adhering by old firm adhesions. The lower part of the lung was broken and torn away.

The left lung was intact. It was adherent at the

apex and there were a few adhesions on the side. In the substance of the lung were several products of consolidation.

The pericardium has open fibres and the heart absent.

In the abdominal cavity was some partly digested food of fish and potatoes and similar food was found in the remains of the stomach attached to the intestines.'

Although the fact that Kelly's heart was missing was withheld from the public, the information was almost leaked by Dr Gabe, who had viewed the body at Miller's Court and had initially told the press that 'a certain organ' was missing.[22] Evidently he was reprimanded for saying this, for he told a different story the very next day: 'In reply to a question put to him,' Lloyd's reported, '[Dr Gabe] declined to give any details. He merely said that he had seen a great deal in dissecting rooms, but that he had never, in all his life, seen such a horrible sight as the murdered woman presented.'[23] A report in the People that same day contained the official version: 'The latest account states, upon what professes to be indisputable authority, that no portion of the murdered woman's body was taken away by the murderer. As already stated, the post-mortem examination was of the most exhaustive character, and the surgeons did not quit their work until every organ was accounted for, and placed as closely as possible in its natural position.'[24]

Nevertheless, both The Times and the Daily Telegraph insisted otherwise. 'We are enabled to state,' said the latter, 'that notwithstanding all that has been said to the contrary, a portion of the bodily organs was missing.'[25] No doubt those inclined to speculate about precisely which organ had gone missing assumed that it was either the uterus, which had been removed from both Chapman's and

Eddowes' bodies, or, perhaps, a kidney, which had been taken from Eddowes' corpse. It's doubtful that anyone guessed that even Jack the Ripper would commit so fiendish and macabre an act as to make off with his victim's heart.

19

'Witness spoke with a stutter, and evidently laboured under great emotion'

At 11.00 a.m. on Monday, 12 November, Dr Roderick MacDonald, the coroner for the North-Eastern district of Middlesex County, opened the inquest into the death of Mary Jane Kelly, at Shoreditch Town Hall. Immediately there was a protest from a couple of jurors who claimed that the proceedings ought to be held in the Spitalfields district where Kelly had been killed, rather than in Shoreditch where the body now lay. This provoked an angry response from Dr MacDonald. 'Do you think that we do not know what we are doing here?' he chided the dissenters. 'Jurisdiction lies where the body lies, not where it was found.'

The matter thus settled, the jury – 'twelve very respectable men' according to the *Pall Mall Gazette*[1] – was taken by Inspector Abberline to view the remains. A reporter from the *Gazette* described the emotive scene as he

195

accompanied them: 'By this time, quite a crowd had gathered around the hall, and followed us quietly to the gloomy gate of Shoreditch Church. The little rusty iron wicket was guarded by a policeman, who held it open as we passed into the melancholy churchyard, with an acre of grey, soot covered gravestones, and sorrowful grass and weeds. The path ran alongside the church, and as we turned sharp round to the left there was a little brick mortuary, a red oasis in the desert of tombstones and soft, dank soil ... There, in a coarse wooden shell lay the body of the Ripper's latest victim. Only her face was visible; the hideous and disembowelled trunk was concealed by the dirty grey cloth, which had probably served to cover many a corpse. The face resembled one of those horrible wax anatomical specimens which may be seen in surgical shops. The eyes were the only vestiges of humanity; the rest was so scored and slashed that it was impossible to say where the flesh began and the cuts ended.'

The jury was then escorted to Dorset Street. 'Here another crowd held possession of the field, towzy women with babies in their arm, drunken men recovering from their orgies, and a whole regiment of children, all openmouthed and commenting on the Jury. The entrance of the Court was held by a couple of policemen, and it was so narrow that we could only pass up in a single file. It was only about three yards long, and then we were at the door which is numbered 13 ...

'The room was surveyed in batches. The inspector [Abberline], holding a candle stuck in a bottle, stood at the head of the filthy, bloodstained bed, and repeated the horrible details with appalling minuteness. He indicated with one hand the bloodstains on the wall, and pointed with the other to the pools which had ebbed out on to the mattress ... A farthing dip in a bottle did not serve to illuminate the fearful gloom, but I was able to see what a wretched hole the poor murdered woman called "home".'[2]

Back at Shoreditch Town Hall, Joseph Barnett was the first witness called to give testimony, his well-groomed appearance – neatly trimmed moustache, top hat, coat and cravat, perhaps his clay pipe in hand – prompting the *Star* to remark that he looked 'very respectable for one of his class'. Barnett was now staying with his sister and her family at 21 Portpool Lane, Leather Lane, Holborn, as so many people had sought him out at Buller's Lodging House that the proprietor had asked him to leave.

In the witness box, Barnett was asked numerous questions about Kelly's past history and their life together. It proved to be something of an ordeal for him, an extremely upsetting experience that so unnerved Barnett that he seems to have lost his composure and displayed some very peculiar behavioural quirks. The press noted his stress, remarking that 'Witness [Barnett] spoke with a stutter, and evidently laboured under great emotion',[3] while one paper saw fit to include in its report Barnett's curious habit of beginning each of his answers by repeating the last word of every question asked.[4] As previously indicated, this is recognized today as the psychological disorder common to autistics known as echolalia, which may be symptomatic of schizophrenia and can also occur as a personality mannerism or at times of high anxiety. Barnett also contradicted a key statement he had made just a few days earlier, but rather than being viewed with suspicion, Barnett's curious behaviour was evidently regarded as being the intense grief of a man whose former 'wife' had just met a most horrible death, and he even seems to have provoked some sympathy from the coroner. 'You have given your evidence very well,' Dr MacDonald reassured Barnett at the conclusion of his testimony.[5]

Inspector Abberline, however, should have known better, for Barnett had given the inquest jury a different reason for his separation from Kelly from the one he had earlier given to Abberline. On the afternoon of 9 November, only about twelve hours after she had been murdered, Barnett claimed that he had left Kelly 'in consequence of not earning sufficient money to give her, and her resorting to prostitution'.[6] It was a perceptive remark, providing some insight into the nature of Barnett and Kelly's relationship, as it pinpointed the true, underlying cause of their separation. Yet, testifying at Kelly's inquest, in front of Inspector Abberline, when Barnett was asked why he had left Kelly, he replied, 'Because she took in an immoral woman.' Then, possibly prompted, he added, 'My being out of work had nothing to do with it.'[7] In essence, this was the very opposite of what he had earlier told Abberline.

In fact, Barnett had already changed his original story shortly after he first told it, putting the blame for his separation from Kelly entirely on the prostitutes she had taken in. On the evening of 9 November, only hours after he had been interviewed by Inspector Abberline, a reporter from the *Star* tracked Barnett down to a pub, where he interviewed him. 'He had lived with [Kelly] for a year and a half, [Barnett] said,' the *Star* wrote, 'and should not have left her except for her violent habits ... Barnett said he and the deceased were very happy and comfortable together, until another woman came to sleep in their room, to which he strongly objected. Finally after the woman had been there two or three nights, he quarrelled with the woman whom he called his wife and left her.'[8] The next day, Saturday, 10 November, Barnett spoke to the Central News Agency and told them a similar story, except this time he revealed that Kelly had taken in *two* prostitute friends to stay with them. 'We lived comfortably until Marie allowed a prostitute named Julia to sleep in the same room,' he explained. 'I objected, and as Mrs Harvey afterwards came and stayed there, I left and took lodgings elsewhere. I told her I would come back if [Mrs Harvey] would go and live somewhere else... Marie never went on the streets when she lived with me. She would never have gone wrong again, and I should never have left, if it had not been for the prostitutes stopping in the house. She only let them in the house because she was good-hearted, and did not like to refuse them shelter on cold, bitter nights.'[9]

While such inconsistencies weren't necessarily indicative of guilt, neither should they have just been dismissed or ignored as they were, or allowed to go unchallenged. At the very least, Barnett's contradictory statements and curious behaviour should have alerted Abberline that something was wrong, prompting him to take a closer look at Barnett. Had he done so, he would have realized just how snugly and precisely Joseph Barnett fitted the mould of Jack the Ripper: here was a man reared all over the East End who now lived in the very heart of it and knew the area extremely well, whose job had given him both some expertise with a knife and a rough knowledge of anatomy (as well as the strength to overpower his victims quickly). Barnett had been to school and could therefore read and write (enabling him to have written the first Jack the Ripper letters) and he disliked prostitutes. He had lived with the latest victim until their violent quarrel ten days earlier and he perfectly fitted some of the eyewitness descriptions, most particularly the one that the police themselves believed to be accurate. Abberline might have also made the connection between the ginger beer bottles found in Kelly's room and those mentioned in the 'Dear Boss' letter, and he might have considered the implications of Julia Venturney's inquest statement that Kelly 'could not bear' Joseph Barnett. But Abberline had evidently already satisfied himself of Barnett's innocence after their previous interrogation, and with no hard evidence against him (indeed, none really existed) and the numerous testimonials forthcoming during the inquest confirming Barnett's good character, the opportunity was allowed to pass and Joseph Barnett was not considered a proper suspect until 1982 when I first identified him as Jack the Ripper.[10]

But what made Barnett change his story in the first place? On the surface, there didn't seem to be anything incriminating in his statement that he had left Kelly 'in consequence of not earning sufficient money to give her', yet Barnett felt it necessary to make it clearly known that that hadn't been the case after all, and that his 'being out of work had nothing to do with it'. Barnett may have feared that to admit that their relationship had come to an end because he was no longer of any use to Kelly would cast him in a suspicious light, possibly in the role of the spurned and bitter lover who, motivated by anger, jealousy or revenge, kills his deceitful spouse. At the same time, it seems to have been very important for Barnett to establish that Kelly loved him as he had loved her; to admit that their long cohabitation had been little more than a convenient arrangement would be to negate any real substance or validity that, in his eyes, their relationship had had, and to expose their time together as a sham and a fraud. This was something that Barnett could not accept.

It wouldn't have been the first time Barnett deluded himself. He insisted that he and Kelly had lived together happily and comfortably, when in fact Kelly was miserable and couldn't bear him (and apparently had another lover), and they had constant, heated rows. While everyone else spoke of Kelly's frequent drunkenness and Julia Venturney told how her intoxication would trigger the rows with Barnett, he said that Kelly was generally sober in his presence. He insisted that Kelly never walked the streets when she was with him, when the evidence indicated otherwise. When Kelly did return to the streets, Barnett blamed it on the influence of her prostitute friends, conveniently neglecting to consider that the loss of his income had anything to do with it.

Otherwise, in response to questioning, Barnett briefly recalled what he claimed was his last meeting with Kelly, early in the evening of 8 November when he told her that he hadn't been working and therefore could not give her any money. He discussed her drinking and went on to relate Kelly's past history, as he knew it, through to their first meeting. Lastly, Barnett told of Kelly's heightened fear of the Whitechapel Murderer and how she would ask him to read her the latest developments on the case from the papers.

Next called was Thomas Bowyer, the landlord's employee, who told of being sent to Kelly's room to try to collect some back rent, and how he discovered her body by peering through the window. He recalled having once seen Kelly drunk.

John McCarthy, Kelly's 'gentlemanly looking', 39-year-old landlord,[11] followed Bowyer on to the witness stand. He told of seeing the body and stated that he had no doubt that it was Kelly's, whom he had frequently seen drunk. He claimed that he hadn't known whether she and Barnett had been married but that they seemed to have lived together comfortably until they had the row which resulted in the broken window panes. The furniture was all his, said McCarthy.

The widowed Mary Ann Cox, the neighbour of Kelly's whom the *Star* described as 'a wretched specimen of East

End womanhood',[12] was next up. Cox, who lived at 5 Miller's Court and admitted to being a prostitute, testified that she knew Kelly as Mary Jane (as did everyone except for Barnett) and had been acquainted with her for about eight or nine months, or approximately since Kelly and Barnett had first come to Miller's Court. Cox recalled that she had often seen Kelly drunk, the last time being near midnight on the night of 8 November, when Kelly was singing 'Sweet Violets' as she let an unidentified man into her room (apparently a customer, who presumably left afterwards). Cox told of her own comings and goings that evening and despite having passed a sleepless night, heard nothing unusual, other than the footsteps of a man leaving the Court at 6.15 a.m. Cox noted the sound because it was too late for any of the residents to have been leaving for work in one of the various markets. Had there been any cries or disturbances, as others had heard, Cox was certain that she would have heard them herself.

Elizabeth Prater, who testified next, said that although she lived in the room above Kelly's, she had only been casually acquainted with her. Prater had been married to a boot machinist who had deserted her five years earlier, since which time she evidently made her living as a prostitute. Having been out since late in the afternoon of Thursday, 9 November, Prater returned to the Court at around 1.00 the next morning, stopping briefly in McCarthy's chandler's shop which was still open even at that late hour. Prater returned to her room at around 1.30 a.m. at which time she noticed no light or sound coming from Kelly's room. Such was Prater's fear of the killer that she barricaded her door with two tables before falling quickly asleep as she had been drinking. Between 3.30 and 4.00 a.m. she was awakened when her pet kitten crawled onto her face only moments before she heard a faint cry of

'Oh, murder!' Prater chose to ignore it, and as she heard no follow-up cries or sounds, she went back to sleep until 5.00 a.m. Less than an hour later she was in the Ten Bells pub in Commercial Street, starting the day off with some rum. Returning home, she slept until eleven when she was apparently awakened by the commotion accompanying the discovery of Kelly's body.

The next to testify was Caroline Maxwell, the wife of a lodging house deputy, with her curious tale of having chatted with Kelly on Friday morning, 9 November, several hours after Kelly had been killed. Despite being warned by the coroner to consider very carefully what she was saying as it differed so blatantly from the facts as they knew them, Maxwell stuck to her story. Otherwise, she described Kelly as having been quiet and aloof, and although she had seen her in drink, she didn't think that Kelly was an habitual drunkard. 'She was not a notorious character,' Maxwell said.

Sarah Lewis,[13] a laundress, who coincidentally lived next door to where Joseph Barnett had once lived in Great Pearl Street, testified next. Following an argument at home, Lewis went to visit a friend in Miller's Court in the early hours of Friday morning. At around 2.30 a.m., she noticed a 'stout looking man, not very tall', loitering around Crossingham's Lodging House, who gave Lewis the impression that he was waiting for someone to come out of Miller's Court. Nearby was another man and a drunken woman.

In her friend Mrs Keyler's room, Lewis dozed off until about half past three, and shortly before 4.00 a.m. she too heard a female voice cry out 'Murder!' though as there was only that single cry she too ignored it. Lewis also told of having encountered a suspicious man in Bethnal Green Road, who tried to lure herself and her companion into a close. She described the man as having been around 40 years old, short and pale, with a black moustache and carrying the obligatory black bag. Lewis claimed to have seen the same man drinking with a woman in the Britannia on the night of the murder.

Dr George Bagster Phillips, the police surgeon, followed Lewis in the witness box. On the basis of his examination of the remains, Dr Phillips determined that although Kelly's body was lying close to the near side of the bed, she had actually been killed on the far side of the bed, the top corner of which was soaked in blood. The immediate cause of death was the severance of the right carotid artery. At that point, according to *The Times*, Coroner MacDonald halted Dr Phillips' testimony, saying that there was no need for him to go into further detail at the moment, though if necessary he might be recalled at a later time.[14] MacDonald then called a brief adjournment.

Julia Venturney, who described herself as a charwoman, living at 1 Miller's Court, was the first witness called after the break.[15] Alluding to Kelly's aloofness, she recalled that it had been some time before she made Kelly's acquaintance. She also knew Barnett, she said, and told of how he objected to Kelly going on the streets. She thought the couple lived together happily, but then went on to describe how Kelly's frequent drunkenness led to rows with Barnett. She also told the jury how Kelly had said that although Barnett had been good to her, she could no longer bear him and was instead fond of another man named Joe (evidently Joseph Fleming) whom Venturney had never met.

On the night of 8 November, Venturney had gone to bed early but like Mary Ann Cox she passed a sleepless night. Although she had heard Kelly singing Irish songs in the past, she didn't hear any that night, and other than hearing a 'strange sound with some door', the court had been very quiet.

Kelly's friend Maria Harvey then took the stand, amusing the audience with her 'decisive, dogmatic manner', according to the *Daily News*.[16] She had slept in Kelly's room on Monday and Tuesday nights, 5 and 6 November, and had last seen her friend on the evening of 8 November when they had been together in Kelly's room. She left when Barnett came to visit, leaving behind several items of clothing, only one of which had since turned up. As far as Harvey knew, there was no one in particular whom Kelly feared.

Inspector Walter Beck, the first policeman to arrive on the scene, testified briefly how he had sent for the doctor before sealing off the court and ordering a search of the area. As far as he knew, Kelly hadn't been known to the police.

The final witness was Inspector Abberline, who stated that he was in charge of the case. After telling of the non-arrival of the bloodhounds and the subsequent forced entry into Kelly's room, he told how a large fire had raged so fiercely in the grate that it had melted the spout off a kettle. An examination of the ashes had revealed that several items of clothing had been burned, evidently including Mrs Harvey's missing garments. As the room had otherwise contained only a single, small candle atop a broken wine glass, Abberline concluded that the purpose of the fire had been to enable the killer to see what he was doing. Abberline also told of the missing key and of the alternative method of entry that Barnett and Kelly had devised, and he explained that Barnett had told him that a clay pipe found in the room had belonged to him.

Coroner MacDonald then surprised everyone by informing the jury that so far as he was concerned there was no longer any need for the proceedings to continue or for the jury to review the evidence. The purpose of the inquest, he said, was simply to determine the cause of death and as he believed that the jury was now sufficiently qualified to do so, he saw no reason for the unnecessary expense and trouble of further sessions. Anything else, he told the jury, such as considering possible suspects, was the job of the police. After a brief consultation, the jury agreed to turn in their verdict which, as expected, was 'wilful murder against some person or persons unknown'.

There has been a good deal of speculation about why Coroner MacDonald chose to terminate the proceedings so abruptly. The various inquests into the deaths of previous Ripper victims had each dragged on for several weeks, keeping the case in the public eye, which contributed to the growing public unrest and the mounting dissatisfaction with how the authorities were handling the case. The Home Office and police were coming under increasing pressure and criticism from the public and press alike. There had already been outbreaks of violence and there was an atmosphere in the streets bordering at times on chaos and anarchy. In view of this, MacDonald may have been persuaded by the authorities to wrap up his inquest as quickly as possible, in the hope of quelling further disturbances. Evidence that he had at least consulted with the police is contained in his statement to the jury that, 'From what I learn, the police are content to take the future conduct of the case.' At any rate, as the jury had indeed fulfilled its purpose, MacDonald may have genuinely felt that there was no point in needlessly dragging the proceedings on.

Just after the inquest concluded, a down-on-his-luck former groom called George Hutchinson came to the police with a fantastic story which, if true, would have provided them with an excellent description of Mary Kelly's killer. Unfortunately, his story appears to have been made up, probably so as to bring the destitute Hutchinson a modicum of self-importance and local celebrity, which he could no doubt milk for at least a few drinks at his local pub.

According to what he told the police and later the press, at around 2.00 a.m. Hutchinson was wandering the streets, penniless, with nowhere to go, when he ran into Kelly, whom he knew well as he had 'been in her company a number of times'.[17] Hutchinson said that Kelly asked him to lend her sixpence, and when he explained that he had no money, she headed towards Thrawl Street where she was approached by a well-dressed man whom she then took back to Miller's Court, Hutchinson following. He claimed to have waited outside Miller's Court for forty-five minutes for the man to come out, before resuming his wanderings.

Although Hutchinson said it never occurred to him that the man might be the killer, his suspicions had nevertheless been aroused by the presence of so respectable looking a man in the neighbourhood at that hour, and he was thus able to furnish the police with a minutely detailed description of the man that would have done Sherlock Holmes proud. 'The man was about 5ft 6ins in height,' the press reported, 'and about 34 or 35 years of age, with a dark complexion, and dark moustache turned up at the ends. He was wearing a long, dark coat, trimmed with astrakhan, a white collar with black necktie, in which was affixed a horseshoe pin. He wore a pair of dark "spats", with light buttons, over button boots, and displayed from his waistcoat a massive gold chain. His watch chain had a big seal, with a red stone hanging from it. He had a heavy moustache, curled up, dark eyes, and bushy eyebrows. He had no side whiskers, and his chin was clean shaven. He looked like a foreigner.'[18] He was also carrying a small parcel in his left hand and had a stern glare.

Needless to say, for Hutchinson's story to have been genuine, he would have had to be possessed of the most extraordinary powers of observation and memory, in that his account was so precise as to include a detailed description of the man's watch chain. Hutchinson's credibility was further strained by the fact that he had waited almost four full days before going to the police, surfacing just after the inquest into Kelly's death had concluded. Presumably this was so he wouldn't be called to testify under oath, as his story might not hold up under close scrutiny. And lest anyone doubt that the man Hutchinson saw had indeed been Jack the Ripper, Hutchinson gave him several known or imagined attributes of the killer, such as a soft tread, a stern glare and a foreign or Jewish appearance, along with the *de rigueur* sinister parcel to carry which, no doubt, contained his deadly knife.[19]

Not long after Hutchinson came forward, Matthew Packer, the grape seller who claimed to have sold Elizabeth Stride and a male companion some grapes shortly before her murder, surfaced again with a tale even more incredible than Hutchinson's. According to *Reynolds Newspaper*, Packer claimed that two men approached him a few days after Kelly's murder, asking for a description of the man to whom he had sold the grapes, as they had reason to believe that he was their cousin and that he might be the killer. This man had recently returned from America, they explained, where he had picked up the word 'boss' which he used constantly. 'I found that he was very much altered upon his return,' one of the men allegedly told Packer, 'for he was a thorough harum scarum. We met a lot of Whitechapel women, and when we passed them he used to say to me,

"Do you see those [whores]? How do you think we used to serve them where I came from? Why we used to cut their throats and rip them up. I could rip one of them and cut her inside out in no time. We Jack Rippers killed lots of women over there."' The men had initially dismissed their cousin's talk as drunken ramblings, Packer explained, but their suspicions were piqued after the killings had begun and the 'Dear Boss' letters had appeared. Said *Reynolds*, 'Packer states he feels sure the men are speaking the truth, as they seemed very much concerned, and hardly knew what to do in the matter'.[20]

On 12 November, as the inquest into Kelly's death was wrapping up, the *Star* and the other evening newspapers announced that 'the report is current at Scotland Yard today that Sir Charles Warren has sent in his resignation. No official confirmation or denial can be obtained. Information has been brought to the *Star* office tending strongly to confirm this rumour.'[21]

The impression was that the horrific circumstances of the latest murder had sounded the death knell for the beleaguered commissioner, but in fact Warren had already tendered his resignation the morning before Kelly had been killed. Besides having alienated much of the public and press, Warren had clashed repeatedly with Home Secretary Matthews and other officials, so that when Warren breached regulations by publishing an article about the Metropolitan Police in the November issue of *Murray's Magazine* without first clearing the material with his superiors, Matthews availed himself of the opportunity to be rid of his foe once and for all. Warren, for his part, professed ignorance of the rule, and claimed in his res gnation letter that he would not have accepted the post of Police Commissioner had he been aware of any such policy.

The *Murray's* article was typical Warren bluster, a

patronising and overly defensive piece with a blanket condemnation of anyone who dared to be critical of the police. 'Across the channel,' he wrote, 'the police are masters of the situation, the public give way before them, and the press does not venture to ... embarrass and hinder their enquiries.' Warren went on to blame the law for restricting the powers of the police, and he criticized the penal system for imposing too lenient sentences on felons. He also had a go at the public for what he termed their 'poverty of originality' in their suggestions on how the police might best catch the Whitechapel Murderer – as if the police themselves had any better ideas!

The press for the most part welcomed Warren's departure. 'Sir Charles Warren has resigned at last,' declared the *Pall Mall Gazette*,[22] while the *Morning Post* spoke for many in stating that 'It would be idle to pretend that [Warren's] administration ... has been so successful as to occasion any great regret for his departure.'[23] The *Irish Times* noted that 'Had Sir C. Warren been lucky enough rapidly to find the miscreant maniac of the East End, he would have been proclaimed the best police officer in Christendom'.[24]

Warren was succeeded by the former Assistant Police Commissioner James Monro. Typically, the last document to bear Warren's name was the announcement of a pardon 'to any accomplice, not being a person who contrived or actually committed the murder' – in reality, little more than a token gesture and hardly the reward offer that the public was clamouring for.

A devout Christian, Warren spent much of the remainder of his life writing articles and he was actively involved in the Boy Scout movement. He died in 1927 at the age of 87.

As before, the police made several arrests which proved to be for nought. One recent immigrant found himself in custody for the third time since the murders had begun.

'What with his odd face, his deprecating shrugs and posturings, and his broken English,' explained the *People*, 'his examination [by the police] was irresistably comic.' When asked why he thought he kept getting arrested, the 'unlucky fellow' reportedly spread the palms of his hands and shrugged his shoulders, and replied, '"Dat is ze zing ... Zat is what I like to know."'[25]

Also arrested was a man who had blackened his face with charcoal, and allegedly announced that he was Jack the Ripper. He was immediately engulfed by a large crowd, who screamed for him to be lynched and it took a cordon of police to rescue him. Once in custody, the man claimed that he was a doctor at St George's Hospital and it was later confirmed that he was, indeed, one Dr Holt. Fancying himself something of an amateur detective, Holt had been prowling about Whitechapel in various disguises in the hope of finding the killer.

Mary Kelly was buried on Monday, 19 November, after attempts to locate her family had failed. Joseph Barnett and John McCarthy reportedly saw to it that Kelly received a proper Catholic burial, and she was interred in Leytonstone Cemetery, East London.[26] Expenses were covered by the undertaker, Henry Wilton, who provided an elm and oak coffin replete with metal fittings. The inscription on the casket read 'Marie Jeannette Kelly, died 9 November 1888, aged 25 years'.

By late morning, several thousand people had gathered around Shoreditch Church and they watched in respectful silence as the coffin was placed in an open hearse, borne by two horses. Two mourning carriages, one containing Joseph Barnett, followed as it slowly began the six-mile trek to Leytonstone, its progress slowed by the dense crowds that lined the route. 'It was a very touching sight,'

the *Daily Chronicle* noted, 'to witness many poor women of
the class to which the deceased belonged greatly affected.'[27]
It was only when the cortège reached the suburbs that the
crowds began to thin, enabling the horses to break into a
trot.

At 2.00 p.m., the procession reached the cemetery,
where the Revd Father Columbant conducted the service,
as Barnett and several of Kelly's women friends knelt on
the cold, clay ground. 'The coffin was incensed, lowered,
and then sprinkled with holy water,' the *Daily Chronicle*
reported, 'and the simple ceremony ended.'

Two wreaths were placed on Kelly's casket, along with a
floral crown paid for by Kelly's 'associates' in Dorset
Street. On it was a large card which bore the inscription 'A
last tribute of respect to Mary Kelly. May she rest in peace,
and may her murderer be brought to justice.'

This, of course, never happened, and although there
would be other murders over the next few years that raised
the grim spectre of his return, Jack the Ripper himself was
never heard from again. He passed into the realm of myth
and legend, leaving behind a mystery that would take
almost 100 years to solve and a name that would endure
forever after as symbolic of pure, bloodcurdling evil.
Joseph Barnett, meanwhile, having survived both the
police and inquest interrogations, found his demons exor-
cised with the death of Mary Kelly, and faded back into
the anonymity of the East End from whence he came,
where he apparently lived a quiet and uneventful life.

Appendix I

The case against Joseph Barnett: A summation

Joseph Barnett precisely fits the contemporary mould of Jack the Ripper.

1. Jack the Ripper knew the East End streets well as demonstrated by his ability to avoid detection, in particular his two narrow escapes on the night of the double murder.

Joseph Barnett was born in the East End and lived there his for his entire life. By 1888, he had lived near all of the murder sites. On the night of the double murder, police followed Jack the Ripper's trail to Dorset Street, where Barnett then lived with Mary Kelly.

2. Jack the Ripper was probably known to his victims, given the ease with which he was able to approach them without alarming them, even after the first few murders made prostitutes very wary of whom they went with. All the victims were taken by surprise and died without putting up a struggle.

As a lifelong East Ender, Joseph Barnett was a familiar local figure and as Mary Kelly's boyfriend may have been known to her fellow prostitutes. One of the victims, Annie Chapman, was reported to have been a friend of Kelly's, while three of the first four victims had lived in Dorset Street around the time of their deaths, where Barnett and Kelly lived. One of them, Catherine Eddowes, had in fact sometimes slept in a room adjoining Barnett's and Kelly's.

3. Jack the Ripper was physically strong, proficient with a knife, and evidently had some sort of basic anatomical knowledge.

Joseph Barnett's job as a fish porter required considerable strength, while years of cleaning fish made him handy with a knife and provided him with a rudimentary knowledge of anatomy. As Dr Halsted pointed out, the alleged surgical skill possessed by Jack the Ripper could easily have been acquired by someone accustomed to boning and filleting fish.

4. Eyewitness reports that the police themselves believed to be accurate described Jack the Ripper as being 30 years old, standing 5ft 7ins or 5ft 8ins tall, of medium build, with a fair complexion and a moustache.

Joseph Barnett was 30 years old at the time of the murders, 5ft 7ins tall, of medium build, with a fair complexion and a moustache.

5. Testifying at Mary Kelly's inquest, Joseph Barnett blatantly contradicted himself, recanting what he had told the police three days earlier about why he left Mary Kelly.

The press noted Barnett's nervousness and anxiety in the witness box, remarking that he spoke with a stutter and 'evidently laboured under great emotion'. It was here that he displayed symptoms of the psychological disorder known as echolalia.

6. Catherine Eddowes was killed next to an orange market where Barnett, an occasional orange seller, may have worked; he may have even been heading there when he ran into Eddowes, a sometime neighbour from Dorset Street. As a known market porter, Barnett could explain his presence on the streets in the early morning hours, if need be.

7. Somehow, Jack the Ripper may have come into possession of the key to Mary Kelly's room, as he apparently locked the door behind him when he left.

The key to the room evidently disappeared on the night Barnett moved out. It was never found.

8. All of the Ripper victims (with the possible exception of Catherine Eddowes who may have appeared to be one), were known prostitutes. Jack the Ripper singled out prostitutes as his intended targets in the first Jack the Ripper letter.

Joseph Barnett was known strongly to dislike prostitutes and blamed them for what he perceived to be Mary Kelly's 'downfall'.

9. The author of the initial, genuine Jack the Ripper letter had been to school as evidenced by the letter's neat hand and relatively grammatically correct wording and the

fact that it was written in the copperplate style taught in the schools of the day. Ginger beer bottles were mentioned in the letter.

Joseph Barnett had been to school and could read and write. Ginger beer bottles were found in the room he had shared with Mary Kelly.

10. Joseph Barnett had compelling – and powerful – motives for killing Mary Kelly: sexual jealousy and rejection. Only ten days after Barnett moved out following a violent row, Mary Kelly was killed by Jack the Ripper. Barnett had expected to move back in but Kelly was evidently glad to be rid of him. She could no longer bear Barnett with whom she had frequently quarrelled. Since the loss of his well paying job, she had resorted to prostitution against his wishes, and had little use for him.

On the night of her death, Kelly was visited by both Barnett's brother and by Barnett himself, who knew how to slip into the locked room. After Kelly was killed, Jack the Ripper was never heard from again. Even today, it is not uncommon to hear of men killing their wives or girlfriends in similar circumstances.

Joseph Barnett precisely fits the mould of the modern day serial killer.

As discussed earlier, the former FBI agent and instructor Robert K. Ressler is perhaps the world's foremost expert on serial killers – it was he, in fact, who coined the term. Before his retirement he had become the FBI's top criminologist and most experienced practitioner of criminal psychological profiling – a science he himself helped to develop and refine. In an attempt to gain much needed insight into the mind of the serial killer, Ressler interviewed more multiple murderers than anyone else, before or since, and as result of his studies, was able to isolate certain fundamental characteristics common to the large majority of serial killers.

Although the Jack the Ripper murders occurred during the previous century, they were in fact the prototype of modern day serial killings. In hindsight, Joseph Barnett precisely fits Ressler's profile of the typical serial killer, particularly in the five key points listed below. Certain of Ressler's criteria, such as the emotional and or sexual abuse suffered by many serial killers, and the presence of alcohol and or drugs in their families, have of necessity been omitted from the list, as there is no way of determining how they might be relevant to Joseph Barnett.

1. Most serial killers are white males in their twenties and thirties; most sexual killers are under 35.

Joseph Barnett was 30 years old at the time of the Ripper murders (which fall into the category of sexual murders, even though no sexual abuse took place).

2. Most serial killers come from dysfunctional families, marked by cold, distant and unloving mothers and absentee fathers. According to Ressler, 'potential murderers became solidified in their loneliness first during the age period of eight to 12; such isolation is considered the single most important aspect of their psychological make up. Many factors go into fashioning this isolation. *Among the most important is the absence of a father* (my italics).

Joseph Barnett was six years old when his father died, and

his mother had disappeared by the time he was 13, possibly having abandoned her family.

3. Many serial killers are intelligent men, often employed in menial jobs far below their true intellectual capabilities.

Unlike many of his peers, Joseph Barnett had been to school, was well spoken and appears to have been fairly intelligent; he certainly seemed capable of doing something more than the backbreaking labour required of a fish porter.

4. Many serial killers suffer from physical ailments or disabilities.

Joseph Barnett had a speech impediment.

5. The initial murderous impulse is often triggered by some sort of pre-crime stress, such as the loss of a job, the break up of a relationship, money problems, etc.

The Jack the Ripper murders began shortly after Joseph Barnett lost his long-time, well paying job, which forced Mary Kelly to return to prostitution, against Barnett's wishes.

The Ripper Project

The stated aim of the Ripper Project was to find a solution to the Jack the Ripper murders through the application of modern scientific detection techniques. Among the various experts in forensics and relevant fields was Supervisory Special Agent of the FBI John E. Douglas, a former protégé of Robert Ressler, who adapted the latest FBI techniques to compose a psychological profile of Jack the Ripper. As with Ressler's profile, some of Douglas's 'perpetrator characteristics' have been omitted from the list where the relevant information about Joseph Barnett was not known, such as his mother's drinking habits or her relationships with other men. In only one instance does a characteristic *not* apply to Barnett, and that is where it is suggested that Jack the Ripper would not be expected to have been married at the time (as Barnett essentially was).

However, as Ressler points out in his book, the various attributes are not meant to be taken as absolute conditions, but rather are generally applicable to most serial killers. Several well-known serial killers, in fact, were married at the time they committed their crimes, including Peter Sutcliffe (the Yorkshire Ripper), Albert DeSalvo (the Boston strangler), and Juan Corona, the Californian farmworker who was found guilty of killing twenty-five men over a six week period. But the main 'perpetrator characteristics' as determined by Douglas precisely fit Joseph Barnett, in this instance to such an extraordinary degree as to pinpoint specific characteristics unique to Barnett, such as his speech impediment. This can be said of no other Ripper suspect thus far presented. Although the Ripper Project concluded that Aaron Kosminski was most likely to have been Jack the Ripper, they only considered a small field of five suspects, the others being 'Prince Eddy' the Duke of Clarence, Sir William Gull, Montague Druitt, and Dr Roslyn O'Donston. As Joseph Barnett at that point had yet to be presented as a suspect, he was not included in the study. Douglas's findings were as follows:

1. Jack the Ripper was a white male, aged 28–36, who lived or worked in the Whitechapel area.

Joseph Barnett was 30 years old at the time of the Ripper murders, and had lived and worked for his entire life in and around the Whitechapel area.

2. Jack the Ripper would have come from a family with a weak, passive or absentee father.

Joseph Barnett was six years old when his father died.

3. Jack the Ripper would have sought a job where he could vicariously experience his destructive fantasies, such as a butcher, mortician's helper, medical examiner's assistant, or hospital attendant.

Joseph Barnett's job boning and gutting fish provided the necessary atmosphere wherein he could indulge in his morbid fantasies.

4. Jack the Ripper would probably have had some type of physical abnormality that, although not severe, he would perceive as psychologically crippling *[such as] a speech impediment* (my italics).

Joseph Barnett had a speech impediment.

5. Jack the Ripper would have been interviewed during the course of the investigations, but would have been overlooked and/or eliminated as a suspect, in part because his ordinary appearance would not have fitted the preconception that both the police and local populace held of Jack the Ripper being an odd or 'ghoulish' looking man.

Joseph Barnett was interviewed by Inspector Abberline on the afternoon Kelly's body was found and cleared of any involvement in her murder. He did not look out of the ordinary and was not of an odd or 'ghoulish' appearance.

6. Jack the Ripper would be perceived as being quiet, a loner, shy, slightly withdrawn, obedient, and neat and orderly in appearance. He would drink at the local pubs.

Joseph Barnett was described by one source as looking 'very respectable for one of his class', and the two published contemporary illustrations of him show a well-dressed man, who took obvious pride in his appearance. Following Kelly's death, he was found by a reporter in a local pub. The room Barnett shared with Kelly was rented in her name, probably at her request, even though he alone paid the rent. Barnett may indeed have been quiet, shy and somewhat withdrawn, as people with speech impediments tend to be; we don't know.

7. Jack the Ripper would not have committed suicide after his last homicide. Generally, crimes such as these cease because the perpetrator has come close to being identified, has been interviewed by the police, or has been arrested for some other offence. We would be surprised if Jack the Ripper suddenly stopped killing, except for one of these reasons.

The police took Barnett in for questioning after Mary Kelly's murder and held him for up to four hours. Barnett's severe nervousness and anxiety while testifying at Kelly's inquest was noted by the press. After Kelly's death, Jack the Ripper was never heard from again; Joseph Barnett lived for another thirty-eight years.

8. Jack the Ripper believed that the homicides were justified – that he was only eliminating vermin.

Joseph Barnett had a strong dislike of prostitutes and blamed them for Mary Kelly's 'downfall'. The mutilations inflicted to Kelly's face – which was virtually obliterated – have been seen to represent the killer's hatred of women, which, in Barnett's case, might be traced back to the rejection he must have felt following his abandonment by his mother.

Copies of the report on the Ripper Project are available from William G. Eckert, MD, Milton Helpern International Centre, Wichita State University, PO Box 8282, Wichita, Kansas 67208, USA. Thanks to Paul Begg for supplying me with a copy.

Appendix II

What became of Joseph Barnett

There are no immediate records of Joseph Barnett's where-abouts following his appearance at the inquest into Mary Kelly's death – but why should there be? By all out-ward appearances, Barnett was a rather insignificant, ordinary man who, for all intents and purposes, led a seemingly average and unremarkable life, save for briefly playing what appeared to be a bit part in a great drama. Such people leave few traces behind – no one records their deeds, saves their pay stubs, school records, letters or rent receipts; no one interviews their relatives or neighbours, or attempts to find out anything about them except in instances such as this, by which time most physical traces of the person have long since vanished. That I have uncovered seventeen different addresses for Barnett seems quite remarkable to me, though virtually all come from the same four sources: birth and death certificates, on file at St Catherine's House, London; census reports, kept at the Public Record Office, London; records of Billingsgate Market fish porters, deposited at the Guildhall Record Room, London; and press reports from newspapers housed in the Newspaper Library in Colindale, London.

As there is no reason to suppose that Joseph Barnett ever left the East End, he probably continued to work around the local fruit markets, and took whatever available labouring jobs he could find, perhaps at the docks, a popular local employer. He may also have found work at Shadwell Fish Market, a rival to Billingsgate, which lasted until 1914, and was situated near New Gravel Lane, where Barnett lived for a time. But there are no known official records of Barnett until 1906[1] when he was given a new porter's licence at Billingsgate Market – whatever offence he committed in 1888 that caused him to lose his licence having long since been forgotten. In 1919, he is listed in the electoral rolls, having taken advantage of a recent change in the law that gave the vote to any male who met a six-month residential requirement, and any female over 30 who was a householder or married to the householder. At that time, he is listed as living with a Louisa Barnett, identified as his wife, though as there is no record of any such marriage she was evidently his common law wife who took his surname for the sake of convenience. Nothing whatsoever is known about this woman except that she died on 3 November 1926 at the age of 70, three and a half weeks before Joseph died. There appears to be no record of any children born to the couple, or to Joseph Barnett at any time previously.

At the end of his life, Barnett finally settled down; up to the time of her death, he and Louisa were still together and still lived at the same address in Shadwell where they had been living at least since 1919, if not earlier – the longest Barnett is known to have stayed in any one place or with any one woman. His death certificate gives the cause of death as oedema of the lungs and bronchitis, and lists his occupation as a dockworker. He was 68 years old, and apparently took his great secret to the grave with him.

JOSEPH BARNETT'S KNOWN ADDRESSES
(source in brackets)

1858   4 Hairbrain Court, Whitechapel [birth certificate].

1861   2 Cartwright Street, Whitechapel [census report].

1864   8 Walton's Court, Cartwright Street, Whitechapel [father's death certificate].

1871   24 1/2 Great Pearl Street, Whitechapel [census report].

1878+ Osborne Street, Whitechapel [Billingsgate porter's licence].*

1878+ St Thomas' Chamber, Heneage Street, Spitalfields [porter's licence].*

1878+ North East Passage, Wellclose Square, St George in the East [porter's licence].*

1887   George Street, with Mary Kelly [Joseph Barnett inquest testimony, press statement].

1887   Paternoster Court, Dorset Street, Whitechapel, with Mary Kelly [press statement].

1887–8 Brick Lane, Whitechapel, with Mary Kelly [press statement].

1888   13 Miller's Court, 26 Dorset Street, Whitechapel, with Mary Kelly [inquest testimony, press statement, press reports].

1888   Buller's Lodging House, New Street, Bishopsgate Street [inquest testimony].

1888   21 Portpool Lane, Leather Lane, Holborn, with sister [inquest testimony].

1906   18 New Gravel Lane, Shadwell, with brother Daniel [new Billingsgate porter's licence, Daniel's death certificate].

1907   60 Red Lion Street, Shadwell [porter's licence].
1908   Tench Street, Wapping [porter's licence].
1919–26 106 Red Lion Street, Shadwell, with 'wife' Louisa
       [electoral rolls, Joseph and Louisa Barnett death
       certificates].

* Exact year unknown.

A partial bibliography

There have been dozens of Jack the Ripper books since the 1929 publication of Leonard Matters's *The Mystery of Jack the Ripper*, and at some point I've made use of them all. Most had something to offer, though many tended to cover the same ground over and over again, and several contained false or misleading information. Some, however, are excellent. These are:

Autumn of Terror, Tom Cullen (Bodley Head, 1965).

The Complete Jack the Ripper, Donald Rumbelow (W. H. Allen, 1975, Penguin, 1975).

The Jack the Ripper A–Z, Paul Begg, Martin Fido, Keith Skinner (Headline, 1991).

Jack the Ripper in Fact and Fiction, Robin Odell (Harrap, 1965).

Jack the Ripper: Summing up and Verdict, Colin Wilson and Robin Odell (Bantam, 1987).

Jack the Ripper: The Uncensored Facts, Paul Begg (Robson, 1988).

Related Works:

From Constable to Commissioner: The Story of Sixty Years, Most of Them Misspent, Major Henry Smith (Chatto & Windus, 1910).

Days of My Life, Sir Melville Macnaghten (Arnold, 1914).

The Lighter Side of my Life, Dr Robert Anderson (originally serialized by *Blackwood's Magazine*, 1910).

For books on serial killers and murderers in general, Robert K. Ressler's *Whoever Fights Monsters* (Simon & Schuster, 1993) proved invaluable, while Colin Wilson's many books on criminology are all highly informative and painstakingly detailed, among them *A Criminal History of Mankind* (Granada, 1984), *Encyclopedia of Murder*, with Donald Seaman (Pan, 1989), *The Serial Killers*, with Donald Seaman (W. H. Allen, 1990), and *Written in Blood* (Equation, 1989). Also very worthwhile are *Criminal Shadows*, Professor David Canter (HarperCollins, 1994), and *Hunting Humans*, Elliot Leyton (Penguin, 1989).

Several books provided essential background details and information, among them:

Annual Report on the Sanitary Conditions of Whitechapel, Joseph Loane, the Medical Officer for Health (1886–90).

The Bitter Cry of Outcast London, Andrew Mearns a.k.a. William C. Preston (Leicester University Press, 1883, reprinted 1970).

British Historical Facts 1830–1900, Chris Cook and Brendan Keith (MacMillan, 1975).

A partial bibliography

Doctor in the Nineties, D. G. Halsted (Christopher Johnson, 1959).

East End 1888, William J. Fishman (Duckworth, 1988).

Grandfather's London, O. J. Morris (Putnam, 1956).

The Great Dock Strike 1889, David Wasp and Allen Davis (Longman, 1974).

Hops and Hop Picking, Richard Filmer (Shire, 1982).

How the Poor Live/Horrible London, George Robert Sims (Chatto & Windus, 1889).

Life and Labour of the People in London, Charles Booth (Macmillan, 1891, 1896).

London Labour and the London Poor, Henry Mayhew (1851, 1852, 1861).

Mid-Victorian Britain 1851–1875, Geoffrey Best (Weidenfeld & Nicholson, 1971).

Ordinary Lives 100 Years Ago, Carol Adams (Virago, 1982).

The People of the Abyss, Jack London (Macmillan, 1903).

The Victorian Underworld, Kellow Chesney (Pelican, 1972).

The What it Cost the day Before Yesterday Book 1850 to the Present, Harold Priestly (Kenneth Mason Publications, 1979).

The liveliest and most valuable sources of information were the wealth of newspapers available at the time, most of which have been largely overlooked or ignored by previous researchers. Of the less frequently consulted newspapers, the *Daily Chronicle*, the *Echo*, *Lloyds Weekly London Newspaper* (which claimed the largest circulation of any paper in the world), the *People*, *Reynolds Newspaper*, the *Standard* and the *Star* all provided particularly thorough and animated coverage of the Whitechapel murders, often with details not found in the five or six newspapers relied upon exclusively by most other Ripper books. Of the better known papers, I found the *Daily Telegraph* to be the most informative and reliable.

All the following have been consulted, and can be found at the British Library Newspaper Library, Colindale, London (telephone: 0171-412 7356): *Cardiff Times & South Wales Weekly News, Daily Chronicle, Daily Graphic, Daily News, Daily Telegraph, East End News, East London Advertiser, East London Observer, Eastern Post and City Chronicle, Echo, Evening News, Globe, Halfpenny Weekly, Illustrated Police News, Illustrated Weekly Telegraph, Jersey Weekly Press and Independent, London, Lloyds Weekly London Newspaper, Morning Advertiser, Morning Post, Observer, Pall Mall Budget, Pall Mall Gazette, Penny Illustrated, People, Pictorial News, Pictorial World, Public Opinion, Reynolds Newspaper, Standard, Star, The Times.*

London's most extensive collection of new and second-hand true crime books can be found at the specialist bookshop, Grey House Books, 60 Portobello Road, London W11 (telephone: 0171-221 0269). Those interested in keeping up to date with the latest goings on in the Jack the Ripper world might consider subscribing to Nick Warren's quarterly *Ripperana*, 16 Costons Avenue, Greenford, Middlesex UB6 8RJ.

Sources and notes

Details of book publishers and dates of publication can be found in the bibliography, if not included here.

CHAPTER 1

1 The 1861 census put the population of England and Wales at 20,066,224.

2 Birth certificates exist for three of the five Barnett children and are on file in St Catherine's House, London WC2. Wary of 'interference' from the authorities, families didn't always report the birth of a child, even after it became mandatory to do so. See also census reports for 1861 and 1871.

3 Press reports noted that Joseph Barnett stammered during his testimony at the inquest held into the death of Mary Kelly, among them those in the *Standard*, 13 November 1888, and the *Illustrated Police News* of 17 November 1888. The *Daily Chronicle* of 13 November 1888, reported that he stammered 'slightly'. A press agency report from the *Cardiff Times & South Wales Weekly News*, 17 November 1888, reporting on the

same inquest, told how 'a curious effect was produced by the witness [Barnett] beginning every answer by repeating the last word of every question asked'.

4 Robert K. Ressler, *Whoever Fights Monsters*, Pocket Books, 1993. Ressler's work is discussed in more detail in Appendix I.

5 Billingsgate porters' licences are on file in the Guildhall, London EC2.

6 Joseph Barnett statement to Central News Agency, carried in *Lloyds Weekly London Newspaper*, 11 November 1888.

7 According to the 'Annual Report on the Sanitary Conditions of Whitechapel' by Joseph Loane, the Medical Officer for Health.

8 The two were published together in book form in 1889.

9 A pseudonym for William C. Preston.

10 In 1888 the borough of Tower Hamlets included Whitechapel, Stepney, St George in the East, Wapping, Limehouse, Poplar, Mile End Old Town and New Town, Bromley and Bow.

11 See *East End 1888*, William Fishman, for further details.

12 Copies of Booth's map can be purchased from the Guildhall Book Shop, London EC2.

CHAPTER 2

1 *Mid Victorian Britain, 1851–1875*, Geoffrey Best.

2 *How the Poor Live*, George Sims.

3 *Link Magazine*, June 1888.

4 *London Labour and the London Poor*, Henry Mayhew (1851).

5 *In Darkest England*, William Booth (International Headquarters [of the Salvation Army], 1890). See also

East End 1888, William Fishman; *The Victorian Underworld*, Kellow Chesney; and *Ordinary Lives 100 Years ago*, Carol Adams.

6 *The Bitter Cry of Outcast London*, Andrew Mearns. The *Pall Mail Gazette*, under the editorship of W. T. Stead, ran a sensational exposé of child prostitution in 1885.

7 *London Labour and the London Poor*, Henry Mayhew (reprinted 1861).

8 Elisabeth Prater, the *Star*, 10 November.

9 Elizabeth Phoenix, statement carried in the *Star*, the *Daily News* and other papers, 12 November. One newspaper reported that Kelly was known as 'Ginger', due to the colour of her hair.

10 *Daily Telegraph*, 10 November.

11 Barnett, Central News Agency statement, *Lloyds Newspaper*, 11 November.

12 *The People of the Abyss*, Jack London.

13 Beatrice Potter, as quoted in *The Great Dock Strike 1889*, David Wasp and Allen Davis.

14 Barnett was the sole source for much of Kelly's background, relating what he said she had told him during their time together.

15 According to her friend Maria Harvey, Kelly's education was 'much superior to that of most persons in her position in life'.

16 Barnett testimony at Kelly's inquest, *Daily Telegraph*, 13 November. In the days before tape recorders, newspapers were less concerned with providing a word-for-word account, than they were in relating the gist of a statement, particularly when it came to lengthy testimonies, when an exact transcript was difficult to record. As such, the wording of Barnett's inquest testimony varies from paper to paper, and while the various

statements are essentially identical, there are nevertheless some significant differences, as writers and
editors chose to omit what they considered to be
inconsequential details. Not every inquest report, for
instance, contained mention of Barnett's stammer, and
only one, apparently, saw fit to tell its readers of
Barnett's habit of repeating the last word of every
question asked – traits which are now seen as significant
to Barnett's character. (See also source note 3 for
Chapter 1.) The fullest versions of Barnett's inquest
testimony appeared in the *Daily Telegraph* and the
Standard, both Tuesday, 13 November, and in the
coroner's files (ref. MJ/SPC NE 1888, Box 3, 12
November, Corporation of London, Greater London
Archives). Quotes taken from these accounts are each
specifically identified.

17 Inquest, *Daily Telegraph*. It has been suggested that
Kelly may have romanticized certain episodes of her
past, such as her trip to France, but there is little reason
to doubt that a young, attractive woman in Kelly's
position would have caught the eye of a gentleman and
been taken on such a trip. Paul Begg, in *Jack the Ripper:
The Uncensored Facts*, proposes that Kelly may have
been lured abroad with false promises of well-paid work
in a brothel.

18 Statement by Elizabeth Phoenix, the *Star*, 12 November.

19 Paul Begg quotes Mrs Carthy as saying so as reported in
the *Western Mail*, 13 November.

20 Barnett and Venturney inquest testimonies, *Daily
Telegraph* and others. In these, Venturney is quoted as
saying that Kelly was 'fond' of Fleming, though in the
version contained in the Coroner's files the term 'very
fond' is used.

21 Inquest, *Daily Telegraph*.

22 Elizabeth Phoenix, the *Star*, 12 November.
23 Inquest, *Daily Telegraph*.
24 Inquest, *Standard*. In the *Daily Telegraph* version, Barnett is quoted as having said that Kelly had been drunk 'several times' in his presence.
25 Inquest, *Daily Telegraph*.
26 Joseph Barnett was born 25 May 1858.
27 Julia Venturney, inquest, Coroner's files.
28 Inquest, *Standard*.
29 Julia Venturney, inquest, Coroner's files.
30 The *Star*, 12 November.
31 Sketches of Barnett appeared in the *Pictorial News*, 17 November, and the *Illustrated Police News*, 24 November.
32 Inspector Abberline later testified that Barnett had informed him that a clay pipe found in the room he shared with Kelly, was his. (Kelly inquest, *Daily Telegraph*, 13 November.)
33 Caroline Maxwell of 14 Dorset Street, inquest, *Daily Telegraph*.
34 Julia Venturney, testifying at Kelly's inquest, *Standard*, 13 November.
35 According to the inquest testimony of Kelly's friend Julia Venturney, *Standard*, 13 November.

CHAPTER 3

1 Barnett, inquest, Coroner's files.
2 Barnett, Central News Agency statement, *Lloyds Newspaper*, 11 November.
3 According to the Medical Officer for Health's 'Annual Report on the Sanitary Conditions of Whitechapel', Flower and Dean Street contained thirty registered lodging houses. After Dorset Street's thirteen, George Street, Thrawl Street and Wentworth Street were next

with ten each. All of these streets were within a few hundred yards of Dorset Street.

4 The *Observer*, 11 November.

5 *East London Observer*, 10 November.

6 Detective Sergeant Leeson, as quoted in *Autumn of Terror*, Tom Cullen.

7 *Daily Telegraph*, 10 November.

8 The *Pall Mall Gazette*, 12 November, identified it as a print entitled 'The Fisherman's Widow', possibly 'The Fisherman's Wife', by F. W. Poole.

9 The *Star*, 12 November.

10 *Daily Telegraph*, 10 November.

11 The *Star*, 10 November.

12 It has been suggested, not unreasonably, that there may have been some sort of impropriety going on between McCarthy and Mary Kelly, as it would have been unusual for him to let one of his tenants fall so far behind in the rent, as Kelly later did.

13 Venturney, inquest, *Standard*.

14 McCarthy, the *Star*, 10 November.

15 Barnett, inquest, *Standard*.

16 Barnett, inquest, *Standard*; Central News Agency statement, *Lloyd's Newspaper*, 11 November; and inquest, *Daily Telegraph*, respectively.

17 Barnett statement to Inspector Frederick Abberline, included in Coroner's files.

18 Central News Agency statement, *Lloyds Newspaper*, 11 November.

19 Barnett, inquest, *Standard*.

CHAPTER 4

1 *The Complete Jack the Ripper*, Donald Rumbelow.

2 In a statement made to Inspector Frederick Abberline on 9 November, Barnett said that he had been out of

work for 'three or four months', or any time from the
beginning of July to the beginning of August. A
compromise figure of three and a half months places the
date of his dismissal somewhere in the final week of
July. Martha Tabram was killed on 7 August.

3 Quoted from an actual licence on file at the Guildhall,
London EC2. According to Charles Booth, market
porters were notorious for using foul language.

4 At Kelly's inquest, Barnett described himself as a fruit
porter and a labourer. The *Daily News*, 10 November,
said Barnett sold oranges on the streets. On his death certificate in 1926, his occupation was listed as a dockworker.

5 *Daily Telegraph*, 10 November.

CHAPTER 5

1 Barnett statement to Inspector Abberline, 9 November
1888, Coroner's files.

2 Inquest, *Standard*, 13 November.

CHAPTER 6

1 A woman living on Brady Street claimed to have heard
cries of 'Murder! and the sounds of someone running
away, but this seems unlikely as she was further away
from the scene of the crime than the two Bucks Row
residents, who had heard no such thing. As the murders
continued, more and more people came forward with
dubious statements and accounts.

2 *East London Advertiser*, 8 September.

3 *Daily News*, 3 September.

4 Such a person would be seen time and again throughout
the case.

CHAPTER 7

1 As reported in the *People*, 11 November

2 *Daily Telegraph*, 10 September.

3 *Daily Telegraph*, 11 September.

4 Ibid.

5 Ibid.

6 Ibid.

7 Chapman and Edward Stanley shared an 8d double bed on weekends, which she liked to keep during the week when she could afford it.

8 *Daily Telegraph*, 11 September.

9 Thanks to Nick Warren FRCS, editor of the quarterly journal *Ripperana*, for his diagnosis.

10 *Daily Telegraph*, 10 September.

11 Others put the number of East End Jews at 33,000. See *East End 1888*, William Fishman, for further details.

12 *East London Observer*, 15 September.

13 *Lloyd's Newspaper*, 9 September. Some other papers carrying the same wire story, such as the *Pall Mall Gazette*, chose to delete any direct references to Leather Apron's Judaism.

14 *Daily Telegraph*, 11 September.

15 This according to Piser's stepmother, *Daily Telegraph*, 11 September.

16 *Jack the Ripper: The Uncensored Facts*, Paul Begg.

17 *East London Observer*, 17 September.

18 Cat's meat shops and vendors sold wafers of horse and other types of meats for a penny a dozen. Cats were a favourite pet of poorer families who couldn't afford to keep dogs, and there were an estimated seven million cats in the UK at the time, a million of them in London.

19 *Daily Telegraph*, 10 September.

20 *Daily Telegraph*, 13 September.

21 *Lloyd's Newspaper*, 6 September.

22 The *Observer*, 9 September.

23 *Daily Telegraph*, 14 September.

24 The *Standard*, 10 September.

25 The *Lancet*, 29 September, as quoted in *A Casebook on Jack the Ripper*, Richard Whittington-Egan (Wildy & Sons, 1975).

26 *Daily Telegraph*, 14 September.

27 *Doctor in the Nineties*, D. G. Halsted (Christopher Johnson, 1959).

CHAPTER 8

1 This too seems a surprisingly low number; despite some of the worst living conditions in all of England, the Whitechapel suicide rate was only about a quarter of that for London as a whole, lending some credence perhaps to claims of the cockney's celebrated heartiness of character and resolution.

2 The *Pall Mall Gazette* chose to tell this tale to its readers at the height of the Ripper frenzy. See also *The Legend of Sawney Bean*, by Ronald Holmes (Frederick Muller, 1975).

3 *Reynolds Newspaper*, 9 September.

4 The *Standard*, 10 September.

5 An alternative version had the message saying 'Five: fifteen more and I give myself up'. It may have been that these phoney messages inspired the subsequent Jack the Ripper letters, which came about three and a half weeks later.

6 *Reynolds Newspaper*, 9 September.

7 *Lloyds Newspaper*, 16 September. The madness seemed to be contagious. The same edition carried the story of a 63-year-old tailor who had tried to cut his daughter's throat with a razor. The man had bought the weapon intending to slice open his own belly, believing that he had animals crawling about inside him.

8 *Daily Telegraph*, 10 September.

9 *Standard*, 10 September.

10 *Daily Telegraph*, 12 September.

11 *Standard*, 17 September.

12 *Lloyds Newspaper*, 16 September.

13 Ibid.

14 Ibid.

15 *Pall Mall Budget*, 6 September.

16 *Lloyds Newspaper*, 16 September.

CHAPTER 9

1 *London Labour and the London Poor*, Henry Mayhew (1851), as quoted in *Autumn of Terror*, Tom Cullen.

2 The first use of fingerprints in a criminal case was in Argentina in 1892. See *Written in Blood*, Colin Wilson for a history of forensic science.

3 *East London Advertiser*, 6 October. While the Ripper, of course, was never caught, chance and happenstance would lead to the capture of several latter-day serial killers, such as David Berkowitz, Peter Sutcliffe, Dennis Neilsen and Jeffrey Dahmer.

4 *Lloyds Newspaper*, 23 September. It has been suggested that Dr Winslow was 'batty' and self-promoting. While that might be true in part, some of his proposals were very sensible and showed a deeper understanding of the case than the police appeared to have.

5 *East London Advertiser*, 6 October.

6 *Punch*, 22 September.

7 *Lloyds Newspaper*, 16 September.

8 *Reynolds Newspaper*, 16 September.

9 According to *The Crimes, Detection and Death of Jack the Ripper*, Martin Fido (Weidenfeld & Nicolson, 1987). See also *The Jack the Ripper A–Z*, Paul Begg, Martin Fido and Keith Skinner.

10 *Daily Telegraph*, 19 September.
11 *Daily News*, 1 October.
12 *Pail Mall Budget*, 20 September.
13 *Standard*, 17 September.
14 As printed in *Lloyds Newspaper*, 23 September.
15 *Pall Mall Budget*, 20 September.

CHAPTER 10

1 Britain's leading criminal 'psychological profiler', Professor David Canter, has established in his book *Criminal Shadows* that 'a large percentage of [serial killers] live within a few minutes walk of their crimes'. Canter discusses in considerable detail the significance of familiarity and convenience in the locations a wrongdoer chooses for his criminal activities. He illustrates this through use of what he calls his 'circle hypothesis', wherein the culprit is often found to be living within an area circumscribed by his crimes. 'One of our firmest hypotheses about a criminal's actions,' writes Canter, 'an hypothesis growing in strength and clarity as our studies unfold, is that knowledge of and familiarity with an area is a prerequisite for many violent criminals. Like a person going shopping, a criminal will also go to locations that are convenient.' Of all the Ripper suspects thus far presented, only Barnett can be shown to fit the requirements of the 'circle hypothesis', and none can be shown to have a documented familiarity with the East End and the Ripper murder sites even remotely akin to that which has been demonstrated for Joseph Barnett.

2 The aforementioned addresses do not take into account the many years for which there are no records for Joseph Barnett. The eleven addresses I have managed to find for him up to that point are all in the East End

and seem to be mostly short term residences, such as the four different places Barnett lived with Mary Kelly during their twenty months together. Previous to that, there are seven listed addresses for Barnett, but even if he had lived at each of them for a year apiece, that would still leave over twenty years during that period for which his exact whereabouts are unknown. Of the seventeen addresses I have for Barnett all but one are in the East End, the single exception being the brief period he stayed with his sister in Holborn following Mary Kelly's death. All indications are that Barnett spent virtually his entire life in the East End, so there is every possibility that he may have lived even closer to some of the murder sites than is already known.

3 *Daily Chronicle*, 1 October.

4 *I caught Crippen*, Chief Inspector Walter Dew (Blackie, 1938).

5 *Daily Chronicle*, 1 October.

6 See *Jack the Ripper: The Uncensored Facts*, Paul Begg, and *The Crimes, Detection, and Death of Jack the Ripper*, Martin Fido, (Weidenfeld & Nicholson, 1987) for more detailed accounts of Stride's background.

7 Some sources give Kidney's address as 33 Dorset Street.

8 Quotes from the *Daily Chronicle*, 2 and 4 October respectively.

9 According to a story in *The Times*, 1 October, which also reported that Stride may have suffered from fits.

10 *The Times*, 4 October.

11 For a detailed account of these sightings see *Jack the Ripper: The Uncensored Facts*, Paul Begg, Chapter seven.

12 According to his inquest testimony, as carried in *The Times*, 6 October.

13 *Daily Chronicle*, 1 October. Israel Lipski was a recent Jewish immigrant who poisoned a fellow lodger in 1887. Some claim that his name subsequently became an anti-Semitic swear word.

14 The various individual accounts concerning the discovery of Stride's body and the procedures followed thereafter, have been combined into a cohesive chronological narrative. Although some editing has been done to avoid redundancies and irrelevant details, the words are all those of the people involved. Louis Diemschutz's story is culled from his inquest testimony as reported by the *Daily Chronicle*, 2 October, and a statement carried in that same paper on the previous day. Mrs Diemschutz's and Morris Eagle's accounts also come from the *Daily Chronicle* of 2 October, while the statements of PC Lamb, Dr Blackwell and Dr Bagster Phillips all come from their inquest testimonies as transcribed by the *Daily Chronicle* of 3 and 4 October.

15 This may not have been entirely true, as neighbours complained about the loud singing coming from the club.

16 At Mary Kelly's inquest, Barnett described himself as a fruit porter and a labourer, *Daily Telegraph* 13 November. The *Daily News*, 10 November, said that Barnett worked as a drover or hawker of oranges in the street.

CHAPTER 11

1 Mrs Elizabeth Fisher, as quoted in the *Daily Chronicle*, 6 October.

2 William Eddowes, *Daily Chronicle*, 5 October.

3 There are conflicting versions of Eddowes' background. See *Jack the Ripper: The Uncensored Facts*, Paul Begg, Chapter eight, for further details.

4 Annie Phillips, *Daily Chronicle*, 6 October.

5 *Daily Chronicle*, 4 October, and *Evening News*, 10 October, respectively.

6 *Daily Chronicle*, 4 October.

7 Wilkinson inquest testimony, *Daily Chronicle*, 5 October.

8 *The Pall Mall Budget*, 4 October, quoting John Kelly.

9 Mrs Walker, as quoted by the *Daily Chronicle*, 5 October.

10 *Lloyds Newspaper*, 7 October.

11 *Daily Telegraph*, 10 November.

12 *Lloyds Newspaper*, 11 November.

13 *Evening News*, 9 October.

14 *From Constable to Commissioner: The Story of Sixty Years, Most of Them Misspent*, Major Henry Smith.

15 *Daily Telegraph*, 13 November.

16 Joseph Barnett's statistics come from his porter's licences for Billingsgate Market. The first of these, obtained in 1878 when he was 20 years old, lists him as being 5ft 7ins tall and of fair complexion. The two published illustrations of Barnett testifying at Mary Kelly's inquest show that he had a moustache and he appears to be of about average build. A second porter's licence, issued in 1906 when he was 48, gives Barnett's height as 5ft 7½ins, with hair then turned grey. Lawende's description of the man he saw comes from Major Smith's memoirs and the Home Office files on the case, stored at the Public Record Office, Kew, Surrey. See also *Jack the Ripper: The Uncensored Facts*, page 120, and *The Jack the Ripper A–Z*, under 'Jack the Ripper, descriptions of'. *The Times*, 2 October, gives a slightly different description of the man: 'He is described as of shabby appearance, about 30 years of age and 5ft 9ins in height, of fair complexion, having a small, fair

moustache, and wearing a red neckerchief and a cap with a peak.'

CHAPTER 12

1 Morris's statement carried by *Lloyds Newspaper*, 7 October.

2 There is some confusion about the precise wording of the message and there are numerous versions of it, such as 'The Juwes are not the men that will be blamed for nothing'. For further details, see *A Casebook on Jack the Ripper*, Richard Whittington-Egan (Wildy & Sons, 1975) and *The Jack the Ripper A–Z*.

3 The size and type of hand was described by the *People*, 14 October.

4 Surely Warren could have had the immediate area cordoned off?

5 Warren's letter is reproduced in *The Ripper File*, Elwyn Jones and John Lloyd (Futura, 1975).

6 Stephen Knight, in *Jack the Ripper: The Final Solution* (Harrap, 1976), built his popular but erroneous and dis-credited Masonic theory largely around the word 'Juwes'.

7 At any rate, the jumbled syntax of the 'Juwes' message was at odds with the initial, largely grammatically correct, Jack the Ripper letter.

8 Smith's memoirs, which were published in 1910, have been criticized for containing inaccuracies, and while this is true, they are largely insignificant, the product of a faulty memory in recalling the details of a case over two decades later. But there is no disputing Smith's dealings with Joseph Lawende, or the fact that unlike Robert Anderson, Melville Macnaghten or any other official of similar rank, he himself was out on the streets in pursuit of the Ripper. Begg points out that Smith

gives the impression that he discovered the blood-stained sink in the wake of Mary Kelly's murder, rather than Eddowes', but as Kelly had been killed outside of his jurisdiction, it's unlikely that Smith would have been involved in the immediate investigation into her death. Furthermore, on page 153, Smith makes it clear that the discovery of the sink had indeed occurred on the night of Eddowes' death, after which, 'completely defeated', he spent the rest of the night vainly checking various police stations for further developments.

9 *Daily Chronicle*, 5 October.
10 Or cleaning large fish, perhaps? Others, such as Dr Sequeira and Dr Sedgewick Saunders, the City public analyst, disagreed with Brown's assessment. See the *Daily Chronicle*, 5 October, and *The Crimes, Detection and Death of Jack the Ripper*, Martin Fido, pages 70–74, for Dr Brown's full post-mortem report.

CHAPTER 13

1 *Daily Chronicle*, 4 October.
2 Press report carried in the *People*, 7 October, and other papers.
3 In *The Complete Jack the Ripper*, Donald Rumbelow supplies the figure of 1,000 letters per week. In *The Identity of Jack the Ripper*, Donald McCormick (John Long, 1959, revised 1970) cites a letter sent to the police in 1969, in which the writer identified his father as having been the Ripper.
4 The Jack the Ripper letters are on file in the Public Record Office, Kew, Surrey, though over the years the files have been pilfered by members of the public.
5 *Illustrated Weekly Telegraph*, 13 October.
6 For the opposing view, see Nick Warren, 'A Postal Kidney', in the *Criminologist*, Spring, 1989.

7 It's not known if the killer wrote any more letters, as
   they would have been lost in the unforeseen flood of
   copycat letters received by the press and police in the
   wake of the initial 'Dear Boss' correspondence.

8 This fact seems to have been overlooked by most
   theorists seeking to discredit the letters.

9 The *People*, 7 October.

10 As will be seen, neither Anderson nor Macnaghten
    was actively involved in the everyday details of the
    case, and for them to expect their unsubstantiated
    claims to be accepted solely on the basis of the
    authority of their office is ludicrous and irresponsible,
    as is Anderson's insinuation that the police knew who
    the Ripper was at the time but were restrained from
    acting due to legal technicalities. Anderson's memoirs,
    The Lighter Side of my Life, were first serialized in
    Blackwood's Magazine in 1910, while Macnaghten's
    autobiography, *Days of my Life*, was published in
    1914. Researchers have concluded that Anderson's
    suspect, a 'low-class Polish Jew', was Aaron Kosminski,
    while Macnaghten apparently believed the Ripper
    to have been Montague J. Druitt, the Blackheath
    barrister who committed suicide shortly after the Mary
    Kelly killing. See *The Jack the Ripper A–Z* for further
    details.

11 Macnaghten didn't even join the force until mid-1889,
    while Anderson first joined Scotland Yard on the day of
    the Nichols murder, after which he promptly took
    leave, departing for Switzerland on the day of Annie
    Chapman's death and not returning to London until
    several days after the double murder and the reception
    of the letters. Macnaghten criticized Sir Henry Smith's
    account of his involvement in the Ripper murders
    because of inaccuracies, but of the three, only Smith

had actually been out on the streets literally in pursuit of the murderer himself.

12 See the entry under 'Best' in *The Jack the Ripper A–Z*.

13 It has been suggested that only an 'insider' would have known of the workings of the Central News Agency, but in fact any regular newspaper reader – such as Joseph Barnett – would have been aware of its function, as many stories of the day began 'The Central News Agency reports...'. Furthermore, the writer of the 'Dear Boss' letter and the follow-up postcard didn't know the agency's precise location, addressing his letter to 'The Central News Office, London, City'. Certainly a reporter would have known and used the proper address, as assurance that his letter would arrive unimpeded.

14 *East London Advertiser*, 6 October.

15 According to the *People*, 11 November.

16 Inquest, *Standard*, 13 November.

17 *Daily Chronicle*, 5 October.

18 The *Star*, 9 October.

19 The *Echo*, 9 October.

20 The *Star*, 18 October.

21 *The Times*, 12 November.

CHAPTER 14

1 The *Star*, 1 October.

2 The *People*, 7 October.

3 The *Star*, 1 October.

4 Letter published in *The Times*, 2 October.

5 As reported by the *Daily Chronicle*, 19 October.

6 As reported in *The Times*, 2 October.

7 Carried in *The Times*, 4 October.

8 The *Echo*, 8 October.

9 The *People*, 21 October.

10 *Daily Chronicle*, 4 October.
11 Charles Booth, the creator of the London poverty map, also saw the dispersal of slum inhabitants as a way of easing conditions in the East End, proposing that cheap transport might facilitate their relocation to the suburbs.
12 *Pall Mall Gazette*, 10 September.
13 Letter published in the *Daily Chronicle*, 5 October.
14 The *Echo*, 8 October.
15 *Daily Chronicle*, 19 October.
16 The *People*, 7 October.
17 'The Lighter Side of my Official Life', Dr Robert Anderson, *Blackwood's Magazine*. Anderson toned down some of the defamatory content of his remarks in the subsequent book editions of his memoirs. See *The Jack the Ripper A–Z* for further discussion.
18 See *The Jack the Ripper A–Z* for a detailed discussion of the matter; also the *Star*, 10 October.
19 Report carried in the *Echo*, 8 October.
20 The *Star*, 17 October.
21 *Daily Chronicle*, 18 October.

CHAPTER 15

1 Report carried in the *People*, 14 October.
2 The *Echo*, 8 October. Unfortunately the suspect's name was not given.
3 The *Echo*, 8 October.
4 See *Jack the Ripper: One Hundred Years of Mystery*, Peter Underwood (Javelin Books, 1987), for a fuller account of Robert Lees' involvement in the case.
5 Stride inquest, *Daily Chronicle*, 3 October.
6 Ibid.
7 Statement carried in the *People*, 14 October.
8 *Daily Chronicle*, 5 October.

9 The *Echo*, 8 October.
10 *Daily Chronicle*, 5 October.

CHAPTER 16

1 Shaw's remarks taken from a letter to the *Star*, 24 September.
2 *Morning Post*, 12 September.
3 S.G.O. was the pen name of the Reverend Lord Sidney Godolphin Osborn. In the same letter to *The Times*, published 18 September, he proposed that the Whitechapel Murderer was a woman and that pornography may have been involved.
4 *Morning Advertiser*, 19 September.
5 Letter published in *The Times*, 19 September.
6 Letter in the *Star*, 9 October.
7 As reported in the *Daily Chronicle*, 19 October.
8 The *Echo*, 15 October.

CHAPTER 17

1 Julia was Kelly's friend Julia Venturney, who testified at her inquest. Barnett referred to her as a prostitute in his Central News Agency statement, carried in *Lloyds Newspaper*, 11 November.
2 Tom Cullen first raised the possibility in *Autumn of Terror*.
3 Julia Venturney told Inspector Abberline that Kelly was drunk at the time of the quarrel (Coroner's files), while *The Times*, 10 November, reported that blows had been struck.
4 Following Kelly's death, Barnett made four different statements. The first of these, contained in the Coroner's files, was given to Inspector Abberline on the afternoon of 9 November, shortly after Kelly's body was found. Secondly, Barnett talked to a reporter from

the *Star*, apparently that same evening as his story was published in that paper the next day, 10 November. Barnett's third statement was to the Central News Agency, and was carried in some of the Sunday papers on 11 November, including *Lloyds Weekly London Newspaper* and the *Observer*. Last is Barnett's inquest testimony, which was published in numerous papers on 12 and 13 November, along with a version contained in the Coroner's files. See also source note 16 for Chapter 2.

5 Barnett statement to the Central News Agency, *Lloyds Newspaper*, 11 November.

6 Inquest, Coroner's files.

7 Barnett Central News Agency statement, *Lloyds Newspaper*, 11 November. The discrepancies in Barnett's statements are examined in greater detail in Chapter 18.

8 Inquest, *Standard*.

9 Maria Harvey statement to Inspector Abberline, 9 November, Coroner's files.

10 Lizzie Albrook, quoted in *Lloyds Newspaper*, 11 November, and other papers.

11 See *Jack the Ripper: The Uncensored Facts*, page 152, for the sources of Margaret's story.

12 It has long been rumoured that Mary Kelly was in the third month of pregnancy at the time of her death. Although the full post-mortem report by Dr Thomas Bond (recovered by Scotland Yard in 1987, and reproduced in *The Jack the Ripper A–Z*) makes no mention of such a condition, it is possible that, given the severity of the abdominal mutilations, Dr Bond missed the evidence, particularly if it wasn't something that he was looking for. The possibility also exists that the information was deliberately withheld for any number of

reasons, not the least of which would have been the calamitous public reaction that such a disclosure may have elicited. Although Dr Bond mentions in his report the fact that Kelly's heart was missing, which was also withheld from the public, there had been prior reports regarding the other victims that various body organs had been missing, and it may have been decided that mention of Kelly's condition was just too shocking to include in his report. If so, then this decision may have come from the Home Office, as it's known that Dr George Bagster Phillips, who presided over Kelly's inquest, met with the Under Secretary Mr Stuart Wortley at the Home Office on the evening of 9 November, according to the *Daily Telegraph* (10 November).

The first mention of Kelly's alleged pregnancy appears to be in William Stewart's 1939 book, *Jack the Ripper*. Twenty years later, Donald McCormick wrote in *The Identity of Jack the Ripper* (John Long, 1959) that he had seen a report by Dr Bagster Phillips revealing that Kelly 'was in the early stages of pregnancy'. Colin Wilson, in his writings, has mentioned seeing such a document as well, though there no longer seems to be any trace of it. Caroline Maxwell, a neighbour of Kelly's, testified at her inquest that she had seen Kelly throwing up on the morning of Friday, 9 November (morning sickness is commonly associated with pregnancy). Although Kelly had been killed several hours before Maxwell claimed to have seen her, it may have been that her story was true but that Maxwell simply got the days mixed up. Although it wouldn't have been at all surprising for Kelly to have become pregnant (possibly by Barnett, or Joseph Fleming, or someone else entirely), there remains no concrete proof either to support or refute the claims, though further research might turn up more information.

13 Mrs Harvey's press statement was printed in *Lloyds Newspaper*, 11 November.

14 Inquest, *Daily Telegraph*, 13 November.

15 *Lloyds Newspaper*, 11 November. Adding to the confusion is a Press Association report carried in the *Jersey Weekly Press*, 17 November, in which an alleged friend of Kelly's named Elizabeth Foster, who lived in a Dorset Street doss house, claimed to have been drinking with Kelly in the Ten Bells pub that evening until 7.05 p.m. Two people even claimed to have seen Mary Kelly the morning after she was murdered. Both Caroline Maxwell, of 14 Dorset Street, and Maurice Lewis, a tailor who claimed to have known Kelly for several years, said that they saw her in or about Ringers' Britannia pub on the morning of Friday, 9 November. Both seemed sincere in their accounts, though they must have either seen a woman who looked like Kelly or simply got the days confused, for Kelly was certainly dead by then. Their reports have prompted speculation that someone other than Kelly may have been killed in her room, but this doesn't take into account the fact that both Joseph Barnett and John McCarthy, the landlord, identified the body as Kelly's, and for it to have been otherwise would mean the existence of a conspiracy of Ludlumesque proportions.

16 Barnett statement to Inspector Abberline, Coroner's files.

17 There is no record of Barnett having been asked about why he never moved back in with Kelly, as he had said he would. As will be seen, several discrepancies in Barnett's various testimonies went unchallenged.

18 Barnett mentioned the meeting in his statement to the *Star*, 10 November.

19 According to what Prater told the *Star*, 10 November.

20 Maurice Lewis's statement was carried in *Lloyds Newspaper*, 11 November.

21 Neither Lewis nor Elizabeth Foster, who claimed to have seen Kelly earlier that night drinking at the Ten Bells pub, was called to testify at Kelly's inquest, which was abruptly concluded.

22 Margaret's statement to the Press Association, printed in the *People*, 11 November.

23 Mary Ann Cox, inquest, *Daily Telegraph*, 13 November. Kelly was singing an Irish song called 'Sweet Violets'.

24 Following Kelly's death, a reporter from the *Star* found Barnett in a pub, and he later told the Central News Agency that he and Kelly had been evicted from one of their lodgings for going 'on a drunk' (*Lloyds Newspaper*, 11 November), so he wasn't a teetotaller.

25 Elizabeth Prater, inquest, *Daily Telegraph*, 13 November. The other woman who heard the murder cry was Sarah Lewis, who may have also been known in newspaper reports as Mrs Kennedy, according to *The Jack the Ripper A–Z*.

26 Inquest, *Daily Telegraph*, 13 November.

CHAPTER 18

1 Inquest, *Daily Telegraph*, 13 November.

2 Ibid.

3 Ibid.

4 Ibid.

5 The *People*, 11 November.

6 Barnett Central News Agency statement, *Lloyds Newspaper*, 11 November. Only Barnett would refer to Kelly as 'Marie'.

7 The *Star*, 10 November, told how Barnett looked through the open window. At the inquest, Barnett said he identified Kelly's body by her hair and eyes, though most papers didn't take into account Barnett's cockney accent and apparent habit of dropping his 'h's, and printed this as '*ear* and eyes'.

8 Barnett Central News Agency statement, *Lloyds Newspaper*, 11 November. Speaking to the *Star*, Barnett said that the police had kept him for two and a half hours.

9 *Daily Telegraph*, 10 November. Unfortunately, this is the only existing contemporary reference to Barnett's alibi. If the police kept any records of their interview with him or of their investigation into Barnett's activities, they have not survived, so there is no way of knowing how thoroughly the police checked out Barnett's story. The fact that they held him for up to four hours suggests that the police may have initially been rather suspicious of Barnett, but in the end he was able to convince them of his innocence.

10 *Eastern Post and City Chronicle*, 10 November.

11 The *Star*, 12 November.

12 *Daily Telegraph*, 13 November.

13 Inquest, *Daily Telegraph*, 13 November.

14 *The Complete Jack the Ripper*, Donald Rumbelow. The confusion is compounded by the lack of specific information about what kind of lock was on the door. The *Daily News*, 10 November, reported that the door had been secured with a spring lock, the common sort of device that automatically locks when the door is shut, but other papers reported that a key had been used which the murderer took with him when he left. Perhaps Robin Odell hit upon the likely solution when he suggested that there was both a mortise type lock, which can only be opened with a key, as well as a bolt,

which Barnett and Kelly used after the key to the other lock had vanished (*Jack the Ripper in Fact & Fiction*).

15 The *Standard*, 10 November, and the *Pall Mall Gazette*, 12 November, respectively.

16 The *Standard*, 12 November. Other newspapers reported a dirty muslin curtain hanging over the window, which may been replaced by the coat.

17 The *Pall Mall Gazette*, 12 November. It should be pointed out that the 'Dear Boss' letter also referred to ginger beer bottles.

18 Inquest, *Daily Telegraph*, 13 November.

19 Scotland Yard files, Public Record Office, Kew, MEPO 3.140; HO 144/220/A49301 C subs. 21. See *The Jack the Ripper A–Z* for a detailed listing of the holdings at the Public Record Office.

20 The *Times*, 10 November

21 The *People*, 11 November.

22 Report carried in the *Halfpenny Weekly*, 10 November.

23 *Lloyds Newspaper*, 11 November.

24 The *People*, 11 November.

25 *Daily Telegraph*, 13 November.

CHAPTER 19

1 *Pall Mall Gazette*, 12 November.

2 Ibid.

3 Press agency report, carried in the *Standard*, 13 November, and the *Illustrated Police News*, 17 November, among other papers. As previously noted, the *Daily Chronicle* of 13 November said that Barnett stammered 'slightly'.

4 Press agency report from the *Cardiff Times & South Wales Weekly News*, 17 November. Other papers carrying the same news agency report apparently chose to omit this last detail.

5 Inquest, *Daily Telegraph*, 13 November.

6 Statement to Inspector Abberline, Coroner's files.

7 Inquest, *Standard*, 13 November. Unless otherwise indicated, subsequent inquest testimonies are taken from the version published in the *Daily Telegraph*, 13 November. The version in the *Star*, 12 November, notes that Barnett's statement that 'being out of work had nothing to do with it' was in response to a question, though the versions in the *Standard* and the *Daily Telegraph* give the impression that the remark was unprompted.

8 The *Star*, 10 November.

9 Barnett Central News Agency statement, *Lloyds Newspaper*, 11 November.

10 Bruce Paley, 'We Name Jack the Ripper', *True Crime*, April, 1982.

11 As described by the *Star*, 12 November.

12 The *Star*, 12 November.

13 Because of the similarities in their stories, Paul Begg believes that Sarah Lewis was the same woman who *Lloyds Newspaper* (11 November) and other papers identified as Mrs Kennedy.

14 The *Times*, 13 November.

15 The *Standard* provides a much more detailed account of Venturney's testimony.

16 The *Daily News*, 13 November.

17 Hutchinson's story was carried in the *Pall Mall Budget*, 15 November, and others, the implication being that Hutchinson had in the past paid for Kelly's favours.

18 'Foreigner' was the common euphemism for a Jewish person, and *The Jack the Ripper A–Z* says that Hutchinson used the term Jew, rather that foreigner, in his initial statement to the police.

19 If Hutchinson wasn't lying, then he may have seen Kelly with the same well-dressed man both her friend Margaret

and Maurice Lewis reported seeing her with at around 10.30 p.m., in which case Hutchinson was either mistaken about the time or moved his story forward a few hours so as to make it more plausible that he had actually seen Kelly with Jack the Ripper.

20 *Reynolds Newspaper*, 18 November.

21 The *Star*, 12 November.

22 *Pall Mall Gazette*, 13 November.

23 The *Morning Post*, 13 November.

24 *Irish Times*, 13 November.

25 The *People*, 11 November.

26 There was no marker on Kelly's grave until 1986, when Ripperologist John Morrison had one erected.

27 Funeral details are taken largely from the report in the *Daily Chronicle*, 20 November.

APPENDIX II

1 Barnett would, of course, appear somewhere in the 1891 census, but as there is no name index of entries, a known address would be necessary to locate him, the alternative being a street-by-street search of the East End.

Index

More True Crime from Headline

THE ENCYCLOPEDIA OF MASS MURDER

OVER 200 OF THE MOST NOTORIOUS CASES

BRIAN LANE AND WILFRED GREGG

The most comprehensive file of the world's worst mass murderers ever published

INCLUDES:

- Ronald 'Butch' DeFeo: the bloody slaughter of his family at Amityville initiated a lucrative spate of books and films

- Wade Frankum: infamous 'Coffee Pot Killer' who went on a shooting rampage in a Sydney shopping plaza

- Julio Gonzalez: arsonist who torched the Happy Land social club killing eighty-seven people after a row with his girlfriend

- Marc Lepine: who shot up a class of women students because he 'hated feminists'

- Michael Ryan: perpetrator of the notorious 'Hungerford Massacre'

- Brenda Spencer: sixteen-year-old student who opened fire with a semi-automatic rifle at a junior school because 'I don't like Mondays'

NON-FICTION / TRUE CRIME 0 7472 4282 8

A selection of non-fiction from Headline

THE NEXT 500 YEARS	Adrian Berry	£7.99 ☐
FIGHT FOR THE TIGER	Michael Day	£7.99 ☐
LEFT FOOT FORWARD	Garry Nelson	£5.99 ☐
THE NATWEST PLAYFAIR CRICKET ANNUAL	Bill Frindall	£4.99 ☐
THE JACK THE RIPPER A–Z	Paul Begg, Martin Fido & Keith Skinner	£8.99 ☐
VEGETARIAN GRUB ON A GRANT	Cas Clarke	£5.99 ☐
PURE FRED	Rupert Fawcett	£6.99 ☐
THE SUPERNATURAL A–Z	James Randi	£6.99 ☐
ERIC CANTONA: MY STORY	Eric Cantona	£6.99 ☐
THE TRUTH IN THE LIGHT	Peter and Elizabeth Fenwick	£6.99 ☐
GOODBYE BAFANA	James Gregory	£6.99 ☐
MY OLD MAN AND THE SEA	Daniel Hayes and David Hayes	£5.99 ☐

All Headline books are available at your local bookshop or newsagent, or can be ordered direct from the publisher. Just tick the titles you want and fill in the form below. Prices and availability subject to change without notice.

Headline Book Publishing, Cash Sales Department, Bookpoint, 39 Milton Park, Abingdon, OXON, OX14 4TD, UK. If you have a credit card you may order by telephone – 01235 400400.

Please enclose a cheque or postal order made payable to Bookpoint Ltd to the value of the cover price and allow the following for postage and packing:

UK & BFPO: £1.00 for the first book, 50p for the second book and 30p for each additional book ordered up to a maximum charge of £3.00.

OVERSEAS & EIRE: £2.00 for the first book, £1.00 for the second book and 50p for each additional book.

Name ....

Address ....

....

....

If you would prefer to pay by credit card, please complete:
Please debit my Visa/Access/Diner's Card/American Express (delete as applicable) card no:

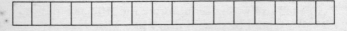

Signature .... Expiry Date ....